W9-BKS-445

ODD JOB MAN

Also by Jonathon Green

Chasing the Sun: Dictionary Makers and the Dictionaries They Made
The Encyclopedia of Censorship
All Dressed Up: The Sixties and the Counterculture
Cutting it Fine: Inside the Restaurant Business (with Andrew Parkinson)
Cannabis: The Story of a Weed That Rocked the World

LANGUAGE: DICTIONARIES AND RELATED PUBLICATIONS

Newspeak: A Dictionary of Jargon
The Dictionary of Contemporary Slang
The Slang Thesaurus
The Dictionary of Jargon
Neologisms
Slang Down the Ages: the Historical Development of Slang
Words Apart: the Language of Prejudice
Cassell Dictionary of Slang
Chambers Slang Dictionary
Green's Dictionary of Slang

DICTIONARIES OF QUOTATIONS

Book of Rock Quotes
Famous Last Words
Book of Sports Quotes
Don't Quote Me: The Other Famous Last Words
Book of Political Quotes
Contemporary Dictionary of Quotations
Sweet Nothings: A Book of Love Quotes
Consuming Passions: A Book of Food Quotes
Cassell Dictionary of Cynical Quotations
Cassell Dictionary of Insulting Quotations

ORAL HISTORIES

It: Sex Since the Sixties
Them
Days in the Life: Voices from the English Underground 1961–1971

ODD JOB MAN

Some Confessions of a Slang Lexicographer

Jonathon Green

JONATHAN CAPE
LONDON

Published by Jonathan Cape 2014

2 4 6 8 10 9 7 5 3 1

First published in Great Britain in 2014 by
Jonathan Cape
Random House, 20 Vauxhall Bridge Road,
London SW1V 2SA

www.vintage-books.co.uk

Addresses for companies within The Random House Group Limited can be found at: www.randomhouse.co.uk/offices.htm

The Random House Group Limited Reg. No. 954009

A CIP catalogue record for this book is available from the British Library

ISBN 9780224097581

The Random House Group Limited supports the Forest Stewardship Council® (FSC®), the leading international forest-certification organisation. Our books carrying the FSC label are printed on FSC®-certified paper. FSC is the only forest-certification scheme supported by the leading environmental organisations, including Greenpeace. Our paper procurement policy can be found at www.randomhouse.co.uk/environment

Typeset in Adobe Caslon by Palimpsest Book Production Limited, Falkirk, Stirlingshire

Printed and bound in Great Britain by Clays Ltd, St Ives PLC

For Patrick Hanks

Introduction

I am the Odd Job Man. This is a book about that job and inevitably, since the job and the life long since became indistinguishable, about the person who does it.

It is my job: lexicography, the making of dictionaries. Specifically dictionaries of slang. It is not a common job, though it is a valuable one, and I suspect that for most of those who use its products it is an almost invisible one.

Invisible? I would say so. Because the dictionary itself – for all its traditional bulk and utility – is something that is created almost wholly by nameless individuals. I am something of an exception in having chosen to place my name on the cover of my work, the covers of which conveniently represent the colour that is also that same name.

I am also an exception in that I know and prize the names of some of those who do the job. Living and dead. They are people I admire and respect and in some cases they are my friends.

The job, which I have done for thirty years and have every intention of doing until my death (though I doubt that even in the best of cases I shall do it for thirty more), is changing. Its traditional form must bend before technology. Fortunately that technology suits the job and will almost certainly improve its quality.

It is a simple job by definition. We tell people what words mean, where they came from and when they arrived in the language.

We do not say why. That is a task for linguists and while they and lexicographers tread the same path, they walk on opposite sides of the street.

I cannot claim to speak for all my colleagues – and the colleagues who are currently working on slang can be counted on a single hand – but it is my hope and intention to portray the job faithfully.

This is not a book that has been written before as far as I am aware. Or not in this way. That, if nothing else, is one justification. The other is, as it must be for all those fortunate enough to have lives as inextricably bound up with their occupation as is mine, that it cannot be categorised as work.

It is the best job I can imagine.

This is what I do and what I intend to do, audience and body willing, until on some unspecified day I crash forward into the keyboard – or whatever equivalent technology throws up in its place. Retirement is not a term in any of my dictionaries.

What I do is sit alone in a room, a screen in front of me, a book more than likely to my left, held open by the weight of a discarded piece of chain. To my right, a wall full of more books that are not just books, but tools, and both extensions of and bastions for my existence. Some of them I have even made myself. With this screen and books and book-shaped tools I chase down words. And by placing these words in alphabetical order, by naming, defining and providing a word-based background for their existence and more words that illustrate examples of their use, I create another book that is designated to be a tool in its turn. A work of reference that is based in hard work and scholarship and even a degree of serendipity, and that provides information which, at its best and most utile, is both trustworthy and authoritative.

Such is the intent. Such, I trust, is the end product.

Introduction

What I do is not intellectual, by which I mean based on reasoning alone. I am certainly no intellectual myself, though reasoning must enter the game: slang is constantly asking questions and the lexicographer's job is to answer them. But it is based on scholarship, by which I mean learning, research, deduction, elucidation and the passing on of such discoveries. I suppose that might make me a scholar, although one must never take scholarship as a synonym for infallibility. The work is based first and foremost on reading, which may be an example of unashamed possession of the cake and eating it too. It deals with a marginal area of language, which appeals personally to me since my background is itself less than wholly mainstream, though both slang and I are pretty much assimilated.

If looked at objectively – indeed if looked at subjectively, that is in that cruel 3 A.M. distorting mirror that renders all our dreams into waking nightmares – what I do is . . . let us be kind and say *odd.* Its best known definition is based on the word drudgery, or rather on 'drudge', the individual him- or herself. To make the vilification even more crushing in these can-do, get-a-life days, the drudge in question is *harmless.* The man who coined the description, if one is to characterise him by the work for which he will be primarily remembered, was just such a drudge, but few individuals were ever less enslaved to drudgery nor honestly considered themselves as such. And when I look at what he did, and I do, I feel no more a drudge (harmless or otherwise) than did Samuel Johnson when in 1755, he included this definition in the published fruits of his seven years' labour: the *Dictionary of the English Language.* This is not to compare myself to Johnson. But it is to set myself in his tradition, to claim my place among his heirs. And of that I am unashamedly proud.

Johnson was not the first – there had been a century and a half of English dictionaries before his – but he was the first to impress himself so hugely on public consciousness. His book would remain the authoritative dictionary, the ultimate court of linguistic appeal, until the *New* and renamed *Oxford English Dictionary* (*OED*) began appearing in 1884. His dictionary earned him an eponym (and only two others have achieved such grandeur: America's *Webster;* and *Partridge*, the twentieth-century British slang dictionary).* But the writers of dictionaries – even before the modern domination of teams rather than individuals – have usually been anonymous figures. And especially so those whose efforts concentrated on slang. A marginal lexis, compounded by marginal individuals. And thus, other than to those, like me, who number themselves among their successors, unknown.

If I consider my predecessors I see nothing that links them, their dictionaries excepted. That said I see the dozen or so slang collectors – whose names I can recite at the least prompting – as my surrogate family, the only genealogy to which I can realistically attach myself.

The first, *c.*1530, was a printer who had allegedly been apprenticed to William Caxton. The second, thirty years later, defies all biography. The third a magistrate. After him a pair of playwrights. Later on we encounter the antiquary and captain of militia Francis Grose, a man whose physique satisfactorily matched his surname. It was said that butchers begged him to allow them to advertise his patronage of their shops, so customers might be persuaded to enjoy the meat that had contributed to his splendid girth. So fat was this acquaintance of Johnson and friend of Robert Burns that after a night's slang-gathering in London's taverns, his servant had to secure him to his bed with a large leather strap. It was feared that otherwise in his tossing and turning the Captain's

* I, quite shamelessly have included my own surname in the title of my most substantial work. But eponymity, at which I seem to grasp, must of course be earned.

belly might overflow the mattress and his whole body follow it to the floor. (This may be apocryphal: I shall still print the legend.) Grose's successor, Pierce Egan, was a sporting journalist and creator of the best-selling *Life in London*. His contemporary and rival John Badcock (as 'Jon B.') devoted himself to plagiarising Egan, including the penning of his own slang dictionary the same year that Egan's had appeared. The mid-nineteenth-century's John Camden Hotten wrote pornography (sometimes in partnership with the poet Swinburne); he termed it his 'flower garden' and titles included *Romance of the Rod*. John S. Farmer, perpetually impoverished, doubled as a leading spiritualist; Albert Barrère taught French to the embryo subalterns of Sandhurst and Eric Partridge, after leaving New Zealand to fight in Flanders, intended to be a publisher in his own right, rather than to serve one. Finally my contemporary Tom Dalzell, working from California, is a labor leader. In a way I am an exception: what my aims were when I left university in 1969 I cannot really say. But they definitely involved words. There are more of us, of course, but not many: we are not an abundant crew.

Looking back from an age so glutted with images, we are quite literally invisible. B. E., Gent., whose *New Dictionary of the Canting Crew* appeared around 1698, left us nothing but his initials and self-proclaimed membership of the upper middle classes. The similarly titled *New Canting Dictionary* claims no author whatsoever. Until the late nineteenth-century's John S. Farmer, born into an era of photography, they are almost invariably faceless. Johnson had his friend Joshua Reynolds to portray him, not to mention David Garrick to immortalise him in verse; his slang coevals – focused not on the standard tongue but on that of Johnson's 'lower employments of life' – are harder to picture. Richard Head, author of *The English Rogue* (1665), looks like a Puritan divine, but for the giggling devil who holds the laurel crown above his head. A portrait of Francis Grose appears as the frontispiece of the 1823 revision of his work, but with its emphasis on the Captain's substantial stomach, suggests caricature rather than reality. We have Charles Turner's engraving of Pierce Egan, holding his prize-fighting journal, *Boxiana*, but there is no allusion to slang and, while both tailor and barber have worked wonders, the background – quill, study, en-leathered quartos – is over-sanitised for the man who hymned the sweet science and revised Captain Grose. As for John Camden Hotten – piratic publisher, pornographer and an outstanding slang collector – we have only the books, his own and those he published, a sympathetic obituary published by a friend, and the poet-sociologist George R. Sims' bitchy – and inaccurate – dismissal: 'Hotten, rotten, forgotten.' Collectors and codifiers of a disdained lexis, their biographies are generally thin at best, and they exist only in their words – or rather those of other people.

Nor, even if the *OED*'s editor Sir James Murray enlisted his children as helpers, sorting citation slips at 1d per hour, does lexicography produce dynasties. There are no generations of dictionary makers as there are those of doctors, lawyers, sportsmen and women. The odd job is not one for which the offspring volunteer. Slang lexicographers are made, or rather become; they are not born – unless one feels that the job to which one has dedicated one's life for so many years must, surely or at least syllogistically, have been that which one was born to do.

And what is it, this odd job to which each of us has dedicated himself?* We find words or phrases that by their very nature are far more often spoken than committed to print; we set them in alphabetical order; we define them; we offer an etymology (the root or story behind the word); we add variant spellings; and, if

* And it truly is 'himself'. Slang's foremost lexicologist, Professor Julie Coleman, is a woman, but its dictionary-making has always been a male preserve.

like me (and only a very tiny subset of us have worked on slang in this way) we work 'on historical principles',* we illustrate our findings with usage examples – citations – that show as best they and we are capable the way in which the slang word works. And with that completed we make and have published our dictionaries. It is not so different from making any other dictionary, but if Standard English is the language of the establishment, then slang is its antithesis, what I call a 'counter-language', and it plays by its own rules. We, its collectors and codifiers, must always take note.

Yet if the lexicographer really is a drudge as we perform our selection, our defining, our etymologising and our gathering of citations (and who is to deny that some stages of dictionary preparation can be nothing if not wearing), the dowdy chrysalis turns butterfly once the work is published and begins to be used. The concept of *the dictionary* – no name is necessary, just the idea of the lexical diktat – as the repository of linguistic authority is long established. Even typographically: how better to imply 'the truth' than to fake up some word plus definition in cod-dictionary layout. Slang dictionaries too. The finished work transcends its making and the users, by offering their trust and thus conferring such authority upon the maker, render the lexicographer, however anonymous, a minor deity. Very minor and, like all the figureheads of faith, such deity is an incontrovertible myth. Nor do lexicographers, unlike the endlessly declarative dictators of 'good' or 'correct' usage, volunteer for the role. It arrives merely by default. An omnipotence that may be respected, but is quite spurious. Dictionaries are made by humans. Surely we all know what that implies.

* The technical name for which is 'diachronic': from Greek 'through time'; uncited dictionaries seeking to list and describe only words in current use are 'synchronic'.

If one is not born but becomes, if one knows the how, the where, the when, the who – what about the why? The why remains the great unanswered. I do answer it. Jocularly: 'It's the whore's excuse – first I did it for myself, then I did it for my friends, now I do it for money,' and add some crack about lexicographical poverty. Self-mockingly: 'I always wanted to say "fuck" in front of my parents.' Self-pityingly: 'No one will let me do anything else.' Confessionally: 'I'm in love with the language.' Maybe, maybe, and there are doubtless elements of them all. But I don't really believe any of them. Thirty years, well over half one's working life, ferreting around for yet another synonym for 'drunk' or 'masturbation' or 'excrement'? There must be more.

Every book that I have written, it seems to me, is a means of answering my own questions. Not perhaps the softcore and pseudonymous *Diary of a Masseuse* (1976), although the jury's still out on *The Big Book of Filth*, but definitely *Days in the Life* (tell me about my Sixties' youth), *It* (tell me about sex), *Them* (tell me about being an immigrant or at least an immigrant's child) or *Chasing the Sun* (tell me about what I do). Maybe even the collection of *Famous Last Words* (tell me how to die). This book began life as a pun – 'Life in Words' – and while the name has changed still offers questions – mine and the readers' – and hopefully answers too, though only mine. It is about what I do and how I came to do it. And how I do it now. Its aim is both to demystify 'the dictionary' and to give some glory to slang, one of language's most disdained of subsets. Asking the question why, I find it impossible to avoid a degree of autobiography. After all, if one's project becomes a life's work, expanding to fill every cranny of one's existence, the life and the work become so entangled that it seems impossible to offer one without the other. Though autobiography is really about what gets left out, and what you may find, with its overriding promotion of the soloist and the marginal, may be merely a fantasy self, a sedentary, peaceable version of that which fifty years ago had me dreaming of life as a teenage assassin, all vodka, Gitanes and telescopic sights, crouching at a window in the flashing glow of neon in a seedy street.

Slang lexicography is not a much sought-after occupation. What brought me there? Why do I keep doing it? Why, indeed, would I resist any alternative employment. I do not pretend that my life is the stuff of anyone's dreams, but if I am to explain what I do, then I need to explain the person who does it. Slang matters to me, deeply. It seems to be the most logical place for me to be. It fits. Did it 'fit' thirty years ago when I started? I believe so, since the fascination – acknowledged or not – had been there for many years already. Only the codifying remained.

Moving to the end of *Chasing the Sun*, my attempt to write an accessible history of lexicography, I wrote this of my predecessor in slang collection: 'To sum up [Eric] Partridge and in so doing to offer a tribute to the many lexicographers who preceded him and worked, like him, very much on their own, one can do worse than borrow from the detective writer Raymond Chandler. Describing his own efforts in a letter of 1957, Chandler suggested that "To accept a mediocre form and make something like literature out of it is in itself rather an accomplishment." In the hierarchy of language, slang is that 'mediocre form'; what Partridge did was make, if not literature, then something profoundly literate out of his spurned lexicon.'

I was also, consciously or otherwise, writing about myself, and find little changed, although another sixteen years have passed, my commitment has deepened and my knowledge expanded.

Lexicographers, I know, are not meant to write, or not beyond the brevity of definitions. This is not self-pity but an acknowledgement of all those carefully crafted and unread texts that preface dictionaries.

The users wish to use what's in the box, not examine its label. But this is not a dictionary, but a dictionary maker's exploration. Please consider it as metadata, as a footnote.

If this book is to be anything then it is my celebration of slang. My own role is almost coincidental, but, as I have tried to explain, the one is intimately bound up with the other. By explaining myself, I want to bring my profession out of the relative darkness in which my predecessors tend to exist. I am fortunate enough to enjoy my work – which tends to lessen its role as 'work' – and wish to celebrate it here. I do not expect to gain any converts – slang lexicography is a tiny moon circling the already small world of general lexicography – but I would hope to inform. Like a dictionary I want to set down the words, define them, explain where they came from and offer pertinent examples.

And I think, I fear, that there may be, however spectral a presence, something of an act of mourning for the very thing with which I work, that I create and above all that I love: the printed book. The last 'death of the book' scare came around the time of the dot-com boom; like that boom it fizzled out. This time it seems serious. I, for one, regret the current obeisance to digits. Technology is useful, but as a servant, not a master.

One last thing before I move on. If that is what I do, what has doing it made? What have I done? My dictionaries. Not, if I cut my eyes across the room and count, that many, but what do you want? If one takes seventeen years, another five and the whole enterprise is wrapped up into more than three decades, how many am I supposed to manage? The great German *Deutsches Wörterbuch*, launched by the Grimm brothers, took over 140 years to be completed. Then, like the *OED*, which took around fifty, it immediately set off towards revision. My three volumes are but a split second in comparison even if they too are being reworked, amended, expanded and improved.*

There are in fact just three titles: *The Contemporary Dictionary of Slang*, which came out in 1984 via Pan Books (latterly Pan Macmillan, who added two revisions); the *Cassell Dictionary of Slang*, published eponymously in 1998, in a revised, expanded edition in 2005 and, now, bending to a new colophon, the *Chambers Slang Dictionary* in 2008. Then there is *Green's Dictionary of Slang*, the big one, of 2010. With the exception of the first, which restricted itself to material published between 1945–84 and ran to a mere 11,500 headwords, all have aimed to take in the entirety of anglophone slang, with a start date of *c.*1500. In addition, since something has to justify Martin Amis's footnoted nickname of 'Mr Slang' (since then paraded shamelessly in all publicity), there have been a variety of ancillary, slang-based works. *The Slang Thesaurus* (Hamish Hamilton, 1986), *Slang Down the Ages* (Kyle Cathie, 1993 and, for reasons that no one has yet been able to explain, republished in America as *Slang Through the Ages*), which was for me a pioneering journey into slang's thematic self-recreation. There was *Words Apart* (Kyle Cathie, 1996), an attempt to illumine the depressing world of racial and national insults and which once more turned to the predominance of recurrent themes in such abuse. And in the aftermath of the first Cassell book, four – three would have been more sensible but one invariably goes a step too far – jolly volumes of lists, starting with the *Big Book of Filth* (small, naturally, and with a stray pubic hair lurking on the front endpaper) and followed by similar 'big books' of *Bodily Functions*,

* The fact that within two years of publication I have already applied at least one of these changes to 40 per cent of the entries elicits mixed emotions. On the one hand: way to go, what else should I be doing; on the other: how could I ever have allowed the thing out with so much yet to be done?

Insults and *Talking Dirty*, the last of which dealt with phraseology. My name is not on any cover, but it follows each introduction. Since then I have added another couple of essentially thematic titles: *Getting Off at Gateshead* (Quercus, 2010) which ran the gamut of taboo terms, and *Crooked Talk* (Random House, 2011) which deals with cant, the language of crime. At the time of writing, *Language!*, a history of slang, is in preparation for Atlantic Books. And of course there is this.

And there is also this: once upon a time, when publishing was something very different, it was possible to set off on a project, however long, let's say seventeen years, and be assured that the colophon on the book's spine would be the same on publication day as that which adorns the contract signed on day one. Starting work in 1993 on what would become *Green's Dictionary of Slang* (*GDoS*), it would never have crossed my mind that a world that had not changed very much for two centuries would undergo the radical alterations that would soon follow. There had, naturally, been changes: publishers, once combining their role with that of booksellers, had become an industry of their own, leaving the bookshops to their own devices. Authors, who once sold their copyrights to those same publishers, now sold what was effectively a licence, received first an advance and then, if fortunate and their book was popular, royalties derived from sales. Of course editors might not stay for ever, better jobs might lure them elsewhere, they might retire, but the structure remained constant, even if there was the occasional paint job.

That was not the story of *GDoS*. When the book finally appeared, in 2010, I was first congratulated not on its content, but on the simple fact, or what would once have seemed a simple fact: that it had actually appeared in print. A three-volume dictionary, published in the early twenty-first century: remarkable, barely conceivable even. I was almost reduced to touching it to make sure that it was truly there.

'Have you ever thought of writing a slang dictionary,' an editor asked in 1993 and although I had, a decade earlier, and published it, I said only 'Yes'. And had a publisher. The problem, in these globalising days, is keeping them. I managed a single-volume dictionary for this first supporter five years later and on the back of that they commissioned my monster. Half a millennium's slang, culled from the entire anglophone world.

Two years later they were taken over. The men who had agreed to commission the book departed. My editor was stripped of his department and left to work on alone. I sympathised but it didn't really impinge on my ongoing researches. Perhaps naively, for it was a time of accelerating change even before the Internet began pushing for even greater novelty, I still assumed that my commissioning publisher would last the course. Time passed. A second edition followed, even if this displayed in its title a publisher's name that no longer existed and on the spine a quite different label. More takeovers followed. My editor departed. The new owner lacked interest. It is not good, twelve years into a life-consuming project to have one's only link to the reading world declare, 'Well, we'll publish it if we really have to.' I cast around for greater enthusiasm. Enter a Very Important Reference Publisher. Took me to high places, showed me the world. Two years passed. A whirlwind of emotional ups and downs. How we flirted, how we courted, how we danced. Almost to the altar, that near, but I checked the pre-nup and frankly they wanted too much. Let's put it this way: I was not willing, as was demanded for certain circumstances, to pay for the use of my own work. Another suitor appeared. Keen, oh-so-very keen. I surrendered. I gained a new editor as well as a new logo, and under that published another revised, expanded single-volume work: effectively a third edition. Just a year to go and the big book would follow. The database was frozen, the lengthy editing commenced. Then an email: my new partner had vanished, binned by its über-corporation, its office empty, its personnel, my new editor included, dismissed. But the über-corp has many mansions. My work is now attached to one of them, although it took three twitchy months to be told which it might be. It is their first slang dictionary. I sense their last, too. They were not, and in my more altruistic moments, I sympathise, especially keen, but had no more choice than had I. The book came out in the UK in late 2010; US distribution followed. Three volumes, 6,200 pages, 110,000 headwords, 415,000 citations. I wept.

Beginning

What we need now is structure. In other words a beginning, though perhaps not a plot and certainly not an end. My life and my work have long since been indissoluble, but once upon a time there was no slang, no words for that matter, and so let us return to day one. Otherwise what follows – and perhaps I do not mind this, but others may – resembles a succession of lemmas, linked together because they appear in a book, between a pair of unifying covers, but otherwise quite discrete disquisitions linked only by the arbitrary order of the English alphabet.

So whatever happens later we must start at the beginning. If it can dovetail with what follows, or at least seem to predict it, so much the better. This is in no way a conventional memoir, but some things must be said. Or so it seems to me, whose working life is so committed to searching the past for origins and roots. It is a beginning that, without the memories that those from more settled lineages have on tap, has always seemed abrupt. Perhaps, like newly arrived immigrants looking forward to their future and rushing to move beyond the past, the young have no interest in asking questions about 'before'? Perhaps that was merely me? I failed to ask and remain in ignorance. And since the past was quite literally another country, and that country no longer exists remotely as it was, I am not going to find out. I have been trying to make up for it, by proxy, ever since.

'In a box of the stone jug I was born / Of a hempen widow, the kid forlorn.'* Perhaps not, but the event if not the historical background is true and if perhaps not wholly necessary, then for what follows, inevitable: you are born. Nobody asked me, as they say, but it happens. It is long and for your mother painful and you bear the scars. 1948: high forceps. Your father is informed: we can't save them both. He begs to differ. Fortunately or otherwise he prevails. There are three months in an incubator. A box and if not of stone then of plastic or glass. Claustrophobia, a lifelong problem, was presumably established. Your mother, consciously or otherwise, does not forgive you. There will be no more children. You are the best on offer. You are the worst. You are Jonathon: 'god-given' in Hebrew. The Jewish prince. In the beginning was the word. And the word is 'Tod'. Tod Sloan: rhyming slang for alone.

At first the words are always passive. You have none yourself. Your first memories are visual, but you are read to. Beatrix Potter,

* As good a place to start as any. May I translate? 'In a cell at Newgate prison I was born / To a hanged villain's widow, a child forlorn.' Good stuff: four slang terms in half as many lines and if one follows the ballad to its end there are sixty choice examples of early eighteenth-century criminal jargon, properly known as cant. And yes, they are valid, and yes, they were used, and yes, with very few exceptions they are as dead as the man who conjured them up: W. Harrison Ainsworth, in whose *Rookwood*, published 1834, this poem occurs. Wholly confected, wholly illusory, a rip-roaring tale of the highwayman Dick Turpin, in life a rather nasty, inept thug, in Ainsworth's 'Newgate novel', a glorious myth, ride to York and noble Black Bess included. Bulwer Lytton, he of 'It was a dark and stormy night' was a Newgate novelist; so too was Dickens (with *Oliver Twist*) although he was at pains to deny it. They wrote much-read (and thus much vilified) yarns in which the use of slang – then as now – adduced to a villain's 'reality'. With Dickens, the genius, one never saw the joins; with the others, the slang is underlined so heavily that one can feel as if one has been tossed into an animated and often anachronistic glossary.

you especially like *The Tailor of Gloucester* (the 'cherry-coloured twist'). Orlando the Marmalade Cat takes the ferry to northern France across to which your father was not that long ago making his way in uniform with four water bottles, each bearing a different flavour of eau de vie. A better return than his departure: Dunkirk. I do not know if his war was 'good' or 'bad'. Most of it seems to have been spent waiting to re-cross the Channel. The least macho of men, he does not do war stories. There are better ones. He reads you *Just So Stories* ('the great grey-green greasy Limpopo'). At some stage he had met your mother (was she truly driving lorries for the army?) and they marry in 1945. They will stay together until he dies forty-four years later. He manages a chain store, whose welcome-back note is bedecked by a frieze of hats – military caps and civvy derbies. 'You've done your bit – now let's get on with the job.' There is a shelf over your bed, it bears 'your' books. One night it falls. You survive. Your bedroom has a picture-rail level frieze of Disney figures against what look like hills. One nightmare has you seeing witches appearing behind those hills. You will never like Disney: the softness, the curves, animated Mabel Lucie Attwell, menace behind the slop.

You start school, tearfully watching your mother recede from view. 'Music and Movement' on the BBC ('tall as a house . . . small as a mouse'), painting (forget it), reading (aha . . .). 'Janet and John' presumably, though in truth it could have been any tale of monosyllabic life among the tiny. The lengthy, ever-expanding verses of 'The House That Jack Built', which is pleasingly similar to another cumulative song, this one sung at Passover, the Jewish spring festival that arrives each year around the same time as Easter. It starts with a lamb and ends with the Angel of Death joining the party. Within months your father is moved to a better store in a cathedral city. The locals rejoice in the name of 'Yellowbellies.'* It refers to frogs. It is notably flat, other than the bits which are not. The Wolds. It is 1953. You drive across the country to your father's parents to watch a grey 10-inch version of the Coronation, curtains closed, chairs encircling the wooden box. The best bit is the 'natural break': the box shows a factory tower being blown up; the film reverses, the tower is reborn. You know no Freud, you are simply delighted. Other trips are irregular but continue while your grandparents are alive. Your father's family – father, mother, the widowed wife of a brother who died young of leukaemia, one married sister and her husband, a sister who didn't marry – live in a wood-panelled mansion, or so it seems to you, with a garden large enough to have a small, if not a lake, then something bigger than a pond. It hosts a small rowing boat. You make the round of relations, kiss kiss kiss. Grandpa, nearly blind and later wholly so, sits in a chair, do you ever see him rise? Later you realise the blindness must have been from diabetes. (Just you wait and see.) Grandma rules the roost. The widowed sister-in-law is more like a live-in servant. But all the women seem to favour flowered pinafores. There are cousins – older, wholly dull. At some stage there is a golden wedding. You sit at 'the children's table'. You are not happy. Resentful at your perceived demotion. Only children are children in name only. You keep your counsel and eat your jelly.

The brother-in-law deals in fruit and veg and the garage is

* *Yellowbelly*: a dialect name for a native of Lincolnshire. Fair enough: it's the yellow-stomached fenland eels and frogs (frog also meaning those other flatlanders, the Dutch before it meant French, and the southernmost part of the county is known as 'south Holland'); less obvious is the *English Dialect Dictionary*'s second sense: 'a slang name for a knife grinder'. Slang adds a coward and a Mexican.

filled with smells and boxes – and your mother is unimpressed. The feeling, it is clear, is mutual. You feel no kinship. There is food, too much, but of course delicious, or so you are informed. In the sitting room is a glass cupboard of books. For a while you are impressed, but the cupboard is never opened – in time, little snob, you will realise that the books are from a club, and the cupboard too. The best thing about the trips is a mile from the house: the word 'Shufflebotham's' inscribed across the height of a terrace-end.

Real pleasure lies nearer home: the signalman on the village's pre-Beeching branch line permits you entrance to his box. He activates the fog signal. Boom! Bliss. Again! On a mainline station you see the *Mallard*, super-train of its day. You are invited onto the footplate. You are far too scared. Cowardy-custard. Sissy. And later, almost immediately, but far too late, you will regret it. There's a first time for lots of things and this will play a chorus through your life. Cowardice? Of course, but more than that, apprehension. The unknown, the mysterious, do not beckon. At the circus you love watching the gaffers prepare the lions' cage, the drilled creation of the edifice of excitement. The smooth efficiency of a task well done. The lions tamed, the clowns prepare to fire their cannon. Near hysterical you beg to be removed. Not the bang, but the waiting. The tension. The unknown. And yet, in work as in life, you love alleys over main roads, the narrow and crooked over the broad vista. They fill in the map and once mapped become known and thus controlled. Knowledge is power. Knowledge is security.

Wondrously you spend three months in a hotel. For a week you are ill. You vomit over each of the six pairs of pyjamas your father has obtained 'on appro'. You listen to *Children's Favourites* on the BBC's Home Service, 'The Laughing Policeman'. You move to a house, your new room is built over the old garage.

You want it painted red, you get blue. There is a garden, an air raid shelter which becomes a rockery. Later that year you stand in the windows of your father's store waving your Union Jack as the young Queen's limousine processes through the crowds.

There is a new school. St Mary's. You must seem bright; they put you in Mrs Hill's class. She is stern but fair. 'Write down "Christopher Hen",' she requests. You can manage the hen; the Christopher – fittingly? – defeats you. You move back to Mrs Bramley's class. She resembles her name, at least in chubbiness and rosy cheeks. She has a red Parker 51; it writes *AEX* ('A-Excellent') on your work. Halfway up the stairs is a table bearing Arthur Bryant's *Our Island Story* and *Our Empire Story*. They gather dust, though we receive regular doses of a scratchy 'Land of Hope and Glory' played at morning assembly. You have friends, your 'gang'. For one season there is a rash of Davy Crockett hats. For another it is cigarette cards. There are girls, you fall in love. You do not say so. The object of your desire cartwheels, careless of propriety, offering up legs and knickers. You will remain what slang terms a 'leg man'. Later you will blot your copybook: invited to the latest in the season's round of parties you overhear your hostess upbraiding her daughter. You approach, volunteer the services of 'the gang' to 'beat her up'. Your hostess smiles, resists your offer. There will be no more parties that year. It is not your only sin. Walking from school you push a smaller schoolmate into a hedge. You are in bed. The door opens: your parents, furious. They have been rung up by the child's parents, furious. The head-mistress carpets you. She is very stern but not, you feel, especially fair. Your parents do not speak to you for two days. You are not especially ashamed, but your mother is, and for that you must pay.

There are school plays (you play the King in a re-enactment of 'Four-and-Twenty Blackbirds' – the rest of the form – but are not required for the Nativity), picnics (a vast bottle of ginger beer), 'test matches' with your best friend (aping the current stars, you duly bat and bowl left and right handed, and change styles every six balls). You have taken possession, somehow, of the dream catapult, hard forked wood, thick rubber: you are firing stones in your front garden, a cycling youth dismounts, 'I'm a police cadet. That is illegal.' And takes it. You will not like the police.

It is not idyllic but it lacks threat. V-bombers are based nearby and you see them flying shatteringly overhead; and you read the daily papers with growing ability. The *Manchester Guardian* and *News Chronicle* for your father (until one day the latter becomes the *Daily Mail* and delivery is quickly discontinued), the *Daily Express* ('for Granny'), the quality broadsheets on Sunday. Only your titular Aunt, your mother's best friend, takes the *News of the World*. Its strapline declares 'The paper for the young at heart'. Your 'aunt' has no children: for you she is forever young. But you are not bright – or not interested – enough to start putting twos with twos. (Indeed, they will stop you doing maths after O level.) It also lacks a dog for the full scenario but there is a dog too. Briefly. One day you return from school, the dog is not there. It was 'overbred', you are informed. It has been taken to the vet, 'put to sleep'. You will be ashamed, when you properly learn such things, that you accepted so readily the compensatory trip to the toyshop.

There is a parallel scenario. Not bad, but different. It is a cathedral city and, perhaps coincidentally, there is but one other Jewish family – and your mother has declared them *treyfe*, unclean, or at least socially unacceptable. Her own father, or so you have been told, had sold pit ponies to Yorkshire colliers, but there was a maid who read *Peg's Paper* and apparently that must have been different. Indeed you know all too little of your own past. You are a mongrel, a mix of German, Polish, Russian and Lithuanian, with grandparents who had the good sense to leave mainland Europe, though insufficient to carry on to New York. Your mother's mother lives with you – inconceivably old and, as attested by the washing line, bedecked in vast pink bloomers. She drinks cups of boiled water and, on days when your mother is out, makes you perfect egg and chips for lunch. She measures out distances on the basis of her life 'before', with references to places that you will never see. You are too young or too repelled by her age to ask her the right questions. You are twelve when she dies and no one else knows or cares about the answers. There is allegedly a far distant great-great-aunt who ran a brewery and was murdered by her peasant coachman on the way to bank the week's take, her corpse thrown from the troika (or is that just something you presume once, eventually, you've read *War and Peace*?). There is undoubtedly an uncle (and probably many others who neither left nor made their way to Palestine) lined up next to the pit he had just helped dig and shot to death by the vodka-sodden small-town race purifiers of a Nazi *Einsatzkommando*, with enthusiastic help from his recent next-door neighbours. You learn to know your enemies – the poujadist, the peasant; you are urban, you distrust all that is not. It is not just in Frankenstein films that the villagers brandish torches and pitchforks. Then there is the Russian revolutionary Maxim Litvinov who, Granny claims, was a cousin. You find him in your dictionary of quotations: 'Peace is indivisible', or so he says. On your father's side: nothing. You ask, of course, but he cannot help. Not even a name, since Green, unless it was Gryn as found in Poland, was surely an immigrant's compromise. I may know my signature, I have been putting it in my books for over fifty years, but I do not know my own name.

You never feel of here, and you have no sustaining idea of

there. It is not religion as such, but it is undoubtedly Jewishness. Obviously there is no form of community where you live. You eat kosher food – no pig, no shellfish, a different set of cutlery and dishes for cooking and eating *fleishik* and *milchik* (meat dishes and 'milk' which means all the other ones). It does not seem odd; our homelife never does as children. You shop locally, except for meat. For this there is 'the order', a monthly trek by car to a larger Jewish centre, with kosher butchers. You bear home the packages of chickens (roasters with giblets for chopped liver which you learn to make and boilers still holding the shell-less yolks that you love boiled in soup; no more, the EU has long since banned them), tongue, beef, lamb. There is a deli in your city, but the Pole who runs it is a *goy*. He sells everything but smoked salmon. Too much salty smoked fish during his days in the salt mines runs the myth. There is no garlic. Your mother is a good cook, taught by your grandmother. Her soufflés rise miraculously, her gefilte fish bobs unbroken in its broth, her fried fish – matzo meal and beaten eggs not stolid batter – delights.

Of course this adherence was – and to an extent, since to an extent it remains, is – absurd. As absurd as believing in some old man in the sky. On that first day at school they served a round of gelatinous, bright pink meat. I ate one forkful, choked and spat it out. Alien flavour: pig, surely. Spam to be precise. I gazed at the ceiling, awaiting the hand that would surely lower to snuff me out. Nothing. Tearful, infinitely guilty, I reported home. There would be no more Spam. But it is 1953 and I am still offering my (English language) prayers at night, and it will be a while before I start to put these childish things aside.

I am solo now. I was then. Community, that antithesis of self-absorption, is another of my least favoured words. Worried parents ask, 'don't you want to join in?' You don't. You have friends, you are no hermit, no embryo geek, but you do not join. The collection of words, lexicography, might be dismissed as super-geekery, but I would refute that. No cubs, no scouts. No clubs. No hobbies. (There is an urged attempt at stamp collecting; one tries but sometimes one does not try again.) Nor in your teens the fissiparous utopianism of the left. Although once, 1964, you trudge a village knocking on doors and suggesting the dwellers place a picture of Harold Wilson in their window. But that was already compromised; the local 'activist', handing over the stack of posters, wishes you good luck. Would he be joining us? 'Bugger that, lads, it's wet out and football on the telly.' Sixteen year olds learn different lessons: I opted for 'politics is bullshit'. Of the words I continue to loathe, *earnest* is among the most loathsome. Mine has been a voluntary solitude. Doubtless one of the products of a solitary childhood. You can't read en masse. Or not before the current florescence of reading groups, and books appended with jolly topics for earnest discussion over the white wine. You may want to believe in the efficacy of group effort, but you never see it. A crowd, to you, always seems to be gathered exulting round a pile of burning texts. You shun belief and its true believers. That way, you have noticed, lies Auschwitz. You are narcissistic. You are masturbatory. You are up your own arse. You do not argue.

After St Mary's, St Hugh's. Are there no schools bereft of these *goyish* titles? Prep school. You are nearly eleven and by some standards late to leave home. When you still lived in the hotel they had been filming *The Dam Busters* and the stars and crew ate across the dining room. One day the three of you drive out to the set, one of the bomber bases so recently at work for real. The fog has descended. There is no filming. Now, to your delight, your school houses the real Dam Busters base, a village lost among the flat, soggy potato fields ('these potatoes are growing to make Smith's Crisps' announce roadside signs). The local hotel, still standing, once poured Guy Gibson his pre-flight pint and offered a garden where his dog, blithely named Nigger, could pee on the rhododendrons. Now on exeat Sundays you eat brown Windsor soup, equally brown and razor-thin, over-roasted beef and vegetables still swimming in their cooking water. Forty years on the village erects a Dam Busters' memorial. It is available on postcards: a lump of raw granite – the dam – a blue-painted centre strip – proof of the buster.

First night in, the school song: give me a word that rhymes with 'Hugh'. Yes, exactly. And shouldn't you have guessed it from the cap badge: a ball flying over a brick wall. Let us go back seven centuries. Here is little Hugh playing ball in the street. Here is the house of the Jew Aaron. The ball flies over the wall. Hugh flies into the Semitic oven and emerges as unleavened bread. The Semite flies into the Christian wrath and there meets the fire in his turn. Blood libels, how they do persist. Did the school even ponder its origins? Certainly an enlightened master petitioned and won from the Cathedral an official denial of the myth. Nor was there the slightest anti-Semitism. Far worse to be fat or, heaven forfend, with parents in some 'foreign' colonial outpost. No blacks nor browns. Though we were treated to – and laughed at – Sir's impressions of the leaders of the Congo horrors. Lumumba, Kasa-Vubu; aren't those darkies droll?

Hang on. All these victim references. Are you saying that your young and not-so-young life was bedevilled with pogroms, with baying mobs, with Jew hatred? Not at all. Indeed my own slang database contains many more negatives than I ever experienced. Of course there have been occasions: the student paper that branded me 'the best reason for anti-Semitism in Oxford'; the odd slip of what I had assumed were otherwise affectionate tongues; an ancient lion of the Left and father of one of my then closest friends, whose unwarranted loathing for a young man he had met perhaps twice, and who had treated him with nothing but fawning respect, seemed to have no other cause. Or so, years later, I was informed. It was, of course, an anomalous period. A hiccup in the status quo. Still enough post-Holocaust guilt to silence all but the most unreconstructed of vilifiers, Israel still plucky rather than perfidious. But if I am right, then what matters most is that you are wrong and, deprived of Vietnam, of South Africa, of useful monochrome scapegoats the ideologically pure struggle for breath without a useful bogeyman. Am I alone in sensing something akin to a sigh of relief at the opportunity to cast off inconvenient guilt and to put the Jews, sorry, the Israelis, back in their traditional place? The green-red-brown triumvirate dictates the agenda now. The old Christian canards re-born and appropriated by once tolerant and co-habiting Islam. The Left twisting itself into the inevitable contortions of true belief, abasing itself before old enemies, screaming out its frustrations at old friends. The Right delighted to batten on to both.

And perhaps, as a good liberal, I too must look forward to a world bereft of the Jew, which then presumably will be purged of every evil. Except that I, too, shall perforce be purged. *Schtum*! Enough. Back to school.

Except there is one more thing. One little irony. When I arrived at Oxford I was amused by the fact that even then, 1966, I still ranked as 'first Jew' for a surprisingly large proportion of my friends. Loved it, of course. And it was a two-way street. To steal from Harold Macmillan, they met Estonians, I Etonians. But what about me? Tossed onto the boarding school conveyor belt I had hardly opted into the Semitic mainstream. The idea of the one Jewish boarding school of which I knew – Carmel College – where I assumed theology would be the order of the day, simply horrified me. My home was far from any Jewish community, my family existed but I barely knew it. My life and thus my intimacies were those of school. Home soon became a strange world where the food was better, the bed more comfortable, and there was freedom from my twin persecutors: sport in all its forms and the play-soldiering of the compulsory cadet corps. But friends? They were school too. I could hardly have been my own 'first Jew', but in truth, I was pretty much my only one.

Now, please, let us go back. To prep school where food still seemed to play so important a role. Just like in the books we had 'dorm feasts': tinned cling peaches and corned beef. On lucky days you sat next to Sir who kindly cut the crusts from his toast and passed them on. On less lucky ones we received already fertilised eggs, with beaks and bones already formed, or mud-clumped bunches of watercress with worms still present in the pendant earth. I was free – perhaps there was a deity – from the local speciality, brawn, and watched as one poor eight year old, having thrown it up, was forced by shouting masters to eat his vomit. But if there was no compulsory pig neither was there any school-provided substitute, only surreptitiously swallowed Kraft cheese slices, their packet held carefully beneath the table's edge. And food provided dreams: one master, newly home from a trip to Texas, pinned on his wall what must have been a perfectly ordinary diner menu. On it a plate and on that, or rather 'over' it since the monstrous chunk of flesh overflowed every edge, a steak. And a price. One mighty dollar. It was unattainable, mouth-watering, quite beyond us. It was America. So too was the school library's collection of *National Geographic*s. Some opted for the much celebrated naked breasts within – albeit carefully positioned as anthropological phenomena and far from the inflated glories of a *Playboy* magazine that had yet to become easily available in the UK. (We had only such delights as *Parade*, furtively scanned inside a Giles annual in the all-male environment of the barber Mr Elsom, who was so unswervingly attuned to the rhythms of his trade that one afternoon he asked an uncomprehending eight year old, 'Anything for the weekend, sir?') You preferred the back covers, wonderfully technicolor, framing a bright red fridge with beads of icy sweat pointing up its thirst-quenching chilliness, and advertising that other Yankee staple: Coca-Cola. America, that home of interesting surnames, and again something, despite one's fascination with an upcoming election – you go for Kennedy, not wholly understanding why – a growing acknowledgement of things 'across the pond' that one was definitely not.

Food is not words, though you consume them both and the consumption can be a matter of taste – but it seems to have been defining. It tells you what you are and, as importantly, what you are not. Books and their reading tell you what you want to be and, whether or not you yet have the slightest idea, what you might become. For me, quite unaware at the time, they have provided a life. The dictionary is, after all, the end product. Its matter could not exist without the printed words among which one researches.

No hobbies? Is reading permitted? A fierce, all-consuming love of books, Of words on paper. The greatest of all escapes. An addiction as powerful as that to heroin, and with highs and lows that, at least emotionally, are not so different. After all, the first ones were free from the children's library, then you were hooked and it was cash down at the local bookshop and then . . . And my own growing accumulation. It was in the cathedral city that I bought my first book. I would like to say I recall the title – it may have been H. G. Wells' short stories – but it was the act that counts.* A tiny bookshop in the shadow of the cathedral, manned by a hunchback or dwarf or maybe both. But he seemed so to me, just as the shelves of books seemed pleasingly crammed and unassailably high. What I bought, and not that many or often since my pocket money was slim and birthdays are but annual events (fortunately one could browse without interference), were of course Penguins, which cost a shilling or maybe one and sixpence. (Pan Books, bearing lurid covers and their eponymous hedonist's pipes, were beyond my pale.)

What I owned and what I borrowed are all mixed up. Long pre-dating prep school I read E. Nesbit who showed that life is never more fun than when parents are absent and Roger Lancellyn Green's version of the Morte d'Arthur and later T. H. White's take – though I grew bored with the later volumes devoted to Morgan le Fay and Mordred's sexually-laden plotting, Arthur's cuckolding and Lancelot and Guinevere's dalliances and reread only *The Sword in the Stone*. Biographies are always most alluring before our hero makes it – after that it's only name-dropping and picking up prizes. And perhaps adultery and its twin, unhappy marriage. I read the Narnia books until I realised they were all a Christian allegory and tossed them aside, grossly affronted at the con. I read Roman myths and Greek myths and Norse myths and Irish myths and Chinese myths – a whole *Golden Bough* in pre-teen adaptations. (I part

* In 2011, giving a talk in Lincoln, some fifty years since leaving in 1961, and seven days after witnessing my estranged mother's death, I returned to the city for the first time. I made due pilgrimage: the Saracen's Head where we had lived and I had stained all those pyjamas was Waterstone's, St Mary's, within a month of shutting down; as things must, my father's store and our house seemed smaller. The bookshop had gone too though I enquired in neighbouring shops and some recalled it. Or at least indulged my questions. Prevailing wisdom advises against return: it's not so bad but it helps if you know where you're going.

lived, of course, in the Jewish myth.) I read Grimms' *Fairytales* (though naturally knew nothing of their author's lexicography): horror stories with their endlessly impaled robins, tortured children and gloatingly evil adults. They fitted my image of Germany: we boycotted all things Teuton – cars, pencils, brown and white goods; a bottle of Liebfraumilch, carelessly plucked from a charity dance lucky dip, sat untouched in the pantry for years. Thanks to an elder cousin I barely knew I received hand-me-down duplicates of bar mitzvah-given Dickens, published by Collins and bound in some kind of pseudo-leather, Rexine perhaps? Precociously I set out to read *Oliver Twist* and *David Copperfield*. I finished them – it would be decades before I would permit myself the heretical act of leaving any book unfinished – but thereafter left both them and their author alone for thirty years. The penalty for the precocious reader is often thus: one yearns to forge ahead, but the eyes and appetite run far too far beyond the brain. Another result of such enthusiasm, which I now find in a new context – the reading of French *polars* with an inadequate vocabulary and a disinclination to be resorting incessantly to the dictionary – is that one encounters many words for the first time. One uses context and guesswork, and while the one may help, the other often doesn't. Accurate definitions, I suppose, came as a pleasant surprise, though occasionally an embarrassing one.

There was *The Wind in the Willows*, though I struggled with the cod-paganism of the 'Piper at the Gates of Dawn' chapter: Toad was much more fun, and surely a city-dweller at heart. I read Billy Bunter, *101 Dalmatians* (yet, mercifully, to succumb to Disneyfication). I read, quite uncomprehending of its nuances, *Nineteen Eighty-Four*, which was one of the few books my parents had on their shelves. They also had Arnold Bennett's *The Grand Babylon Hotel* which I enjoyed hugely. Returning to it now its protagonist seems to show only gross American arrogance, but one viewed such figures less critically when God's Own Country was also still a Promised Land. I read Edward Lear ('Who, or why, or which, or what, is the Akond of Swat?' and wondered, as a neophyte victim of Hillard and Botting's text books, whether the answer might in some way be connected to the gerund). A trip to Stratford resulted in a Complete Shakespeare, and this time the leather was real. Via LPs came the lyrics of Gilbert and Sullivan. Early on I received the *Children's Encyclopedia*, a mix of outdated information, strange murkily coloured illustrations, technicolor flags from defunct merchant fleets and carefully detailed improving pursuits for boys and girls, such as making fire using only a pair of sticks. I read them, but the chunky volumes also served as useful building blocks for castles, forts, whatever. I tried *The Water Babies* but found it too much of a refugee from Sunday school. On similar lines – where had it come from? – there was a very nasty thing called the *Chatterbox Annual*. It had, among much other fake Victorian moralising, a story in which an over-bookish child was consumed by an 'actual' bookworm. The illustration scared me but I derided the concept. I took this wretched object to the air-raid shelter and, armed with a box of purloined matches, attempted what I instinctively knew to be the greatest of sins: to burn it. It did not catch properly but my disdain was absolute and the dustbin received the slightly scorched remains. In time I read *Emil and the Detectives* which, with much else that I would come to enjoy, had once been burnt by more professional arsonists, the Nazis.

I read of Sherlock Holmes and Beau Geste, both initially gifts of the radio, on which they were serialised. The former needs no introduction, although I cannot remember who 'my' Holmes and Watson were. (I have looked it up: Carleton Hobbs and Norman Shelley; they did the job from 1952–69.) The latter, with names as rib-nudgingly descriptive as those of a Restoration melodrama – the evil Sergeant Lajaune, the debonair Major Henri de Beaujolais, and of course the glorious Beau himself – first thrilled me via the Home Service. The climactic scene, all the fort dead except for the wicked Lajaune and our hero, corpses lodged in every embrasure, the sworn enemies temporarily allied in firing from successive loopholes to impress the encircling Arabs, retains its thrill. The power of cheap literature, *pace* Noel Coward, who apostrophised cheap music, lingers. And from its pages I learned how to crucify a man on a barracks table with bayonets, and of tying him *en crapaudine*: hands and feet lashed together in the small of the back, the mouth filled with sand. You didn't get that in another favourite read: *Eagle*, although the comic's intrepid Luck of the Legion did manage some pleasing French oaths: '*Nom d'un nom d'un nom d'un sacré cochon noir!*' and '*Sapristi!*' among others. *Eagle* even offered a glance at homegrown slang. Space hero Dan Dare's working-class oppo Digby was wont to mutter 'Lumme!' in stressful situations. I took due note.

And there was Kipling. It is useful to read certain authors before one realises – either through one's own or others' critical diktats – that they should not in fact be read. Kipling floats in and out of fashion. When I encountered him I imagine he was pretty much out, but *Just So Stories* and *The Jungle Book* (another book whose destruction by Disney's Huns was still a future tragedy) were still acceptable. I read most of his opus: short stories, the Barrack Room Ballads, *Captains Courageous*, *Kim* and so on, though *Plain Tales from the Hills* came later. Favourite – perhaps more accessible – was *Puck of Pook's Hill*, didactic, nationalistic, but well enough disguised. It is said that everyone has a great, good place to which they wish to return. If I have one it must be a sunny afternoon in a hotel in Bosham on the south coast, a monster humbug striped black and white and tasting of synthetic bananas close to sticky hand and the knowledge that since I had barely started a newly acquired copy of *Rewards and Fairies*, *Puck*'s sequel, there would be paradise and blissful solitude for at least one more day.

There was also *Stalky and Co.*, Kipling's semi-autobiographical tales of school. Looking back, it's interesting how Kipling set the pattern for the school stories of his era. The priggish Tom Brown shied away from slang and what he used was adult. Stalky & Co. could have turned up at Billy Bunter's Greyfriars with their use of 'my aunt!', 'bags I!', 'bait' (a rage), 'biznai', 'blub' (to cry), 'brew' (a study feast), 'cat' (to vomit), 'cave!' (look out!), 'cram' (a tutor or last-minute pre-examination work), 'dicker' (a dictionary), 'impot' (an imposition, for example punishment of lines), 'jammy' (easy), 'padre' (a chaplain), 'pi-jaw' (an earnest, moralising lecture), 'ripping!', 'rot' (to talk nonsense), 'scrag' (to beat up), 'slack' (lazy), 'sneak' (to tell tales), 'swot' as noun or verb, 'tip' (of a parent to pass over money) and 'wigging' (a telling-off). But the slang in Kipling, as it was in the rest of my reading, was incidental. There were other, deeper pleasures. Every biography of Kipling excoriates one story in particular: 'The Moral Reformers', in which Stalky, M'Turk and Beetle become bullies to the bullies, and subject a pair of 'crammers' pups' to such undisclosed but lovingly evoked tortures as 'brush drill' and 'the torture of the key – which has no key at all'. It was the sweet revenge on evil that I enjoyed. My culture does not turn the other cheek: it plucks out the offending eye. I have always loved 'The Moral Reformers'. Similar pleasures were derived from Saki's perfect tale of the biter quite literally bit: 'Sredni Vashtar', the story of a ten year old child, subjected to the caprices and sadistic cruelty of a tyrannical aunt, who, through the agency of his polecat ferret, achieves revenge. Like

Waugh's celebrated 'bat's squeak of sexuality', the final lines are engraved on my mind: '"Whoever will break it to the poor child? I couldn't for the life of me!" exclaimed a shrill voice. And while they debated the matter among themselves, Conradin made himself another piece of toast.'

Saki's stories turned up on television around 1961, during another period of hotel living – my father had finally escaped the yellowbellies' county town, moved to London's northern outskirts, and we were again looking for a house. This time the hotel was in the gin-and-Jag world of Gerrards Cross (a local golf club, apparently, still banned my people), and Sunday lunchtimes might see the descent of figures from nearby Shepperton, home of the guttering stars of the UK film industry. I am haunted by a single episode: the usual Saki country house, daunting dowagers, epicene young men, a sort of (homo)sexualised Blandings? There is a fire, there is a supposedly valuable picture. The young men rush to its rescue, and are consumed by the flames. The picture turns out to have been fake. I was old enough to appreciate that this was an allegory of the First World War (in which Saki died). Very much of its time. (We would do *Oh What a Lovely War* as a school play not much later.) One problem: I have read Saki and that story is not there.

So by 1961 television had a role, but before that, none but borrowed murmurs. Mine is perhaps the last generation for whom an upbringing without television did not, quite, render one a crank. I have drifted away from it again, for well over a decade now, but this was no moral decision, just boredom. (The last thing I watched, thanks to my younger son's screen, was the coverage of 9/11.) And in the 1950s the decision was in any case not mine. We had a large, bakelite 'steam' radio which required a degree of waiting for valves to heat up and offered a dial glowing with such exotica as 'Hilversum' and 'Droitwich'.

We listened to it as religiously as any television addict. And it too, I realise, was a glorious source of language. *Children's Hour* was unashamedly didactic – 'Uncle Mac', 'David' (the story teller David Davis, though listeners were granted no surname), 'Toytown' – and one duly learnt. (Though not, back then, of 'Auntie's' tolerance of some presenters' paedophilia.) Beyond that, perhaps *Journey into Space* and *Educating Archie*, *Take It From Here* and *Ray's a Laugh* don't really fill the bill, but *Hancock's Half Hour* remains an oft-repeated classic and in time there would be *Round the Horne*, with the peerless Julian and Sandy who brought for my nascent profession a strange but hilarious language of nudges, winks and double entendres. It was called, though nobody could tell me then, 'Polari' and offered such exotica as 'omee-palones', 'riah' (backslang, actually, and for hair), 'trolling', 'naff' (which would return for a moment's glory via Princess Anne) and cries of 'fantabulosa!' How did they get away with it? And why did so many of the uninitiated find it so funny. For once ignorance might qualify as bliss.

Prep school generally did a fair imitation of hell but there were some respites: roles in school plays when one drank wine, or properly cherryade; the weekly distribution of a carefully measured ration of sweets; a woman called Miss Potter who gave us strangely comforting mugs of warm milk, hitherto an anathema, after our weekly bath. Its library, if not heaven, was some form of happy ante-chamber. And if I want to unearth at least some of the roots of a life in slang, then those shelves must provide them. Wodehouse, Sapper, Conan Doyle in his non-Holmes books ('Professor Challenger', 'Brigadier Gerard'), other P. C. Wrens (surely not the source, however, of my francophilia), shelf upon shelf of the best (worst?) of popular literature. There were presumably classics, not to mention the imperialist derring-do of G. A. Henty, but not for me. Wodehouse, like Saki a chronicler of aunts, is of course impeccable, and as regards slang his blithe mixture of the defunct language of the late nineteenth century ('oojah-cum-spiff', 'rannygazoo') with much newer coinages ('hotsy-totsy', 'all over bar the shouting') has provided me with many hundreds of citations. He offered a first taste of one of the necessities of slang lexicography: not only need one find the words and define them, but also, in this deliberately secret language, one needs first to find out what they mean. Wodehouse, it was said around the time I was discovering him, offers the mindset of an educated fifteen year old; my problem was that I was three years younger. As for Sapper, whose entry I would eventually write for the new *DNB*, what a card. Nowhere – perhaps in Wodehouse but never so heartily raffish – had I encountered such a vocabulary. A world of 'cads' and 'bounders', 'flappers' and 'freaks', 'bruisers' and 'loonies', of drinkers of 'gargle' and smokers of *flor de cabbagio*. Not to mention 'Bulldog' Drummond, nemesis of alien Huns, Jerries, Japs, coons, niggers, and of course Jews. Sapper's Jews, like Agatha Christie's Jews and the Jews of nearly every popular writer prior to Auschwitz are de facto bad. It is possible that this was not conscious anti-Semitism as such, merely a given in a world in which P.C. still referred only to a member of the police. Orwell does not mention what such writers sneeringly referred to as 'the chosen people' in his taxonomy of alien stereotypes in 'Boys' Weeklies' (did they ever even turn up in such titles?) but they are of the breed. As my only acknowledged hero Lenny Bruce would put it later: 'A Jew, in the dictionary, is one who is descended from the ancient tribes of Judea . . . but you and I know what a Jew is: One Who Killed Our Lord.'

It was not that I didn't notice Sapper's take on Jews – after all, I knew what I was and had my own yellow star, my Kraft cheese slices, to prove it – but if I should have been affronted,

I wasn't. I was too busy deciphering all that beery bonhomie, a mixture of slangs: of the trenches, of the Edwardian 'johnnie', of the 1920s flapper, of the chirpy Cockney sparrer, even of America, at least when certain villains were concerned. And falling in love with his nemesis, the sinuous, sinful Irma ('deadlier than the male'), though certainly not with his vapid home counties wife Mary. The grown-ups' Sapper, although equally consumed by the young, was John Buchan, another glorious discovery. I would choose *Greenmantle*, with the Lawrentian (T. E. not D. H.) Sandy Arbuthnot and its wholly coincident foretaste of Islamic militancy, as a school prize. Of the writer Richard Usborne's trio of *Clubland Heroes*, his tongue-in-cheek study of Sapper, Buchan and Dornford Yates, I never encountered the latter – perhaps there were too many girls involved for our library's consumption? And when I read him, too late for credulousness but spurred on by Usborne's witty commentary, I was deeply unimpressed. But Buchan, among whose Semites might be 'the whitest Jew since Jesus', was usually reliable. He also introduced a new strand of slang: South African, with its *Peruvians* (who were anything but), *kaffirs*, *smouses* and shouts of *voetsak!*

School omitted Nigel Molesworth from its shelves. It was far too close to the bone. An uncle presented me with the 'compleet' works for passing the eleven-plus It seemed pretty much a documentary as would the film *If* half a dozen years later. When I passed a brass plate bearing the words 'Gabbitas and Thring' I realised that I had not been mistaken.

Was I compiling my first database even then? Mentally, unconsciously, no doubt, but nothing so formal as a list. But whatever else I may recall of that grim potato-girt establishment, I have nothing but fond memories of its library. What my consumption of yesterday's popular potboilers made clear, again subconsciously, was that if you wanted interesting language, you weren't going to get it along the straight and narrow. The good stuff was off down the alleyways, alongside the waterfronts, in the back rooms of addresses whose frontages would in real life scare you far away. These were not worlds I was due to encounter, then or later. The slang lexicographer is by very nature a voyeur. The lexis undoubtedly leans towards pimping and prostitution, crime and imprisonment, violence and cruelty, drugged and drunken debauches, but the lexicographer is neither whore nor thief, thug nor prisoner, addict nor drunkard. Or not professionally. They are linguistic reporters, except that unlike the tabloids' traditional formula they make no excuses and they do not leave. The job is to collect knowledge, to explicate it, and to disseminate the information that emerges. As I say, a voyeur, but ideally an informed one. As Burns remarked of his friend Francis Grose, 'there's a chiel' among ye takin' notes / An' faith, he'll print it'.

But if one can suggest that reading popular potboilers gave me a taste for language that only appears in the circumstances of melodrama, is there not a logical antithesis? Had I been more serious, more earnest, above all more clever, would I have turned to serious books, those that demand intellectual effort? Finding slang, perhaps, but dismissing it as is the usual way. Nothing but a larger scale use of what Walter Benjamin termed the 'waste matter of language', the obscenities. And as such disposable. After all does not the clever child eschew stupid things? A contempt for stupid reading may extend into that for what he or she can easily and logically dismiss as stupid language?

Except that I don't believe that differently skilled – better skilled? – I might never have stumbled upon the thing that has made my professional and possibly even emotional life. Because how could that same bright child, or that bright child with an appreciation for language, fail to see the glories of the words that make up slang? For all the pieties protested by religion and its moralising parasites, there is no hierarchy in slang's lexis. No better nor no best, nor no worst either. Were I to be asked to offer a selection of favourite terms, I would find it hard to amass even the most nugatory list. But were the questioner to ask for those terms I despise, there I would have no problem. I offer *earnest*, *wholesome*, the adjectival use of *family*. But back in the dictionary there are only agglomerations of vowels and consonants. And if, it has now been suggested, the kind of words found in slang have the added effect of rendering nanoseconds of pleasurable stimulation to certain areas of the brain, why would anyone but a fool, the literal idiot savant, resist let alone refuse to appreciate such pleasure?

But then I've always failed in self-denial. I find it hard enough – selfish, irredeemable only child that I remain – to sustain any situation in which the denial is a transitive act, at least with any resignation. Someone else doing it to me. And I am sufficiently cynical to believe that most self-deniers are denying only what they don't anyway want in order, cunningly, to obtain that which they do.

One thing that none of the influential trio of authors could offer takes me back to my roots. Yiddish. Hindsight is dangerous. I have had friends whose childhoods were awash with this Germano-Hebrew dialect; mine was not. My father used a certain amount (and among our few books was a German Shakespeare in pre-war Gothic text) but even for him it was fading. My parents might essay a few sentences: and in a Jewish house *nicht bevor der kinder* substitutes for *pas devant les enfants*. As much as either works. They preferred disappearing behind a closed door. Invisibility was also their policy when arguing:

the image of parental unity was preserved at all costs. They were right, no child ought to witness its parents locked in loathing. But these were moments when I would have preferred not to be alone. My loyal father opted for humour, chanting a chorus of 'Mummy's always right' and urging me to pick up the beat. What Yiddish would term a *bittere gelechte*: a humourless joke. My lexicography, abhorring deception, focusing on revelation, prefers its doors left open. (Nor do I work behind a shut door: there is something threatening there.) For me at least ignorance is never bliss and I shrink from the whispered secret and find my life unravelled by the unanswered email. Meanwhile Yiddish has played its role in slang for centuries. When I came to meet it later I would recognise, if not an old friend, then at least an acquaintance: this is mine. So it is Yiddish, or a single instance thereof, that provides yet another part-answer to my question: why? and offers one small string that can be tugged to straighten out the greater tangle.

If, as I have suggested, Lenny Bruce attains heroic status it was not only for his wit, but also for his language, blending black, hipster slang with such coarse Yiddishisms as *fresser* (a fellatrix), *schtup* (to fuck) and *nafka*. This last, I could say, changed my life. If there was a moment when I realised that slang was not the province of a priesthood, that however arcane some of it might be, I too could put in my ten penn'orth, it was encountering Eric Partridge's etymology for *nafka*, as found in his *Dictionary of Slang and Unconventional English*, around 1970. The word, and here the old boy was spot on, means whore. No arguments there. The problem is that as opposed to Partridge's suggested origin: the fusion of *nau*ghty and *gi*rl, *nafka* is really very simple: it is a Yiddish word and it is a perfect synonym. We can presume that it started life in the East End Jewish community, and filtered through to the wider world. I had heard *nafka*, and I knew the whys, the wherefores and the fact that no elisions were required.

I shall resist public school. I did then. A middle ranking institution in the Midlands, chosen by my parents over grander establishments because it was avowedly 'non-denominational' and such other schools as Westminster, with its back door into the Abbey itself, were too 'churchy'. (Compensating, I sent my own sons to Westminster. Only half-Jews and properly atheistic, I assume they worked out their own take on religion. I certainly didn't sense any proselytising and my younger son, walking one afternoon between classes, was prayed over in the street by a pair of roller-skating evangelists.) But there was a vast red chapel of Victorian gothic bricks (as was the main school building itself; it burned down after my time – arson apparently – but a facsimile soon emerged) and all the rites and ritual that accrued to yet another of those former grammar schools that, mid-nineteenth century, had upmarketed itself to provide administrators for the burgeoning empire. I substituted the local deli's black bread and olives for the Kraft cheese slices. I played the role of rebel, thinking it important then, coming in time to realise that it was a long-accepted position, probably as sanctified as that of captain of cricket. I duly earned my place at Oxford, and the school, for a small outlay of tolerance, gained what it had wanted: another academic honour to parade before parents still wondering about the fees.

There were no 'young adult' titles then and I would surely have disdained them had this condescending publishers' invention existed. I also disdained my youthful potboilers (bar Wodehouse, of course) and was keen to move into wider worlds. As adolescence passed there was also rock 'n' roll (Buddy Holly, Eddie Cochran, the Everly Brothers and Elvis had infiltrated prep school but this was serious: Beatles, Dylan, The Who, the Rolling Stones, the Velvet Underground, the Airplane, the Dead and the rest of the Sixties cast list), and an ever optimistic pursuit of members of the town's many girls' schools. This one 'did it', her adventures were recounted. One close friend was notably successful. Usually I played the role of the plain friend – a job opportunity on offer to boys as well as girls. I wrote letters to one girl, and we enjoyed a correspondence, mine composed on a battered typewriter, hers in that rounded schoolgirl hand. It went no further though she borrowed a handkerchief once and I kept it unwashed and deeply perfumed for weeks. One day someone bought some porn – a book – and I read it aloud on the riverbank to my friends as they fished and we all ogled the courting couples writhing enviably. Softer core was *The Passion Flower Hotel*, as cockteasingly frustrating as its heroines. Its male author took a female pseudonym; for the slang aficionado his real name 'Roger Longrigg' sounds even less feasible.*

Equally important were post-school afternoons spent in the room of another intimate, a day-boy and a massively talented graphic designer in the making. He covered the school art room with a vast blow-up of a braided naval arm, then the image that advertised Rothmans King-Size cigarettes, while at home he stockpiled Sunday colour supplements and decorated his walls with photos in prototype clip frames. We smoked Disques Bleus, recited lines from *Beyond the Fringe*, sang along with The Who's

* More recently I have had the same problem with Bruce Rodgers, author of the gay slang dictionary, *The Queens' Vernacular*. 'Bruce' being once filed as a 'typical' gay name and 'Rodgers' seemingly playing on 'roger', the penis and used as such in Urqhart's 1653 translation of Rabelais, and which, as a verb, means 'to fuck'. Yet I am assured that all is coincidence and Mr Rodgers' name is just that.

B-sides ('Daddy Rolling Stone'), and hoped we died before we got old. We read *Private Eye*, still a novelty, and sneaked his mother's gin and tonic.

Back at the bookshop where we had our school accounts I crammed my choice of books between authorised textbooks and the master's necessary signature. Waugh, Huxley and Keith Waterhouse ('What are Poles doing in Russia?' 'Holding up the telegraph wires.' Once I knew *Billy Liar* by heart). I noticed C. S. Lewis' *Screwtape Letters* and was pleased to see that my instincts about Narnia had been correct. I discovered a translated Brecht and wrote an embarrassingly plagiaristic prize essay (it failed to win) in his honour. I was delighted to realise that a hitherto incomprehensible but strangely fascinating television play – we had moved nearer London and had succumbed, supposedly to watch *That Was The Week That Was* – turned out to be *The Caucasian Chalk Circle*. A master played me a scratchy 78 of the original performance of 'Mackie Messer' – Mack the Knife as rendered popular and thus blunted by such as Bobby Darin and Tony Bennett. I made regular pilgrimages to the old Foyles Paperback shop and in time to Better Books, on the other side of Charing Cross Road. I was no richer than the next person and took hours over my choices – Norman Mailer's *Advertisements for Myself*, Martin Meyer's *Madison Avenue USA* were, I recall, the first fruits of such trips. In Better Books I found a Kerouac, but not *On the Road*, just some poems. I was disappointed.

I essayed school journalism; first a house magazine, laboriously typed out on the waxy 'paper' that one needed for the Roneo machine; then a 'proper' magazine, in which I was forbidden to use the punning headline 'Phallusy' (and what, I wonder now, did the piece's text proclaim?). The latter required going to a real print shop. It seemed very romantic. One edition fell foul of the authorities, welcome to censorship. So too did my 'long' hair (lovingly combed forward à la John Lennon). In the official school mag, all rugby matches and *valete*, I wrote on *Lord of the Flies*: 'I am Piggy', irony quite unintended. Hoping to have me inside the tent pissing out, I was offered, in the time-honoured English way, my own authority and its concomitant blue tie (the masses wore black, supposedly still mourning Queen Victoria); enormously pleased with my gesture, I turned it down. Instead I worked in the hope of Oxford, kept vodka behind my study's books (no telltale breath, the ads promised) and rolled into lunch stoned on amyl nitrate. I had encountered it in a book of wild, drug-crazed beatniks, and my study mate, the stud and scientist, had announced 'I can make that', coming back one day with a bottleful. We soaked our handkerchiefs and breathed deep. It was with him I visited my first pub, in the town's poorest area, already peopled by Asian immigrants. Weaving our way home we pissed out our half-pints on the darkened First XV pitch. Oxford said yes to me, but not to him. He visited once, bearing tabs of LSD, but life took him north and me south and that, but for a few more meetings – partners, children, houses – was that.

I have never joined. Perhaps I am incapable of that degree of self-immersion. Perhaps it was reading *Nineteen Eighty-Four* at an impressionable age or noting – nothing very smart there – that life en masse, typically school, was also unrewarding, even unpleasant. I find it hard to use the first person plural in all but the most neutral circumstances. This is nothing for pride, but neither shame. I have never called a sports team 'we', let alone a country, and love Stalin's dismissal of Jews as 'rootless cosmopolitans', even if Christopher Hitchens noted that one cannot claim cosmopolitanism if you don't know where you came from in the first place. In any case, for all that I live between two cities, I am not cosmopolitan and am all too fearfully rooted. I'm simply not sure where. (And my 'cosmopolitan' is only an Edward Gorey wicked uncle, all full-length astrakhan coat and curling moustachios.) I simply lack that bonding gene. I am, as I perceive myself when working, a soloist.

That Jew Thing

I am at home in English, but not in England.

Tony Judt

Slang needs the city, as do I. I no longer much like London but I remain besotted with the archetype of the city and its concrete underpinning, the street. I visit but ultimately shy from Chiantishire, however beautiful, and bypass the Dordogne, where the butcher and baker have long since been expelled and their shops colonised by estate agents whose anglophone names pun on 'frog'. The fantasy, of course, is that Jews = cities and fuck the fiddler and his wretched roof, though read Isaac Bashevis Singer's tales of the *shtetl* and that one starts to crumble. Nothing underlines my self-perception as much as my inability – almost all-encompassing – to give names to nature. For many years I believed that Yiddish boasted but two words for flowers, one for roses, to be given to one's mother, and 'flowers' would do for the rest. Learning eventually that this was wrong I remain disappointed. On the other hand – draw such lessons from this as you may – there is nothing like Yiddish for words that mean fool. The Inuit do not, popular belief notwithstanding, have an especially wide-ranging list of synonyms for snow. But Yiddish undoubtedly knows a fool, and the gradations thereof: *shlub*, *shloomp*, *shmo*, *shlemiel*, *schlimazel*, *schmendrick* . . . Not to mention the ones that also mean penis: *putz, shmuck, schmeckel* and *yutz*.

When they left the Russian pale and the Polish hinterland they gravitated to London, to Paris, to Amsterdam and New York (assuming no one had conned them off the boat at, say, Cardiff and if so maybe they were truly more like peasants than I wish to believe). There are anomalies, but like all immigrants the Jews went where the work or the trade was. The world's greatest slang bibliophile may have grown up in a rabbinical home in Ohio but she has long since been safely ensconced in the West Village. Ghettoes, starting with that of Venice, are not established in sylvan glades. Those would be reserved for extermination camps.

I have no past. I would like one but I cannot conjure one up and thus must start not at an ancestral beginning but merely at my own. I failed to ask the right questions of others when younger. Now there are no others to ask. Or not of my kin. My tragedy, or at least my regret, is that my families got off the boat too early, that they stopped in England and failed to continue on to New York City. I crave the Lower East Side. I want to see my grandfather on Delancey Street in some sepia photo *c.*1900: pushcart, *tallit* and *yarmulke* maybe, or, better still, a well-cut if cheaply purchased suit, a pushy young man on the way up and out. Not Whitechapel – not that mine even stayed there – which lay in a country that was less inclined to allow Jews, however assimilated (and I am), the kind of success that NYC extended to them. The cure for that, of course, being do-it-yourself.

As far as I know there are none of my people among those who hunt down slang. Or not among the canonical listing. Nor do there seem to be many who spring to mind in any form of English-language lexicography, though Marghanita Laski, born to a family of Jewish intellectuals, contributed more citations to *OED2* than any contemporary. (My wife, who continues to labour mightily in the unbounded fields of slang, may well have surpassed her.) Its editor, Robert Burchfield, called Laski the 'lexicographical irregular supreme'. (Burchfield came from New Zealand which seems to be far more fruitful: Eric Partridge, Australia's Sydney Baker and Oxford University Press's Dan Davin originated there.) Although now I think again the names start jumping out, though only one is a hands-on, and indeed distinguished, dictionary man and slang is not his current preoccupation. We are better at conjuring it up.

Yet I cannot escape the belief that my own background, my own rearing, is deeply interwoven with my choice of job. The Jew, in my generalisation – for I am as locked into stereotypes as the most benighted anti-Semite – comes in two flavours: the pedlar and the Talmudic scholar. Assuming they transcend such beginnings, the pedlar tends to move on to more sophisticated and more profitable commodities; the Talmudic scholar, conversely, tends to dump the religion for non-denominational scholarship. The first is beyond me. I inherited money, a lot of money, once. I knew, agonised even, that far from multiply this unforeseen *mitzvah*, I would (may that God in whom I do not believe forgive me) merely spend it. So, shamefully bereft of practical skills, I set myself among the second group. I can live without the wonder rabbis, I lack the spiritual obsessions of the Orthodox and Hasidim, though I quite like the beaver hats or fedoras and definitely go for the long, somewhat nineteenth-century frock coats – Shylock's Jewish gabardine – that go with the *frum* communities of Brownsville and Stamford Hill. But the poring over texts, the analysis of words, the disputes over meanings; oh yes, I can definitely go there.

I was the solo Jew at prep school and one of maybe three – all older and, being seniors, uninterested – at secondary school. I cannot, quite honestly, say that it ever caused me the slightest angst. Quite the opposite though I don't recall pondering it very much. I don't know whether my parents delivered themselves of some kind of sensible advice. If so I do not recall it either. What I recall mainly is that it was only noticeable on two levels: culinary and what assonance would like to call cultural, but was, in fact, religious. I didn't eat pork products and I didn't do prayers (I didn't eat shellfish either but I don't believe you got much of that in British schools of the 1950s). I have dealt with the former already. I saw the latter as a relief. Getting out of things. I knew, from my own annual treks to the synagogue that religion was of its nature boring. Mind-numbingly dull. The story was unexciting, the deity unlikely, and for His alleged Son, the very word Jesus was rivalled only by that of Hitler as a term of menace.* You simply had to look at his pictures: that mournful expression, that blond hair, and, on the very rare occasions on which for whatever reason – maybe a concert or somesuch – we were dragged by coach from school to a church, those bloodied wounds and crown of thorns. Terrifying. Hel-lo? Am I missing something here? Isn't there a second commandment somewhere: Thou Shalt Not Make Graven Images. And the crucifix. I wouldn't claim the idea as my own, but one has to ask: worshipping an image of torture?

So, as the only Jew I got to miss all that. Better still, I didn't have to undergo whatever might have been the equivalent as expounded and imposed by my own lot. Or not as often as my friends seemed to do. At the assembly which started the school day they muttered the Lord's Prayer while you merely bowed your

* Unsurprisingly, Jesus has a variety of Yiddish nicknames, primarily *Yoshke Pandra*, the first part of which combines a diminutive *–ke* and approximates to 'Little Joe' and the second takes on the heretical belief that far from Christ being the son of god, Christ's father was actually a Roman soldier named *Pantera* ('panther'). This in turn can become *Yoshke Pandrek*, wherein part two translates as 'King of Shit'.

head. You knew it – how could you not – but it was nothing of yours. Much the same during hymns – you didn't know them and didn't wish to – and you were relieved when they petered out into silence. Sundays had them trekking to the chapel, an example of that architectural subset: public school gothic. You missed that too, and sat in the boarding house reading the Sunday papers. There were RE lessons – religious education – no probs: down to the library to read, or finished unattended prep. I delved occasionally into old school magazines, especially those of what the school memorial hall still termed the 'Great' War. The transmutation of this year's captain of cricket into a youthful corpse, sometimes it seemed within a matter of mere months, was saddening. Especially to one who was still of an age that in different circumstances might have been eligible, for the death if not the sporting glory. Today's revisionist historians rewrite the clash as being somehow valuable. My memories of those magazines which, for all their jingoistic patriotism retailed in their lists the baldest of facts, make it hard for me to revise my own feelings.

I did not manage, however, to miss out on all religion. There was the one into which I had been born to contend with. Of my parents I think my father might have been more of a believer, my mother the shriller Zionist, though neither shoved it down my throat and observances really were minimal. That said we were technically Orthodox, which should not be confused with the exotic gentry in various combinations of fur hats, silk-faced jackets and curling sidelocks. Not to mention wives with wigs – the Jewish hijab and no more demanded by the Bible than is the Muslim covering in the Q'ran – and large families in larger cars. These are ultra-Orthodox of various hues, live in a seriously fundamentalist world, and are as dismissive of Israel as the most dedicated jihadist – so show me when the Messiah arrived? Promised Land? Hah! On our level Orthodox simply meant that the synagogue to which one went, when one did, was affiliated to a traditional brand of Judaism. We were not Reform, a wishy-washy version of the faith where rituals and prayers, if not actually in English, were seriously attenuated. Nor were we what was then termed Conservative, known today as Masorti, which, far from being fundamentalist, is based in modern intellectual attitudes that wish to conserve rather than reform the religion, or at least it is in the UK; in America it is barely Judaism at all. But all that was irrelevant: if we were anything we were old school and I have yet to slap down my pounds, or indeed euros, for a loin of pork or even, though here I am almost certainly foolish, a slice of Parma ham. Salami, of course, is quite a different ballgame; and as for mussels and oysters . . .

Years later, in one of many rows, your mother derides you as a 'food Jew'. And she is right. If you experienced the ritualistic side of religion it was usually as boredom. So there was Friday night, the start of the Sabbath, at least until I went to boarding school, but that was fun. Good food and minimal religiosity. There were a few festivals: Passover (commemorative of the Exodus from Egypt, a spring festival and thus around Easter), Rosh Hashanah (an autumn festival, the New Year), Hanukkah (which turned up around Christmas-time), but they were fun too and at the last one even received presents, even if in your house one had to wait seven nights of brief but still frustrating prayers before you got there. Yom Kippur, the Day of Atonement, was less amusing. It is the year's great fast. (There are others such as Fast of the Firstborn, which would mean me too, there being no other born in my house but we didn't do them.) Yom Kippur was bad enough. I didn't mind the hunger. I decided to get through the whole day without food when I was ten – you didn't actually have to do it until you were thirteen and officially 'a man' – and once started you couldn't look back. But the boredom. The absolute unredeemed, life-sapping boredom. You look at the *machzor*, the prayer book. It is very big: has to be, there's a day to be disposed of. There had been a smaller, companion volume to wade through on the night before, offering the evening service that follows your final meal for 24 hours. You look at the Hebrew, which you can read, but not understand beyond a few words. Across the page – on the left, since Hebrew reads from right to left and thus takes pride of place on the right-hand pages – there is a translation. No laughs there. Definitely no laughs. How can a book be so dull? The *shul* (synagogue) is full. You cannot understand the constant sotto voce chatter; isn't prayer supposed to be quiet? You know nothing of churches – they supposedly give your mother a headache and are never entered even as tourists – but you can't miss the great cathedral on its hill, and it, you sense, must be quite sepulchral. You are wearing your *yarmulke*, a skullcap, and a *tallit*, a prayer shawl. The scrolls of the law, the Torah, are ritually processed by men who, bizarrely, are wearing gymshoes. You follow your father, pressing a corner of the shawl against the silken cover, then kiss it. Words matter. Especially when holy. You drop a prayer book and on picking it up you kiss that too. I'm sorry, words, forgive me. I'm kissing you better.

Consciously or not, you see this and absorb its lesson: words, seemingly all words, matter. They are, after all, what makes books. Meanwhile we are assimilated into a sports-loving society and your father, thinking perhaps of muscular Zionists and their blooming desert, has occasionally attempted to interest you in the limited team of Jewish sportsmen: you couldn't care less. These are not your role models. Compton, May, Miller, Lindwall – the names you hear on *Test Match Special* have no –bergs or –steins. Not that such omissions often cross your mind. You will never be one for heroes. But if identification's required, television, which you do not have, but which you watch at a friend's, is more rewarding, movie credits in particular: Goldwyn, Segal, Cohen – these are your people.

So. Let us atone. People coming and going. Jewish mothers and Jewish mothers-in-waiting upstairs in a gallery; you can see yours, gazing down. Jewish men and mini-men down here; you are next to your father. It is hot. (One year your father faints. Someone comes over with smelling salts. He recovers. It is frightening and disturbing. It is also the first sign of the diabetes that he will have for the last third of his life.) Since we didn't live anywhere near a Jewish community we know nobody. Any visit to the synagogue required an hour-long drive before and after. The cathedral city in which we lived had dealt with its Jews in the thirteenth century. The congregation, all of whom seem to know each other, move in and out of the *shul*. There are important moments and everyone is there for them; there are also longueurs, many, many longueurs and at those moments there are drifts to the outdoors for cigarettes. Children chatter. You go out too, but you stand alone. Who do you know? School is a world where, however silently, you are always conscious of your difference; here, where you ought not to need it, you choose to assume the alien's role. You look at your watch. If you'd heard of Einstein you might muse on the elasticity of time. You do not. You know only life-destroying, soul-crushing boredom. I am here to acknowledge my sins: fine, let me confess. Let me purge. Let me do penance. Let me be punished. And then let me go. But there is no confession, nor is there penance: you are no Catholic. Nor is there a punishment, not of the mighty, swift sword variety. No angry deity reaching forth to snuff out the wicked. No. The punishment is more . . . subtle. The punishment is slow, the punishment is sure. The punishment is simply being here.

In time, at the far end of yet another of those hour-long drives, you are bar mitzvah, the second of those cultural bookends meted out to Jewish males of which the first had been circumcision. You have learned your 'portion' – the weekly section of the Torah that is ritually chanted by the neophtye 'Jewish man' as his initiation into adulthood – on a makeshift tape recorder at prep school while your peers are off at chapel. At least you only have to do it once; the rest learn something called the collect every week. The headmaster lends you his study: his books include T. S. Eliot's *Macavity* verses. Strange – you know nothing of Eliot other than that he is in some way 'important' though why is another mystery, and certainly nothing of his anti-Semitism – but you are surprised to find him author of what you assume are children's rhymes. On the day you do your stuff. The rabbi places an arm around you, his robes smell of stale tobacco and you yearn for release. He intones some formula: but you are a man today – and you can sniff out the banal. Afterwards there is a lunch, dozens of unknowns who give you gifts – supposed appurtenances of manhood such as silver-backed hairbrushes and pigskin briefcases – that you will never need. There are no books. Your parents – can you in some aberrant moment have actually requested such a thing? – give you golf clubs. (In a few years they provide a passport to get off rugby and gain access to the club's bar.) Later you are sent to bed while your mother dances the twist downstairs. You wake to weeping: a cousin on whom you have been dumped is reading American Jewry's current best-selling weepie *Exodus*. You write forty-nine thank you letters and misspell 'sincerily' in every one. You write forty-nine more. A photo arrives. The traditional line-up: your father, your mother and in the centre you. The negative is returned and recut. It reappears and the trio has been rearranged: your father to one side, you to the other and now, the central focus is your mother.

The Jew Thing. Along with only childhood, it set me up, or so I believe, for what I do. Not so much that slang plays the Jew role – though it can be shoehorned into rebellious and/or victim terminology (or in Zionist terms it is the hard-ass Jabotinsky and the Stern gang: no deserts blooming here, thank you) – but simply the early embrace of solitude. Not, however, of boredom. I hate boredom, my threshold so low that I see it as a pit beneath me, but then slang offers only delight. At least to me. The *OED* has a seventy-strong team, boosted by consultants and external readers, but slang collection has always been a solo gig. There might occasionally be pairs – Barrère and Leland, Farmer and Henley, Wentworth and Flexner, but even there the heavy lifting usually turns out to have been done by one and the other simply chipped in.

Thus the Jewish influence in my profession of choice. I yearn to think at length. To take time, to slap down that jerking knee. I ponder the production of massy periods, of multi-claused juggernauts crushing quibblers and rolling towards sonorous, unarguable conclusions. What I do is other. Because like Art Spiegelman's 'pale, marginal' and ultimately fearful Jew I lack the luxury of slow thinking. Because the priest is always whipping up the Easter congregation, the Cossacks always riding in our direction, the vodka-swigging peasants sharpening their scythes, the Nazis aligning their rows of huts and the barbed wire that surrounds them. To ponder in such circumstances is foolish and dangerous. It is simpler to write definitions than lengthy sentences. The brief summation is more prudent than the worked-over paragraph. I hear my friends laugh and they are right. But don't tell me that's not how I think.

An only child, I retain a certain social claustrophobia. Or at least the ability to spend time alone. Of many whinges, that of loneliness is not among them. 'Community' is another weasel word for me. 'Joining in'. Perhaps that helps with the job. Even the *OED*'s dedicated specialists are forbidden, or at least politely requested not to converse other than in purpose built glass boxes. Slang is the province of the soloist. I am well suited.

Born but not wholly bred, I have no great wish to be English and I cherish the thought that the feeling may be mutual. Englishness to me always seems to require a devotion to mud and trees, not to mention animals – reared, ridden, slaughtered – that I cannot muster. My familiar is the rat. On the other hand I am not Woody Allen, turned orthodox at lunch in *Annie Hall* with Diane Keaton's WASP family. As for echt Jewishness, I want to steal from Kafka who complained 'I have scarcely anything in common with myself. What do I have in common with the Jews?' If I cannot become English any more than, in Paris, I can become French, then neither do I know how to become a Jew. Genetics, were I to check, might tell me that I have the requisite chromosomes and I assume the unknown past contains the usual number of rabbis. I embody the whole 'people of the book' thing. As for religion I echo Jonathan Miller's punning lexical joke: 'not a Jew but Jew-ish'. To the Orthodox I am a Jew only by absence, of those few centimetres of infant flesh that I, and they, are ordained to lack.

My families left the countries of their origin but I wonder if I have yet to truly arrive in the one in which I was born. Like the late Tony Judt I delight in the language but have problems with the country of its origin. That England that I both love and hate, pursue and flee, and can never have nor ever do without. And compensate with its language or at least a vulgar, improper, contrary subset thereof. I have come to live there part-time only, but perversely have chosen as an alternative France, which, as I am often reminded, is far more poisonously – or at least openly – anti-Semitic than the UK. No matter, we must aim even half-heartedly at rootless cosmopolitanism. I am happy with this, proud even, but weary at times at my feeling of exclusion, however self-fantasised it may be. My friends, I assume, see me as wholly assimilated. I do not. I play the game and wonder at that sentence which for Jews can only ever be a question: who will hide me when the . . . come, and reach no happy conclusions. At the same time I revel in having taken a part of their language – the most despised part, language's equivalent of soul food, that confection of parts that none but the very poor would eat – and made it something of value, but fear that they don't care about such craftsmanship. Perhaps to cherish a marginal language you must be yourself marginal.

Words Fail Me

> *Dummy*: A cant phrase for a stupid fellow; a man who has not a word to say for himself. The family of the dummies is very numerous.
>
> Pierce Egan, *Life in London* (1821)

At this point, a little professional candour. I have interviewed for and edited one book, and researched and narrated another, heavily indebted to those interviews, on what has become known as the Sixties. The one assembled between 1986–8, the second written between 1996–8. The first is a collection of interlocking interviews, the second a simple non-fiction narrative. (I did not especially wish to write the second, but did so anyway. Perhaps karma took a hand, as some might have said back then, when, pursued by mediocrity and its ally malice, the book encountered the law of libel and lasted but 48 hours in the shops. A gelded paperback appeared later; I can't say it really lost anything by the excisions.) I also experienced a degree of the period hands-on, from amidst the collection of quasi-news publications known as the 'underground press'. The long-term effect of this is not so much the end of memory, but its confusion. Pondering any event, I immediately wonder: was that me, was it someone else, was it an interview, was it in a book? Did it even happen? I would have believed that I would never experience such confusions. I would have been wrong.

Writing the necessary explication for my dictionaries, I have defined slang as a 'counter-language'. And that use of 'counter' stems directly from one of the social subsets of the Sixties, at least in Western countries – the 'counter-culture'. Otherwise known as 'alternative society' or, epitomising the self-aggrandising fantasies that underpinned the whole fantastical era, the 'underground'. My experiences are summed up in the introduction to my first book and my opinions expanded through the text of the second. I have no interest in theorising about it again. Merely to say that pretty much everything you've heard, especially as filtered through the media, is bullshit. Of course the drugs were fun (although I found LSD a little over-enthusiastic a player at times), and the clothes had a certain clownish charm (I still mourn a particular grey velvet suit: just £17.10.0 from Carnaby Street) and above all the music had its moments, but you can assay them yourself. And for those of us – a far smaller number than myth might suggest – who made our way to the playground it was on the whole enormously enjoyable. For the rest, it's not a matter that, to evoke that tired remark, 'if you remember the Sixties you weren't really there'. Bollocks. If you remember the Sixties, please keep it to yourself.

Except I can't. But I won't theorise. Or not too much.

The Sixties, as I have suggested in one of those books, probably began in the Forties, around the time of my birth, and undoubtedly drew to a close in the Seventies, just about in time for the arrival of our eldest son. They began among the Beats and ended with Punk. A succession of what we were not yet calling youth cults (although 'youth culture' is first recorded for 1958). Looked at from a distance the whole thing resembles just one more way station on the long trek known as 'bohemia', that endless caravan of the alienated, the angry, the wilfully disenfranchised, the egregiously creative – all of whom most often flourish among the young. The word came from Central Europe's Bohemia, home to the gypsies; thus bohemians were 'the gypsies of society', states the *OED*. The Romantics – Shelley and Co. – seem to have set the concept in motion. It continues. Forget the details: texts, polemics, clothes, faces. The ephemeral versions of the great underlying triumvirate of sex, drugs and rock 'n' roll. The writer Nik Cohn, not yet the disco hagiographer (and, it transpires, creative fabulist) of *Saturday Night Fever*, but still the best of the early rock and roll writers, summed it up in his rock chronicle *Awopbopaloobop Alopbamboom* back in 1969: 'Generation to generation, nothing changes in Bohemia.' And added, 'The heroes shift, that's all.'

Slang has no heroes, other than those set up merely to be thrown down. It is, at least in part, the language of Bohemia. Had Cohn wished to take on hippie speech as well as what the contemporary rock business termed 'psychedelia', 'neither does the slang'. A little far-fetched. There is not much slang in Shelley, though Byron, a boxing fan, has bits and bobs such as his own coinages, 'fulke' for fuck and 'drapery miss': 'a pretty, a high-born, a fashionable young female, well-instructed by her friends, and furnished by her milliner with a wardrobe upon credit, to be repaid, when *married*, by her *husband*' (a figure not that distant from contemporary prostitution's 'dress lodger', working in finery hired out by her landlady/bawd). However, if one reins in the wider chronology to start with the 1940s' kick-off date as I suggest for 'the Sixties', then there is some truth.

It is, of course, about being black. American black. It has been about being black since New York college boy Jack Kerouac and his pals began their romancing on and of the road (a synonym for the 'real' or at least less rule-bound world and a precursor of the 'street'; more recently, users of Multicultural London English (MLE), the current form of London youth slang, seem to be reintroducing 'road'). Back to Norman Mailer and his 'white negro'. The hipster, who was cool, and latterly the hippie, a term that was originally used by musicians to delineate those who were anything but. The beat and his mass-marketed successor the beatnik, another figure of fun, though as ever, not to themselves. To jazz. Anthems of doomed youth. To Charlie Parker who embodied the whole vision of the musician as doomed, nihilistic and most importantly drug-addicted rebel. Drugs as rebellion. Irresistible. Thus to Lenny Bruce who ticked all the boxes and seems like a white negro if ever there was one. And on to the counter-culture and all that has followed.

1969. Big gig. Two months out of university and I am interviewing the great cultural commentator – was he wearing the totemic white suit? He took a hit on the joint but despite having just published a best-selling story of LSD, claimed that nothing stronger had tickled his frontal lobes. Britain, he states, has no power, no importance. No relevance. It has but one future: it will become 'a museum of style'. In a way it already was. The counter-culture, amidst which I would find myself, was always pretty ersatz by US standards. The dog that didn't bark: Vietnam, or the lack of it. 'Hell! No! we won't go!' But, dear boy, no one's *asking* you to. If the first anti-war demonstration in Grosvenor Square in March '68 shocked both police and protestors with its vehemence and the violence it elicited, it didn't suggest to anyone, as had Paris during its May *évènements*, that a government might tumble. That a police horse or two had done so was far more productive of British emotion. And come October that year, when both sides were back on the streets, hyped to the gills with six months' posturing, how did it end? They all sang 'Auld Lang Syne'. Our leaders were not assassinated; fortunately for them they weren't important enough. What we did well was the clothes. And of course the music.

What was also ersatz, lexicographically speaking, was our slang. We had a vague idea that if we dug down deep enough the music would find its roots in black America, even if that didn't quite extend to the first exemplar of what was christened the 'English invasion': Herman's Hermits mockney rendering of 'I'm Henery the Eighth I Am'. But what we didn't realise was that this was also the case when it came to those much parodied staples of hippie communication: 'bag', 'groovy', 'thing', 'vibes', 'out of sight', 'something else' and the rest. They had all been here before. The all-purpose 'heavy' could already be found in the 1920s, but really came on strong three decades later. It would become the *echt*-hippie term, a general intensifier that could refer to bad or good, people or drugs, places or things, each use varying as to context and each nuance perfectly understood – to those who understand. The self-referential 'freak', in slang's enduring tradition of taking the mainstream 'bad' and re-rendering it as oppositional 'good', had been plucked from standard use where it had referred, *inter alia*, to the bizarre end of the circus midway (notably the chicken- or snake-consuming 'geek', a use that long predated his keyboard pounding descendants);* but that too had pre-existed in black use where it referred to any woman considered, at least in male terms, to be sexually OTT.

Even 'hippie,' in its jazz-era origin, meant someone who was faking it; some poor plastic saddo who simply wasn't hip. That

* For those who appreciate such things, the 'geek' derived from older dialact 'geck', a fool; modern use was popularised by the notoriety of one Wagner, of Charleston, West Virginia, who had a celebrated touring snake-eating act: his ballyhoo ran in part, 'Come and see Esau / Sitting on a see-saw / Eatin' 'em raw!' The showbiz chronicle *Variety* noted his still novel act on 8 September 1922: 'The old and reliable snake charmer retired to make room for the snake eater, and weird creatures appeared in dens filled with small reptiles, outside of which huge banners proclaimed the fact that "Bosco" or "Esau" "eats 'em alive".'

sneering '–pie' diminutive. The West Coast newspaper columnist Herb Caen had done the same thing when in 1958 he attached '–nik', a nice little Yiddishism (though Caen claimed it had come from the recently launched Russian space probe Sputnik), onto 'beat' and set a thousand bongos beating. 'Cool' was something one desired, but again, it was a black jazz discard. Or was it: cool had meant cold-blooded and dispassionate in the eighteenth century, when it was also found widely to mean relaxed, calm and self-contained. Around 1890 Eton schoolboys talked of 'cool fishes', meaning their cocky, self-possessed peers. ('Fish', used in slang and usually linked unflatteringly to the female, had meant a person since the mid-century.) All of which are strains of the greater, modern use. Best link it to the generally accepted spur: the 'cool jazz' era of Charlie Parker. Today, of course, you can buy it in your local mall.

And it really didn't run to tie-dyes, beads and bells. The reality, words-wise, was that which had already underpinned hippie's predecessor, beatnik: a wholesale adoption of a slightly passé black culture. It wasn't true of mods and rockers, both stalwart British working-class movements – even if the one yearned for Italian suits and the other for Hells Angels colours. But it was the case for the mainly middle-class counter-culture, the 'alternative society', or, least felicitous of all self-descriptions, the 'underground'. A very long way from a world where there really were undergrounds whose leaders had much better things to do than 'manipulate the media' (for which read 'get oneself on the telly').

I refused to classify myself as a hippie then and retrospect does not soften my resistance, though it's as good a shortcut as any. Nuances tend not to survive histories of popular culture and the Sixties has been set in erroneous stone long since. I left Oxford in summer 1969 and was already looking for jobs. Would I cut my hair? No. Would I go outside London? No. No future in the Thomson Organization, then. I wrote to an ad agency: silence until they suddenly summoned me to their achingly trendy offices one Saturday morning. 'No, we don't actually have a job, but we'll bear you in mind.' I was unimpressed too. I auditioned for the gossip column at the London *Evening Standard* (the Kray brothers had just gone down for a thirty year stretch apiece and I carefully mugged up the day's paper): the editor was charming, but there was no job for me. I failed to achieve a traineeship with the BBC, though a year later I played the hippie role for a friend who did get the job, intoning pro-drug mantras for his Uher. I didn't get a job then, I have never had one since. My inability then and ever after to confect the correct tone for that page of the application whereon you have to justify your desire for the appointment has probably played the single greatest role in setting me on a solo career. I mean, what exactly do you fail to understand about the simple and, for Christ's sake, undeniably honest answer: 'because I want the job'? And might I also vouchsafe that other piece of simple honesty: 'because I need the money.'

No matter. I had always admired Charles Foster Kane's justification for investing in the New York *Enquirer*: 'I think it would be fun to run a newspaper.' Which was the direction I duly took. But not on Fleet Street. And certainly not running one. The nearest to that was an aborted interview with the *Sunday Times*' 'Atticus' column. In its pre-Murdoch prime the *Sunday Times* had long since replaced the *Observer* as the chattering classes' heavy Sunday of choice. I was in awe. Reception phoned upstairs to seek out my interviewer. Silence. His PA disclaimed any knowledge of my existence. The receptionist, I could see, was starting to view me as someone who wrote in green ink. I waited a little longer. The receptionist added lined paper to the green ink. I shrugged. I sighed. I left. And thus do we reach life's great forks. Had I waited . . . Later it turned out that the PA was a temp, that my interviewer, a delightful man for whom I did in time do the odd summer relief, kept such appointments in his head, and that he had intended to offer me a job. But by then I was a couple of miles further west, ensconced in Cool HQ, the West End office of *Rolling Stone* UK, whence I had sent a couple of reviews on spec a few weeks earlier. The future beckoned, passed me a joint and promised to pay £20 a week. OK, it was a job, but certainly not as the world knew it. And I am still awaiting my pay. The man who took the 'Atticus' job went on to become a star war correspondent. He was killed on assignment twenty years later.

The underground press was what we called ourselves, and I was thus an 'underground journalist'. Sure. The Václav Havel of Hanover Square, W1, which was where we were, catty-corner from *Vogue*. Over the next five years I worked my way through most of the titles: *Friends* (the erstwhile *Rolling Stone* UK; the San Francisco HQ pulled the plug within three months of my arrival), *Time Out*, *Oz*, which I co-edited while the real stars were embroiled in their trial, *Ink* (the underground's attempt at a grown-up paper) and daddy of them all, *IT*. Fun while it lasted, but hardly remunerative. It certainly didn't count as 'real' journalism. Which was fair, because the 'real' journalists among us could be counted on a single severely mutilated hand. At the time we vaunted it as technically advanced, which it was, compared with Fleet Street's hot metal and old Spanish practices. (Nothing like that for us: the 'revo' stopped a long way short of unions.) We used IBM typesetting machines (very sophisticated typewriters that turned out justified columns), and sought out the biggest Letraset to create our headlines. (Really big ones were created out of house. This caused problems with frustratingly puritan printers: the word 'shit', for instance, had to be sent off as 'hits' and then recut.) Process cameras,

Cow Gum and later hot wax, repro, scalpels. Cutting edge? Positively antediluvian.

OK, we were not underground. Point taken. If any of us were to serve a night, let alone any kind of real time, behind bars then the odds were it would be for dope. Which wouldn't be much to do with what we wrote, unflinchingly pro-drug though of course it was. In the event it turned out that there would be a further stumbling block: censorship, but that was yet to lurch into view. But we were hardly mainstream. And if I look at the paper on which I spent the bulk of my time – the absurdly and embarrassingly named *Friends* – there's no denying that some of the topics that only we would cover, typically what would be known as 'green' issues, were, as yet, sidelined on Fleet Street, but would, in time, become wholly mainstream.

But forget content, what set the counter-cultural press aside was drugs. Its attitude to them, its consumption of them. There were certain pieties – cannabis good, heroin bad – but the overall verdict was no problemo. One title, let it be nameless – who can calculate the lasting vindictiveness of those in power – let the shopfront that doubled as its distribution department double too as a front for cannabis sales. The title in question would suffer all kinds of police harassment, but nary a squeak from the drugs squad. Thinking myself reasonably trained up at Oxford, I found a drug regime that was a good deal more demanding. After a few weeks' wanderings, wanderings that would typify my first few years in London (there were, I think, some twenty-two addresses before I came to rest, thanks to my generous father's severance pay, in a small mansion flat near Maida Vale tube), I found myself on a mattress in my editor's attic home. Quite luxurious – a large sitting room, ditto bedroom, bathroom, kitchen. He, his wife, me, and a regular procession of passing freaks and visiting transatlantic firemen. A bit of free love, or so the tabloids would have termed it, though we omitted to tell her husband. Brown rice and vegetables, which seemed to mean carrots. If nothing else, one lost weight. I cannot recall alcohol, I was one of the few *Friends* staffers who drank. We smoked. Hashish for choice – Black Pak, Afghani, Nepalese Temple Balls, Chitrali, the lowly Moroccan kif – though grass was available, from Thailand or the Caribbean. We would wake and stumble up, maybe 10 o'clock, possibly later. I would make some tea, my editor prepared the wake-up joint. We drank tea and smoked. Eventually dressed, we smoked one for the road and another, pre-rolled, in the cab (and cabs were mandatory). Arrival at the office: of course we need a joint. And so it went as the day moved on until finally, around 3 or 4 A.M., having thrown in a few chillums-full for good measure and complete immersion, we would light a last one for sweet dreams. I will not claim that it was amazing that we managed to work, because the reality was that . . . this was the reality and one hardly considered it. One might suggest that the paucity of real journalism in any of the underground papers was down to the excess of drugs, but the truth was that it was due to the lack of journalistic expertise. I wrote who knows how many thousands of words per week – and had no one but myself to edit them. A good thing for me, since most were composed directly on to the IBM machine and there was no time for major rewrites. Not so good for the readers.

There was also not much in the way of 'stories'. We looked west to America, as did the whole of the counter-culture, and were encouraged to pillage the Underground Press Syndicate (UPS) which ensured that a copy of every underground paper in the States would appear in the office each time they were published. There was little idea of 'reporting'. There weren't any reporters and if I was nominally 'news editor', it was not in the way of my supposed peers in EC4. Not for nothing did I christen the news section 'Newzak'. *Friends*, which had started life as *Friends of Rolling Stone*, took time to shed its links to the music industry. We ran reviews and interviews and were grateful for their ads. Early on, an office still unsettled, we were beached briefly in a flat behind Harrods. The walls were carefully graduated from dark green to white, the monster bed boasted that stud's best friend, a dimmer switch, and the seducer himself allegedly sniffed cocaine. One of those ads gleaned us £70. It seemed logical to get it cashed, proceed directly to the adjacent food hall and feed the staff.

By the end of 1969 we had landed. Portobello Road, just north of the still-new Westway. Colin MacInnes' Napoli. There was a West Indian restaurant, the Backayard, very dry chicken, very hot sauce; there was a clothes shop, 'I Was Lord Kitchener's Valet', mainly for the tourists, such as there were; there was a record store selling something that we were informed was called reggae. We worked above a junkshop. It boasted a fourteen year old refugee from Fagin's Saffron Hill 'bus-napper's academy',* whose father, he informed us, had been a major fence, and whose mother, on his father's death, had found sufficient off-cuts of precious metals to finance a stylish send-off. A bit of street cred in the flesh. The building, 305, was owned by a couple of . . . let us call them hustlers. A regular Stan and Ollie: Mr Tall and Thin, Mr Short and Fat.

* Recorded in 1754, the link to public transport is wholly coincidental and to kidnapping non-existent. The actor-cum-lecturer George Parker explained it thus in his *View of Society* (1781): 'This *Rig* is generally executed by a young fry of boys, who are first pick'd up in the purlieus of St. Giles's, [. . .] they are put into a room, in which there are figures dressed up like a man and a woman, with bells in every pocket for the young ones to practice on [. . .] If they can *make the dive*, take book, handkerchief, or purse, without making the bells speak in the execution of this business, then they are qualified to take their degrees, go out on the *leer* the next *darkey*, and follow the profession of a *Buz-napper*.'

They had the building, they had us, they had a private detective, in the ground floor back they had the graphic designer Barney Bubbles. They also seemed to have a large apartment overlooking Marble Arch. In the end it transpired they had very little: one cheque for £10,000 and a number of bank accounts between which it was shuttled. One of them also had a jail record. The detective, unpaid, tracked that down. Fun, as they say, while they lasted. They also had a band called Brinsley Schwarz and flew a planeload of journos to watch them debut down the bill on a Quicksilver Messenger Service gig at the Fillmore East, New York. The plane stopped off in Shannon for undisclosed reasons, pessimists talked of engine problems. Off we re-lumbered: the underground rolled joints, the Fleet Streeters drank and demanded that the captain have us all arrested. A guy from the *Jewish Chronicle* cornered me: so tell me, this Brinsley Schwarz, he's a Jewish boy?

For me there was always an inbuilt paradox: here we were in the so-called communications industry, and yes, even the counter-cultural press had such pretensions, in a world where the default mode was all too regularly *duh*.

The Sixties were noisy but if one looks back, where were the words that lasted? Gone to rock lyrics and movie scripts every one. My generation had better things to do than write about it. There was certainly no Waugh to run herd on the developing novelties. One read those who were slightly older, and afterwards those who were slightly younger carved out literary stardom. Novel-writing continued, publishing continued, but not from the underground. Our preferred literary form was the manifesto, or in my case the underground newspaper.

There may well be stories based on the era, but I haven't heard of them, and I certainly cannot recall a thing that appeared at the time. I lie: there was *Agro*, by one 'Nick Fury', a wonderful piece of tosh that barely survived publication day due to the author's foolish inability to make sufficiently different the names of his characters and those of real-life freaks. A passage, doubtless a savage indictment of the hypocrisy of the so-called alternative world, which portrayed a barely disguised underground hero dressed in his SS uniform and masturbating before a mirror was not appreciated. Nor was the use of his then girlfriend's real name. Injunctions were served. The book disappeared. Perhaps my copy is valuable?

There was also a popular 'biography' of the leader of the UK Hells Angels. The author, at times a rock manager, moved on to novels soon after; it is possible that he had already begun. There was the confessional *Groupie*, whose protagonist resisted much temptation to go especially far beyond the author's own memoirs, but in this case nobody seemed to mind. She popularised the rhyming slang 'plate': it means fellate, which duly rhymes, but the slang is properly based on 'plate of meat', to eat. One never spells out the whole phrase in this particular slang subset. She also created the 'manny', a drug of which no one had heard, until they thought to add the necessary 'd' and realised that it was a slight sidestep away from 'mandy', or Mandrax, a drug of which everyone had heard and many were regularly consuming. Known as 'randy mandies', they led to falling over and fucking, and not invariably in that order.

There were poets, but they had really come out of the beatnik world, and as one who hopes they know their own limitations, I am unwilling to comment further. Anyway their apogee, the Poetry Reading at the Albert Hall, was long gone by the time I made it to the 'alternative' world. I heard far more about it when I came to assemble *Days in the Life* nearly two decades on.

What I need to admit is this: words were not of importance. This was no fun for me, who couldn't keep their mouth shut, but such was the case. Love, as we knew, was all we needed and woe betide those who might have felt otherwise. As journos we felt ourselves above or at least in some parallel reality to the hippie masses, and we didn't swallow all the guff. Whether we produced it was another story. We hoped not. *Friends* was a gruesome name, but at least it wasn't *Gandalf's Garden*.

The thing is that drugs make you dumb. Literally. As in silent. Not talking. *Shtum*. Well maybe not speed, but certainly cannabis. And the more you take the dumber you are. Or if you wanted to come up with some kind of rationale: cool. Cool did not rabbit on. Cool kept it zipped, or, at best, cool mumbled. It was those drugs again. Like our slang, it started off with the junkie's nodding silence. The vibe was clear: 'I'm just so . . . *fucked up*, man.' Cheech and Chong, Gilbert Shelton's Fabulous Furry Freak Brothers made showbiz flesh, carved a career out of it. Lenny Bruce on song was a rapier, these knuckle-draggers were a club, if, that is, they could be bothered to raise it. Drugs obviated the need for expression. 'Heavy' was perhaps the ultimate descriptor, serving a wide spectrum from very good to truly bad, beauty to ugliness, excitement to tedium. We worshipped at Dylan's wilful obscurantism, but couldn't imitate it. Too stoned to put up, we shut up.

Or we were meant to. Unsurprisingly I found this voluntary lingualectomy remarkably hard. University had seen articulacy as praiseworthy. Words existed to be used, amusingly and well if at all possible, and certainly not stored away in some mental attic. Long nights of joints and music, with rarely a word spoken, could prove seriously dull. Worse still were those who tended to dominate such conversation as there was, the self-appointed gurus, the incarnation not so much of the godhead, but of the dangers (and mind-numbing tedium) of that well known quotient of self-aggrandisement: a little knowledge. If, heaven forfend, they came with a guitar . . . MEGO, as US ad-men abbreviated it: my eyes glaze over.

As far as work was concerned, the default mode of the rock god – there were rock goddesses, too, but they were in very short supply and the best of them, Janis Joplin, lived life too hard to live it very long – remained mumbling inarticulacy. That must-have cool. The early Beatles had offered some cracks, geared to underline their 'wacky Liverpudlian' credentials in London and their 'wacky Brit' ones in the US. Mick Jagger, studiously Mockney long before first Estuary English and later MLE crossed classes and flesh-tones, was always up to asking audiences of adoring young women 'You don't want to see my *trousers* fall off, do you?' preening in the sure knowledge that oh yes they really did, but silence conferred some form of mystery. And for most of them, especially the cornfed Americans from the mid-West, it was so much easier.

1969. I am sitting in NEMS, outpost of Brian Epstein's Liverpool roots and the Beatles' pre-Apple HQ. Stucco, portico, gleaming white gloss. A long way from Penny Lane. The walls of the Mayfair mansion are white, furniture minimal, the PR man obsequious. The star whom I have come to interview, not a Moptop but still of serious psychedelic fame, is standing. Colour-coded, he is also in white. Top to toe. I asked . . . whatever one asked, and awaited the oracle. 'Can you see them,' he not so much responded as intoned, slightly awestruck himself. I followed his eyes: he was gazing at a cornice.

'Can you see them, man?'

'Them?'

'The people, man. The white people up there.'

I looked up, hoping at least to humour him, then asked another question. Same result. I admitted that perhaps I couldn't, suggested that there might be a better time to talk, and left. The PR man attempted to hold me back, almost begging. I was unmoved. I could hear him remonstrating with his client as I slipped away. Words, it appeared, had failed us both.

Or you could get too many of them. It was probably the drugs. Sometimes an interview turned into a form of challenge: how many spliffs could the interviewer consume and still manipulate the tape recorder or recall the last question asked? (Interviewing for *Days in the Life* two decades later certain diehards ran me through the same gauntlet.) One subject kept his Rizlas ready-gummed into the canonical trio, with little piles of pre-mixed tobacco and hashish, and small pre-rolled cardboard filters all ready in a drawer by his chair. Another – back at the office I had been casually tossed an ounce of Afghani hash 'to cool him out' – turned out to be violently anti-dope. And tediously vociferous about it. We were on the ground floor and I glanced through a window. Outside the flat a well-known figure, then a star of some televisual magnitude, staggered (or was it crawled?) up the path: his choice of drugs was palpably alcohol. Who could have guessed, as they say, that a few decades in the future his son-in-law, then but a schoolboy, would rule our waves.

Interviewing the occasional rock god was a new experience for me, and, I imagine, for some of them. Up till about 1967 the typical muso interview effectively reheated the latest press release. This usually involved the performer's mum, and such tastes as his manager ordained that he should enjoy. There would be sanctioned photos. There was one recent exception, the counter-culture's *IT* where Barry Miles made his way through the performers that we had come to know gave us rock (good), and not pop (beyond bad), and let them run. In 1967 *Rolling Stone* had been launched in the US. There, but on an American scale, musicians were allowed to spout. You could see where it was going on day one: big bucks and a slavish desire to please the industry. This wasn't to say they didn't publish great stuff – Tom Wolfe, Hunter S. Thompson for judicious starters – but 'the *Stone*' was basically cut from the same cloth that let mega-corporations run ads declaring 'The Man Can't Bust Our Music'. But those same heavies would never have appeared in the tatty pages of the real underground. It should have surprised no one when, scant months after I joined up, the San Francisco HQ shut down the fun at Hanover Square. I don't think we were selling that much; we certainly didn't have the advertising, the wealth of stars, the depth of writing. But maybe it was the party. Very good party. Bit excessive perhaps: some gatecrashing lefties graffitied the pristine walls, pretty much everything was spiked, and poor Marc Bolan had a *really* bad trip. Personally I was back in someone's flat singing along to Steppenwolf when the hapless former monarch of mod got his motor somewhat overheated. But the party seems to have frightened the Californians. This would not make the industry happy. This would not generate money. This was the end. Someone from the Stones office – Jagger had been a major investor – came to change the locks soon after. Like it or not, we were on the road.

I haven't read the rock press in years (I assume it's all online now anyway) and if I seem to wince when I recall having been a part of it then wince I do, but it was not wholly the musos' fault. Seen by the worried establishment as a possible link to the incomprehensible and thus terrifying young, they had been put up as 'leaders'. Perhaps the model had been established by the ludicrous 'summit meeting', set up by television's *World in Action*, which brought together Jagger, fresh from escaping his 1967 bust, to set the world to rights with a couple of senior clerics and the editor of *The Times*. Jagger was bright; a few others too. The lumpen bulk were not but, as ever, that didn't stop them believing their promo. I encountered very few who had much time for the hippies, and even fewer who would have been very happy had the 'revo' finally happened (though no more would the man who was interviewing them), but on the whole, and with sufficient prompting, they knew what to say. Even if, despite the earnest efforts of such as the *New Left Review*, they had not on the whole replaced 'my favourite chick/car/colour/food' with 'my favourite Althusserian philosopher'. As they did then, they might now prefer the mystique of silence, the default mode for stardom, but both then and now, as their managers undoubtedly pointed out, records don't sell themselves (even for the Fab Four by late in the decade) and as the far-from-hippie Truman Capote had put it in another context, 'a boy's gotta hustle his book.'

Drugs make other people dumb too. Stupid dumb. Hindsight's always spot on and what a stormy teacup it all seems from forty years away. Not so in context. The moral panic substituted for religious censure in a once less terrorised and rather more secular Britain and each successive incarnation of youth triggers a fresh one – even if 'fresh' turns out to be xeroxed. The length of someone's hair, the colour and cut of their clothes, the means they opt for when it comes to damping down reality and enhancing alternative possibilities – such things are pilloried time after tedious time. Nothing much changes outside Bohemia either. The Home Secretary Roy Jenkins, calling for what he hailed as a 'civilised' and what the moralists decried as a 'permissive' society, was gradually piloting through the changes in the country's social control laws: on divorce, abortion and on homosexuality. It was these laws, which have yet to be repealed despite a seemingly endless whine of disapproval, that in sum ran more genuinely counter to the prevailing culture than anything the 'alternative society' achieved. But it was gradual and *IT* had been tried already, on confected charges pertaining to the running of small ads whereby one gay man might encounter another. The revised Obscene Publications Act (with Jenkins as a supportive private member) was already a dozen years old but it was that, plus an act alleging conspiracy last used to attack an eighteenth-century guide to Covent Garden whores, that was aimed at *Oz*, on whose door in 1970 the 'dirty squad' came knocking next.

Maybe the drugs had made its editors dumb as well. Hiring a bunch of schoolchildren to produce the thing, under 'grown-up' editorial direction, probably seemed incredibly cool when they debated it. Weren't schools talking of rebellion too? Of pupils' rights. And hadn't they already run issues on feminism ('cunt power'), various brands of revolution, Vietnam and the contemporary rest? Apparently the editors saw themselves as out of touch: bring in the teenies and get a shot of what's happening. (Why do I see vicars blessing rockers' bikes?) Perhaps they were just bored. Certainly Richard Neville, self-appointed but undeniably articulate star of the show, had much to do touting his polemical book *Play Power*, his version of the necessary hymn to hippiedom and social revolution that was a must for any underground leader worth his television time. The issue, number 28, appeared in May 1970. It was noticed by those who need to search for such things that in the illustration of naked women on the cover, at least one had something protruding from her vagina: a tampon string? a rat's tail? Inside, the conflation of a lubricious Robert Crumb cartoon with one of Rupert Bear, an icon of preschool pap published by the *Daily Express* for decades, cut straight to the sexual chase. Teachers and schools were pilloried, as in any school mag turned over to 'the rebels'. The magazine had been, to an extent, produced *by* schoolkids. Those who attacked it claimed that the issue was *for* them. Even before unfortunate paediatricians dangled like strange fruit from the balconies of the country's council estates, the idea of child abuse – our vulnerable young people: the kiddies, innit – obsessed both establishment and public. *Oz*, however vociferous, was never more than a pinprick. It was selling, what?

Well, it was said 70,000 tops. The tabs at the time were up in the millions. But the pin must have goaded, and this was a world that was much easier to disturb. And disturbed it was.

What fun the *Oz* trial was. And a happy ending too, even if the accused had some nasty moments. Neville had been through it all before – running *Oz* in Australia where it had started life as a student rag and where it had teased the authorities that bit too much. Now he defended himself and would be rewarded in that English establishment way, which always opts for having its perceived threats pissing out from the tent rather than up against it: a column of his own in the *Evening Standard*. The others, gay Jim Anderson and hustling Felix Dennis, were fronted by John Mortimer, his creation Horace Rumpole made flesh but a good deal smarter, and a young Geoffrey Robertson. Parades of great, good and self-aggrandising (often in a single human package) duly graced the witness box. The judge, Michael Argyll, was uncomprehending and transparently prejudiced. Right-wingers dragged their knuckles outside the court. John and Yoko wrote a song; against all the regulations a defence publicity team was formed and there were parades. The papers gave it the full treatment every morning. On sentencing day we piled a lumpy effigy of Argyll into our car, drove up from Fulham Road, then helped burn it outside the Old Bailey on a street where a century earlier Dickens, Thackeray and drunken, brawling crowds had turned up to watch murderers climb the leafless tree and have what slangy wits termed a 'vegetable breakfast' (think 'hearty choke'). 'A wailing wall of weirdos,' said the press, and splashed the pics. The trio were jailed, vengefully shorn of hair although no rule demanded any scissors, then released. Interviewing Dennis in 1987, I was told of a midnight trip from Wandsworth nick to Grays Inn, cutting a deal with the Lord Chief Justice at the Prime Minister's behest. The other principals denied any such thing. But then they would, wouldn't they. What mattered was their speedy return to the world – they had worn schoolgirl uniforms for the committal, now at the appeal they wore long wigs – even if they were temporarily banned from editing and I and two others had to pick up the slack until they were permitted back. Meanwhile the investigative hacks had sunk their teeth into Scotland Yard and soon the 'dirty squad', their hands proven to be deep in gangland's pockets, proved to be as corrupt as their peers in that other agency of social control, the drugs squad. Slang had never had any doubts: detectives were the 'filth'.

The *Oz* gig was a mistake but I was young and undoubtedly foolish and even if the full fifteen minutes wasn't on offer, fifteen seconds had its appeal. The *Mirror* pictured me: *Oz* trial T-shirt, denimed from top to toe, feet on editorial desk. Neville, picking it up in prison, remarked, 'It's an ill wind.' We did three issues. The collecting completists doubtless have to have them but it was a magazine in decline. You couldn't top the trial; but you didn't want to miss out on the sales. Men from Soho arrived in white vans to take away long unsold back copies for sale to punters whose wishful thinking saw school 'girls' rather than simply 'kids'. You'd see the covers in 'bookshop' windows, a tenner apiece. The magazine would limp on until late 1973, back in Dennis' hands. Neville had returned to Australia, Anderson was in Marin County. I was long gone, my final outing was editing a very terminal *IT* a year later. Meanwhile *Oz* died, Dennis moved into comics and then launched *Kung-Fu Monthly*. I wrote issue 2 as Jo Nat Hon. Turning up in the office to deliver my copy I saw him, with a pair of assistants, emptying canvas bags full of responses to the launch issue's mail shot: postal orders in this box, cheques in this, cash in that. Dennis called himself Felix Yen. It remains apposite.

There were a few mumblings, there were always a few

mumblings about the content we included, but the only time I faced the beak, at least as a representative of the counter-culture, came for the most banal of reasons: drunk and disorderly. There was a press party in Covent Garden. It was winding down but the fruit and veg were still being traded and the porters still saw it as 'theirs'. The venue had been the Middle Earth club a few years before (a successor to UFO, the first hippie club). It was lunchtime, there was much to drink and more to smoke and I recall full bottles being dropped into stairwells to see what happened. What happened was that the porters, disliking a bunch of drunken, drugged hippies on their sacred cobbles, weighed in. What little history they knew: Covent Garden had always been a playground for those for whom the greengrocery was merely a backdrop and 'greengrocer' means, as explained in Harris' 1773 *List of Covent Garden Ladies*, a whore. In the eighteenth century Tom King's Coffee House, a shack leaning against the local church and to be found in a Hogarth engraving, was the birthplace of 'flash', a new take on the criminal vocabulary. No matter. Something was said. Something was said back. Suddenly there were the police. Grabbing my friend, the underground journalist-cum-rock star, I essay a rescue mission – drink had been taken. I am grabbed in turn and so are a number of others. How fortunate that the Bow Street nick was so near. Had it not hurt so much I would have admired the skill with which my captor, marching me down to my cell, casually backhanded the side of my head at the precise moment when the opposite temple would have to smash into the corner of a conveniently placed fusebox. I mentioned it in court; he seemed to have forgotten all about it. All pretty minor league stuff, I can't even remember the fines, but I was nominally *Oz* editor and the *Guardian* had a picture. These fifteen seconds' worths do pile up.

Still, outside of what I filtered through the IBM machine, there wasn't a great deal of offing the pigs up against the walls. The Angry Brigade may have been coming on like revolutionary gangbusters, but not me. But I too, I fought the law. And yes, they won.

1973. Midnight. Shepherds Bush Green. Enter left, heading for Portobello Road where they live, a pair of less than stable feet. Or so they must appear, even if their owner sees himself as striding purposefully forward. A white van pulls to a halt. A white van with a stripe down the side. A white van that bears a pair of woodentops who are not in this case characters of a children's TV programme, but uniformed members of Her Majesty's Metropolitan Police. The woodentops come out to play. The feet are led into the rear of the van. The mouth has attempted to suggest a state of absolute sobriety, of unimpeached geographical orientation. But perhaps its message was in some way impaired. Slurred maybe. Mouth, feet and all the rest, plus two bobbies arrive at the local nick, Hammersmith. Out of the van, across a yard, into the station. Hands, those of interested others, into pockets. 'Look at this, then, Sarge.' This is an envelope. Within the envelope is as near to one ounce of high grade hashish as a dozen quid can still get you. 'Told you so,' says bobby to his partner, 'told you I was right to nick him.'

It had been a long evening. Many hours in a fashionable wine bar off Holland Park whose manageress was destined, poor girl, to be my girlfriend for a few months of the next year. I was already getting cut-price bottles. There had been many. Or at least enough. There was also dope to pick up, a task that required a trip to the house wherein lived a former partner, the wound of whose departure remained raw. I arrived. Handed over my dosh, obtained my envelope. Pocketed it. Was there an altercation? I do not recall. Probably. All that remains are the words of one of my replacements in the departed's affections, an American, the son of a more famous and far more talented American: 'I'm gonna kill you with my

Vietnam hold!' Perhaps he was capable. I certainly wasn't. Wiser spirits interceded, it was suggested that I depart. Now. And thence to the Green and thence to the white van.

Once satisfied, my captors were happy, genial. They brought me ten cigarettes and asked, quite kindly, as to the dope's origin. 'Bought it from a black man on Portobello Road.' They seemed happy with this. 'Do you do this often?' I imagine by 1973 it is very hard not to notice that I have not opted for a career in, say, the City. 'No, never. I had broken up with my girlfriend. I wanted to feel better.' They seemed satisfied by that too. Must have missed the scrawl that even drunken I had seen on the envelope: 'Here's your stuff, Jon.' Banged me up. Hell's own hangover in the A.M. Off to the court. Cops told me what best to say. Bailed in my own recognisance. Went home. Recalled that I was giving a party that evening. Two litre bottles of Italian plonk. Huge. Bought a dozen. On the street my friend removed half a dozen more from his coat. Wouldn't believe you could just walk them out of the shop like that. Party time. A carrier-bag bulging with hash cake. Off we go again. Tried a couple of weeks later and pleaded the recent John Lennon defence: don't convict or I shall not be able to pursue my career in the United States. Got away with it, but the costs, it so happened, were exactly the sum of the fine I had escaped.

Still, the provisional discharge was good. Wiped off the books in a year or two, I was assured. Never did pay the costs. Never did get off the books either. Thirty years later, when I was putting up bail for a foolish friend, the solicitor calls. 'Yes, they'll take your bail; the bust in '73 doesn't matter.' Pigs, eh. Never trust anyone under thirty.

I have never been one for go-faster medications. I go too fast already, and what I need is something to calm not cajole. And speed come-downs, tearful, self-recriminating, worse than my worst hangovers, thanks, but I think no thanks. Cocaine, well, occasionally, but I've rarely had top-grade coke in the UK, only in New York, where I must admit it had me sailing through Greenwich Village thinking, 'maybe there is something in this stuff after all.' But all those city boys, all those yuppie puppies. If you've got a line, fine, but I'm not slapping down my dosh. As for crack: just the once. Interviewing an upmarket call-girl for my sex book, *It*, I noticed that she was rolling cigarettes and crumbling in something lumpy and white. Not enough kit for all-out freebasing, so eventually I realised what we had: the latest evil of evils, crack. It is perhaps a testimony to the lightning fast proliferation of this cocaine derivative that the word itself, coined as slang, entered mainstream English almost without breaking stride. And it did seem to work. I left the interview, mounted my bicycle and headed home. The ride usually involved a good milesworth of uphill grind. Amazingly, I hardly noticed it. Halfway up and I paused to visit a bank. Outside stood some wretched homunculus proclaiming his adhesion to a group known as Jews for Jesus. I locked up the bike, walked to meet him. Donned my metaphorical *yarmulke* and informed him that, as a Jew, I found his message and indeed him personally offensive. Didn't I want Our Lord as my saviour? he enquired. I explained that no, I did not and suggested with a certain vigour that he remove himself prior to my return from getting my cash. Out I came. There he was. I approached him again, explained that I had given him fair warning and . . . hit him. He bleated something about forgiveness and took to his heels. I unlocked the bike, saddled up and zoom . . . up the hill and home. It was not until I was back at my desk that I took stock. I, Mr Wimpguts in the trembling flesh, had *hit* a complete stranger in the public street. I was terrified. What in hell? And realised: all those ciggies, all that smoke, I may not have asked, but Scotty had still beamed me up. I was tweaking by proxy. Never again.

Heroin is a filthy and disgusting drug which destroys lives, especially young ones, and encourages crime on both a small and internationally organised scale. Along with other powdered narcotics it is a scourge of our world. This is undeniably true. No wonder a succession of politicians have launched their 'wars' against it. It must also be noted that none of these wars have come within even a long distance of being won. Because, unfortunately, what is equally true is that, unlike all too many popular substances, legal or otherwise, heroin, at least at the beginning, and the beginning is all that is required to acquire the necessary taste, does just what it says on the packet.

1973 again. Early hours. Visiting my muso friends who have a nitrous oxide cylinder stowed beneath their ratty sofa. A far more famous star is ensconced. In front of him is a mirror. What look like lines of coke. He offers, I accept. It feels . . . different. He smiles: 'It's not coke, man.' No it isn't. It is heroin. Chinese white, presumably, since it lacked the browish tinge of Mexican. And it is fantastic. An embrace from a vast down-filled velvet glove. I feel g-r-e-a-t. Yum-my!

It was, at that stage, a one-off. If I knew where to get some more, I resisted looking. But once bitten. Much later, such bad habits behind me, I met a woman for what I believed was the first time. We've met before, she informed me. Oh yes? Yes, you were buying heroin from my brother-in-law. A-a-a-a-h. Yes. She was quite right. When had I rejoined the party? The late '70s I suppose. 1976: Ian Dury's 'Sex & Drugs & Rock & Roll' was playing. And the B side: 'Razzle In My Pocket' – the story of our hero's failure to steal a pornzine. My kind of guy. My indulgence lasted on and off till the mid-'80s. Up to, and shamefully including the birth of my younger son. My dealer gave me a bonus half-gram as a congratulation. I find it hard to look at the photos of me holding his newly born self: eyes unfocused, sloppy smile. I didn't inject, you didn't have to. Just whack it up the nose or, if desirous of a bit of low-tech ritual, chase the dragon with cigarette lighter and kitchen foil. Nor did I nod, if anything it enhanced my work. Not quality, I imagine, but undoubtedly my ability to go on and on. There are at least two books that owe their arrival on deadline to the drug. The other thing, for me at least, was that heroin suppressed my fears. Not for nothing was it named for the word 'hero'. But isn't the hero often the coward gone momentarily mad? Stoned on smack, temporarily fearless, I made decisions, two in particular, that would change my life. For better? for worse? Suffice it to say that I have lived with both.

Was I a junkie? Is it naive to claim that I'm not sure. William Burroughs I wasn't, though I recall a hairy expedition into a pre-gentrification Lower East Side to score 'D' (or 'duji' as the old junkies called it) that gave a certain sense of community (and a burning desire to rush home and tell the tale to certain pals back in London). But for a while I took it regularly enough, I felt that visceral tug to get more and spent too much of our limited money to do so; perhaps most shameful of all, I garbed myself in a boiler suit for most of the day. I found, as one does, that it would require larger doses to achieve the same result, and after a while, just to stay 'normal'. I didn't enjoy stopping, which withdrawal I tried on and off, when a sense of guilt managed to permeate the happy self-denial. In the end I did stop for good. Even put in a fruitless eighteen months yattering on to a shrink on the pretext of 'getting myself over it'. And that really was a waste of money. The last 'hard' drug I took was opium: vilely expensive and more of a romantic pleasure than a narcotic one. It's over thirty years since I last saw one of those alluring little wraps of paper.

Narcotics began their life, and may be considered to have continued even in recreational use, as agents of analgesia: killing the pain. Such auto-analgesia, so the experts suggest, is the motive force of the addictive personality. Of the pain killers to which Wikipedia claims the addictive personality is prey, drugs, drink, gambling, food and sex top the list, though there is also mention of cell phone use, tanning, and exercise. The writing of slang dictionaries is not mentioned. Perhaps it should be.

The Human Factor

We are in the past. Let us stay there for a while. Mine is recent, that of my predecessors more distant. If slang is my family, then these – and unlike the flesh-and-blood ones I actually know their names – represent its members.

It is not only the language that is alive: so too are the lexicographers. Lest we forget, dictionaries remain the products of human beings. Hard-working, distractible, determined, hesitant, biased and discriminating human beings. Humans who reflect the culture within which they live, and in the case of such as Johnson or Noah Webster, also aid in defining it. 'Human' as found in definition 2 of the word as offered in the latest revision of the *OED*: 'Of, relating to, or characteristic of humans as distinguished from God or gods; secular, not divine; (also) of or relating to the abilities or sphere of activity of human as opposed to supernatural beings; mundane, worldly; imperfect, fallible.'

It is perhaps harder to keep this in mind these days, when so many dictionaries are the product not of individuals – more or less obsessive – but of substantial and skilful teams, but even teams are ultimately composed of individuals and somewhere, atop the hierarchy, sits a single editor whose task is to pronounce yea or nay. There are rules, but there are also interpretations. There is even office politics. To take the foremost example, the *OED*, recent scholarship by Lynda Mugglestone, Charlotte Brewer and Sarah

Ogilvie, while focusing on one or another aspect of the creation of the dictionary, still finds it impossible to avoid personalities. Not merely the madmen, of whom the celebrated W. C. Minor was but the best known, but the 'professors' or at least the professional lexicographers.

If I seem to overstress this human aspect of dictionary-making, then it is because, however invisible it may be to the reader, it must always be borne in mind alongside the dictionary's end product: authority. The artist – drunken, adulterous, manipulative, egomaniacal, socially inept in any one of a dozen ways – is still the person who creates the imperishable art. The lexicographer may not be ranked among the artists, but the same contradiction exists. Political correctness has suggested that we elide the two and judge accordingly. I disagree. This duality is hardly unique to lexicography, but that is what I know, and I also know that it runs within me. The language we assess is also the language we use, although I would never claim to use, or even remember, the amount of slang I list. When those dictionaries are published the user comes up against an unavoidable subtext: 'You want to know what X means? Fine, this is what X means – and trust me, I'm a lexicographer.' So while slang may be the impoverished younger sibling of standard, we who define it are subject to the same paradox: drudges then, as I have noted, mini-deities.

Which brings me to another paradox. Alongside the dictionary is the equally authoritative language expert, the language *maven* as some Americans, borrowing the Hebrew term for 'one who possesses expertise through understanding', like to describe such people. The maven is usually associated with questions of usage and tends to the diktat and the ukase. Lexicographers, especially those who pursue slang, are less likely to fulfil this role. It is still there: such is the way dictionaries work. Like the 'before' and 'after' illustrations that accompany some puff for a patent medicine or diet, the lexicographer takes on two opposing roles, each predicted by the state of the dictionary. While the book is still in embryo, during the long years of research, the lexicographer is indeed the drudge. One may love one's work, but however blind that love, there remain undeniable longueurs. But with the dictionary 'born', its creator takes on a new persona: the sanctity, the divinity even, of the trusted expert. The one who possesses expertise through understanding.

It is, never forget, a hard-won expertise. Dictionaries require decades for their construction – and even then remain unfinished – because they require such extensive and time-consuming labour. Some call it nit-picking, others attention to detail. Slang, so determinedly obscure in its origins and, on occasion, its meanings too, allows for less of this, even makes it impossible. It is possible that we have been soloists because the lexis we study doesn't actually require the teams that codify standard languages, but one still makes the effort.

Back in the Sixties we were very big on *demystification*. The first use is currently taken from the *Economist* but we more likely picked it up from the anti-psychiatrist David Cooper, who seems to have promoted the term. It's a synonym for clarification, especially of irrational beliefs. Somewhat unfashionable now, it still serves its purpose and of all the demystifications the most necessary in my context is that of the dictionary itself. The mystique of the dictionary. The Universal Authorising Dictionary of 'Is it in the dictionary?', 'I'll look it up in the dictionary', 'It isn't in the dictionary.' The dictionary? There are dozens, at any one time, and the reality is that 'the dictionary' tends to be the one that resides upon the speaker's shelf. Or, these days, screen. But if all are equal then some are indeed more equal than others. From 1755 to the emergence in the 1880s of the first fascicles of the *New English Dictionary*, soon to be renamed the *Oxford English Dictionary*, it was Samuel Johnson's *Dictionary of the English Language* that was the word-book of final appeal. Not for nothing did Thackeray's Becky Sharp, capricious heroine of *Vanity Fair* and whose surname, in the era's slang, betokened not just intelligence but also cunning and self-motivation, signify her emancipation from the schoolroom by tossing a copy from the coach that bore her away from Miss Pinkerton's Academy for Young Ladies (even if, given the date, it may well have been Todd's later revision). The great lexicographer, as Miss P. apostrophised him, stood for linguistic authority. One needed to enquire no further than his two folio volumes.

Johnson's commission had been to set the English language in stone; there may not have been a British Academy, like that found in France and advocated by such as Jonathan Swift, but at least 'correct' English could be established by isolating the acceptable words in a book. To Johnson's credit he admitted that this was an impossibility. This did not deter his crusade for the establishment, again through his work, of a moral and thus social order. This he did through definitions. These were to be taken as immutable, and any dissent was not simply academic, but a threat to the moral order and as such intolerable. In his own words the definition 'is the only way whereby the meaning of words can be known, without leaving room for *contest* about it.' Harmless drudge? Was ever a lexicographer less so?

Modern dictionary-making does not allow for much in the way of personal projection. The idea of subjective interpretation, of working to promote one's own cultural and social beliefs, as did a Johnson or a Webster, is unacceptable. Those giants were never told. Johnson and Webster did it their way. The old one. Johnson, the high Tory, made sure that any potentially controversial terms – 'liberty', 'freedom', 'Whig' and of course 'Tory' itself – were defined in ways that bolstered the Great Cham's world view. Thus a Tory was 'one who adheres to the ancient constitution of the state, and the apostolical hierarchy of the church of England' while a Whig was no more than 'a faction'. No doubts about who got to wear the white hat. And as I noted in *Chasing the Sun*: 'The *Dictionary* is no tract, but as he skewed individual quotations, so too does Johnson skew his choice of sources. For instance, the political theorist Thomas Hobbes, who had his own attitudes to dictionary-making, is never chosen himself; only in quotations in which he is systematically refuted does he make an appearance. At the same time, many of the political writers Johnson uses are also pillars of the High Church. In this there can be no doubt that he is deliberately standing in the way of progress.' Johnson may have been writing at the heart of the Enlightenment, but the world he promoted continued to prefer religion to reason.

But the great lexicographer, and so of course he was, might equally well have been known as the great fabricator. Johnson's book is a testament to Johnson's personality. He was the first 'modern' to include illustrative citations in his lexicon, their task to back up the definitions of a given word. The concept of 'historical principles', which since the *OED* has been applied to any dictionary (including my own) that displays these examples, had not yet been coined. That was still what Johnson was doing. But it was, to an extent, Johnson's history. It was also strictly ring-fenced: the writers on whom Johnson drew were only to be those that he considered of the first quality. His citations showed how a word had been used, but even more important, how it had been used *properly*. And if the writer had not quite come up to Johnson's mark, then the Doctor saw nothing wrong in tweaking the material to fit his requirements. Similarly his definitions: the concept of disinterested defining, a given of modern dictionaries, does not seem to have worried him. The 'big' concepts: God, liberty, freedom, power, religion, were laid out in terms to which an Anglican Tory such as Johnson could subscribe. As for less portentous definitions – 'oats', 'lexicographer' and 'patron' remain best known – these were all well and good, but again, a little short on the necessary disinterestedness. The first, for instance, was a chestnut well known for centuries; the latter pair seem more like in-jokes, geared to amuse his intellectual friends at their elite meeting-place, The Club.

But there seems to me – and I may of course have misinterpreted him – that Johnson's work contains an essential paradox. In attempting to offer a didactic work, setting out definitions that conformed to a specific point of view, he might be seen as attempting to control the language. And in this he was, of course, following the example of the French Academy, whose own dictionary, the product of its members, the 'Forty Immortals', had taken sixty years to complete and which, in successive editions remains an exemplar of pre- and proscriptiveness. Commissioned in 1632, it had not appeared until 1694. Johnson – and his team, the 'eight drunken Scots' – had taken a mere nine years to do their job and, as his friend David Garrick put it, 'had beat forty French and could beat forty more'. His list of headwords – what goes in and by definition what stays out – reflects his desire to purge the lexis. 'Bamboozle' for instance was quite unacceptable. And as for slang . . . Yet, if one reads his introduction one finds a far more pragmatic figure. When I wrote my history of dictionary-making and dictionary-makers, I chose the title *Chasing the Sun* specifically as a tribute to what seemed to me to be Johnson's open-mindedness. Any attempt to curb the language, he suggested, was equivalent to the futile efforts of those who climb a mountain in order to entrap the sun, only to find that the sun has moved on to the next peak. And ever more shall do so. This to me seemed the essence of descriptive lexicography, the sensible acknowledgement that language is alive and organic and cannot be pinned down between the covers of a book, however skilfully created.

Johnson was not alone in his desire to instruct as well as inform. Noah Webster, who in 1828 provided 'the dictionary' for his American fellows, was determined that his definitions of those same important terms would reflect *his* beliefs, in this case those of an American nationalist and lover of his still new-minted republic. For him Johnson was a yardstick against which he might measure himself, but only insofar as he completely rejected the conservative Englishman. He was determined to record an American language which, while it might have used many of the same words, was to mean something very different to the corrupt syllables of Old England. Like Johnson he promoted a personal programme and, like Johnson, he stood for conservatism. Definitions laid down the law and to argue with them was to expose oneself to social disorder. For both of them unpicking the stated definitions of the language was the last stop before unpicking the world in which that language was used. He was quite open in his prejudices: a Democrat was 'a person who attempts an undue opposition or influence over government by means of private clubs, secret intrigues or by public popular meetings which are extraneous to the Constitution'. Republicans, on the other hand, were 'friends of our representative Governments'. Freedom, other than in subjection to divine laws, was absurd; it is seen as 'violation of the rules of decorum' and as 'license'. As for love, 'the love of God is the first duty of man'. Laws existed simply to 'enjoin the duties of piety and morality'. Education had no relation to learning; education was 'instruction and discipline', it would fit the young for their future stations. And wisdom? 'The fear of the Lord,' he declared, quoting the *Book of Common Prayer*, 'was the beginning of wisdom.' Such religiosity undermined his scholarly skills, since many of his etymologies were based on Biblical rather than linguistic standards. Like much of his new spelling system – which when it appeared in 1808 had proved one of the new nation's first best-sellers, and which was tossed aside in the great revision of his work by Carl Friedrich Mahn that appeared in 1864 – these too had to be expelled.

Neither Johnson nor Webster, it would appear, faced much criticism. Or not beyond the academy. There were others on offer – lexicographers did not simply throw up their hands and give in. Webster's Americanism in particular was engaged in a bitter commercial and theoretical battle with Joseph Worcester's far more anglophile work – but the two great dictionaries, each subjected to a succession of revisions and expansions, captured the bulk of the market and with it the authority. For Johnson the lack of criticism survived until the *OED*; meanwhile Webster, long-dead and vastly rewritten in 1864, had become a generic.

Not all the problems are down to personality. Prevailing cultural standards will have their say. Many of my predecessors found the inclusion of obscenities challenging. Not all slang is 'dirty' words but most 'dirty' words are listed as slang and they have to be included. Thus the abundance of asterisks and hyphens where reality would have placed a vowel. And if, like my predecessor Eric Partridge, one professes due respect for the dictionary, in this case the *OED*, such respect can promote absurdities. Even in the early-twentieth century, *Oxford*, to its credit, offered the word 'shit'. (An old word, with genuine 'Anglo-Saxon', i.e. Old English, antecedents, it remained standard until the late seventeenth century.) So too does Partridge. No blanks required. But the *OED* passes over slang's 'shit-stirrer' or 'shithead', for instance, and thus for these one finds Partridge preferring 'sh-t'. I have no intention of sneering, but one must surely laugh.

Fallibility can also spring from another of lexicography's givens: what the unkind might term plagiarism and the euphemistic research. The need to absorb one's predecessors. Few dictionaries can honestly claim to have been conjured from a clean sheet. Cant, criminal slang, is especially vulnerable, with lexicon after lexicon doing little but reproduce its predecessors. Thus one finds the word 'autem', meaning a church, in twenty-one successive glossaries, but lacking a single 'real-life' example. Again, the original *Oxford* swallowed almost completely whole the work of the contemporary slang experts John S. Farmer and W. E. Henley, whose seven-volume *Slang and Its Analogues* appeared between 1890 and 1904. But Farmer and Henley were largely Farmer, and one man, trust me, cannot hope for perfection even if, in Farmer's case, he was able to submit his proofs to James Murray for a second opinion. But in the book went. Dangerous, to say the least.

Of all registers slang is the least willing to lend itself to control. It can't even present itself in consistent spelling. This on the whole is not the same as the *OED*'s careful progress of forms, tracking change gradually from century to century. The mutability, at least in print, of many words simply reflects a non-standard vocabulary that is used by those who, failing to use the cadences of received standard punctuation, to 'talk proper', make life so much harder for those who attempt to transcribe them. And this, after all, is the first step: we have not arrived at definitions let alone etymologies. The fine tuning of uses – and if the language is meant to be obscure, then who's to say exactly what the user is meaning – multiply the definitions, although one can only go so far on this. Popular fantasies, given new life by an Internet where scholarship is dismissed as elitism, blur the accuracy of etymology, which is hard enough to establish when it comes to slang.

All of which should be borne in mind when reading any dictionary. That every one should carry some kind of lexical health warning: what you are reading here is incontrovertibly correct and wholly trustworthy – until further research improves upon it. This isn't theory, it's fact. I have experienced it, I experience it every day. It is frustrating because the realities of publication mean that at some stage you have to draw a line under your research and the language isn't listening. It keeps moving on. And research, especially in the context of what is, finally, a one-man band, is potentially infinite and far too much for any individual. The ever increasing availability of material, represented by that shorthand term, 'the Net', merely drives the boundaries into an ever more unreachable distance. Range upon range of peaks behind which the unfettered sun, laughing at our feeble efforts at pursuit, dances mockingly ahead. Even the finding of citations and the dates of use that they offer, the proofs of what the headwords and definitions assert, is still essentially serendipitous. Dig and dig and there's always the possibility of finding another layer to excavate. Another Troy beneath the last. The biggest frustration of all, remember, is that as far as slang is concerned we are bound to the limits of its tangible existence. There is not even an attempt at a glossary of English slang prior to the mid-1530s and nothing really useful for another thirty years after that. That glossary, and those that immediately followed, are restricted only to a subset of what must have been a larger slang vocabulary – the occupational jargon of a gang of beggars. Of course John Camden Hotten was right when he asserted that the Babylonians cracked slangy jokes on the steps of Sennacherib's palace. But where's the evidence?

Not so long ago a friend and scholar published a study of slang. It was filled with theories, a dignity that my marginal, disdained topic usually fails to attract. I am rolling no logs, since I offer no details, when I say that I enjoyed it and was delighted to see someone taking what I do seriously. But that, perhaps, was what worried me. The theories needed underpinning and my work, as well as that of my peers, was liberally quoted to back them up. As to my opinions of some of those he quoted, nuf ced. I know the works well and not all of them, let us say, stand up to much scrutiny. But I know my own best of all, and I know that some of his citations – for instance a taxonomy of the terms that make up my database – should not be taken as gospel. Or rather, that's exactly what they should be taken for: a concoction created to persuade. Or in this case to awaken an audience of students who are still young enough to find amusing the enunciation of the odd obscenity within a lecture hall. The broad-brush effect is fine, it's when the figures get quoted that I start to worry. The devil, as we know, is in the detail. In the end I felt that he flattered, and may, although certainly not intentionally, have deceived. But perhaps I worry over-much.

As does slang, I have a problem with ideology, with true belief. If I don't believe in true believers, then with the case of blind faith. If one aspect of this book is for me to answer my own question (why do I do it? and how did I get there?) then a parallel aim, in this case for the reader, is to explain how it's done. A glance at the morning-after nightclub with the cleaners in, or *The Wizard of Oz* bereft of special effects. And, since I have found it impossible to attempt either without offering a degree of autobiography, I have also tried to show who does it. Or at least one person who does it. To put it metaphorically and hugely personally: to open that closed door that seems so greatly to bedevil me.

So it's all nonsense, is it? It's all a con? This great fat tome you expect us to buy, these definitions and etymologies that you promise are to be trusted, this information that you assure us can be retailed without fear of denial? No doubt your beloved slang has a word for it? Several, actually:

Abdabs, ackamarackus, air, alfalfa, all my eye (and Betty Martin), alligator, allsbay, apcray, apple sauce, arkymalarkey, arsehole, ass, b, b.s., baggage, baked wind, balductum, ballocks, balloon, balls, ballyhoo, ballyhooly, baloney, balooey, bamboo, banana, bananas, banter, barney's bull, bat, batshit, Beecham's belly wash, berley, bilge, bilgewater, billy-o, birdseed, blah, blarney, blather, blatherskite blither blither, blithering, bobbins, boogie-joogie, bop, borak, bosh, bottle, Bovril, bowldacks, bubble gum, bughouse, bull, bull-jive, bullo, bullock, bullshit, bum, bum-fluff, bumbee work, bumble, bumf, bunco, bunk, bunkum, bushwa, buzwuz, caca, cack, catshit chepooka, cherry-ripe, chickenfeed, cobblers, cock, cockamamie, cods, codswallop, cow confetti, cowsh, cowshit, cowyard, crack, crap crud, dick doggery, dogshit, doodad, dookie, dope, dripping, drizzle, drool, Dutch fustian, eye, fairydiddle, fandangle, farmyard confetti, fee-faw-fum, fiddledeedee, flam, flannel, flap, flapdoodle, Flemington confetti, flim-flam, flop, flub, fluff, flummadiddle, fox, frogsh, fuckery, gaff, gammon, garbage, garbar, garp, gas, geyser, giffle gaffle, glop, gobshite, gook, goopher feathers, goulash, granny, guff, gunk, hank, hans wurst, hee-haw, heifer, hockie, hogwash, hoke, hokey, hokey-pokey, hokum, hooey, hooha, hootenanny, hornswoggle, horsefeathers, horseshit, hot air, how's-yer-father, hoy, hubba-hubba, hum, humbug, humbuggery, hydraulics, jack an' danny, jackshit, Jackson Pollocks, jerker, jim-jam, jive, Johnnie Rollocks, junk, kak, keech, keg, kibosh, kid, kidstakes, lallygag, load, lunch, macaroni, madam, mahula, malarkey, manure, mash, meadow mayonnaise, mishegaas, moonshine, mother hubbard, moulie, muck, muckty-muck, muggins, mush, Niagara Falls, nitshit, noodle, nyaams, oars (and rollocks), panther piss, pants, parsley, phonus balonus, phooey, pickle, piddle, pigswill, pigshit, pillocks, pillow, pish, pish-posh, pishery-pashery, piss, pony and trap, poo, poop, posh, prune, puke, pulp, punk, raas, raashole, racket, randle, rannygazoo, razzle-dazzle, rebop, rhubarb, rimble-ramble, rollocks, rot, ruck, scam, schlock, schmaltz, schmegegge, schon, screwball, seconds, shenanigan, shit, shite, skite, skittles, slag, slang, slobber, slum, slumgudgeon, smack, snash, spinach, squit, stuff, sweet Fanny Adams, swosh, talk, taradiddle, tats, tilly-vally, tinkerty-tonk, tits, toffee, tomasso di rotto, tommyrot, toodle-pip, tosh, toss, trash, tripe, turtle, twak, waffle, wank, wash, whangdoodle, whim-wham, yang yang, ying-yang.

Ah. Slang as introspection. Two hundred and seventy-one terms for nonsense. More, as it happens than for anger, obesity, vomiting and a good many others.

That's not the point. Nor is it the case. Everything that's in my book is put there because to the best of my and others' efforts and abilities, it is intended to be correct, it is meant to inform, it is even, in the most wide-ranging use of the term, meant to educate. Isn't that what a dictionary is meant to do? Especially a slang one. Don't tell me you're reading it to check the spellings. All I am trying to say, all that this whole book is trying to say, is that the lexicographer is human. That the dictionary is a human product. *Caveat emptor*. That's all.

Thick, Square Books

> Words, words, words. He had lived too much with words and not what the words stood for . . . The real world, where words are glued to things.
>
> Anthony Burgess, *The Doctor Is Sick* (1960)

All my wisdom is received.

The lexicographer does not make many appearances in fiction. Jonathan Meades' short story 'Filthy English' deals with it (twenty years ago he grilled me about the details over two bottles of white in the then-fashionable restaurant 192 and I still feel bad that I had, at the time, so little of use to offer). The most famous appearance is almost invisible: the character of the Water Rat in Kenneth Grahame's *The Wind in the Willows* was based on Frederick Furnivall. He of the Early English Text Society and a score of other learned Victorian literary societies and journals; he of the red tie (so daring), the rowing eight composed of waitresses recruited in the New Bond Street ABC restaurant of which he was a regular; of the Mistress who, like Miss Havisham and a regular roll-call of Victorian unfortunates, died when her dress drifted too near to a flame. Furnivall was among the fathers of the *OED*, and had introduced Grahame to the river. The favour was repaid.

I could warm to Ratty but always preferred Toad, even if he lacked a lexicographical coeval. Is it over-stretching imagery to see slang as the Toad of language? Braggadocio, noise, duplicity, wide-spectrum excess. Even prison and transvestism. Mole (Grahame himself) representing Standard English. And if Furnivall was Ratty, who was Toad? The truth is, apparently, one Colonel Francis Cecil Ricardo CVO CBE (1852–1924), the first owner of a car in Cookham in Berkshire, where Grahame wrote the book. The ultra-patriotic Horatio Bottomley and Oscar Wilde have also been put forward; I would claim him for another bombastic jingo, W. E. Henley, the slang collector John S. Farmer's on-and-off collaborator, but he had already been appropriated by his friend Robert Louis Stevenson, who used him for Long John Silver in *Treasure Island.**

Samuel Johnson had too many other tricks and James Murray, tricycle, Canterbury cap, beard and all, ought to be the paradigm lexicographer, but for non-specialists that role has been grabbed by W. C. Minor, enshrined in Simon Winchester's *The Surgeon of Crowthorne* (aka *The Professor and the Madman*). Minor with his murky past, his murder, his madness, and his book-lined 'study' that just happened to be sealed away alongside the other criminally insane occupants of Broadmoor. What the outside uninitiated world desires of its dictionary-makers. Not scholarship, not drudgery, but craziness. Minor was not the only contributor who was a fascicle short of a full volume. Not so Murray who was wholly sane, other, perhaps, than in his magnificent and necessary commitment to his work. But that is a given and dedication does not equate with lunacy. The State knighted Murray but the University did not honour him. Or not in time. He was no madman

* Henley's shade, perhaps, has descended on the multi-millionaire and popular versifier Felix Dennis, another whose poems stick sedulously to orthodox rhyme schemes, and who has built an entire 'pleasure dome' representing a modern-day homage to the book, complete with *Hispaniola.*

but neither was he a professor and some of those who were, typically Balliol's Master Benjamin Jowett, never ceased to claim that they could do his job faster, better and indeed, as the OUP dearly would have liked, cheaper. If Murray was honoured it was initially in the prophet's way: abroad. Nothing from Oxford until two years before he died. Working: he had just finished T, and was looking forward to U.

And what are we, we who publish word-books, those damned, thick, square tomes? Those monuments, suddenly, to a dead technology. Compilers? Editors? Authors?

The literal translation of 'glossographia' is 'writing about language' and the reader may ask whether putting words in order, however much they are garlanded with extra information, is 'writing'. Lexicography, 'writing word-books' is not lexicology, which translates literally as 'dictionary discourse', in other words writing about dictionaries and their making. There is no obvious narrative. We are not talking 'creative'. Or as some might suggest when encountering our more suppositious etymologies, only its jokey negative: making things up. As in 'creative accounting'. This time the pun is on 'accounting'. Telling stories.

Looking back five centuries to the beginnings of slang collection I have no real idea of how my predecessors saw themselves. The word 'slang' did not exist for the first century-plus of slang collection and no collector used it in a dictionary title until 1859. The craft did not exist, or not as an accepted job description. 'Slang lexicography' still garners barely 250 hits on Google Books and nothing before the 1990s. 'Slang lexicographer' a bare fifty, most of them Eric Partridge and none before 1950.

I doubt that 'author' (which as a precursor of 'novelist', in this sense coined in the eighteenth century, had existed since 1380) entered the equation. Johnson, a century later, undoubtedly saw himself as such but he was a professional already, wrote much more than his dictionary and nixed slang since he eschewed what he termed cant. 'Writer' still meant copyist, the creative sense did not yet exist. Johnson described himself as his dictionary's author, which did refer to books but ultimately meant an originator, inventor and constructor and, in a parallel meaning that he must have relished, an authority. The word 'editor' was used but it had been synonymous with publisher and in his day referred to the annotation and preparation of the editions of such as Shakespeare. It was the antithesis of 'author'. Johnson acknowledged himself as a 'lexicographer' too (that term had existed for a century), but regretted that such was a disappointing reality when his dreams proclaimed him a poet.

But the chain of slang-gatherers, starting back around 1531? The first consideration was money – only in the current world is it assumed that authorship is some kind of charity work, rendering us all what Johnson would have termed fools if, slaves to our obsession, we struggle on – and after that? Educators, guides to the underworld mysteries, entertainers? Their investigations paralleled those of a wider contemporary movement, of looking at the terminology of a variety of occupations – archery, cooking, heraldry – and expounding upon it. Crime was just one more topic, if a little 'sexier'. Some restricted themselves to lists, inevitably bald of excitement; the words must have seemed strange but perhaps no more so than the vocabulary of any closed world. Others preferred narratives, and invented implausibly cant-dense conversations in which their counterfeit villains – all faked up sores and carefully ripped clothing – paraded the glossary: 'Maund of this morte whate bene peck is in her ken' and then translated it, 'Ask of this wyfe what goode meate shee hath in her house.' The ur-form of such confections as 'Put the bracelets on, guv, it's a fair cop', and about as likely. The playwrights of the late sixteenth and early seventeenth century capitalised on the lexis in their scripts, and among them Robert Greene and Thomas Dekker, lexicologists *avant la lettre*, wrote pamphlets about it. My sense is that neither they nor those that followed were over-worried about the justification or effect of what they did, merely that they did it. They recognised a niche and duly catered for it. The playwrights had their day jobs, as had those who would come after. Even the dedicated slang lexicographers tended to start life as something else. Not until the 1930s do we encounter the first full-timer and even he had not set out to write slang dictionaries.

Eric Partridge, that original 'slang lexicographer', writing under his pen-name 'Corrie Dennison' – a name he used for novels but also, since every little helps, to sign congratulatory blurbs on the back covers of certain of his dictionaries – suggested that 'There is far more of imagination and enthusiasm in the making of a good dictionary than in the average novel.' This was doubtless self-referential: like Scholartis Press, his short-lived publishing house, his pseudonymous novels missed the cut, while his dictionaries made his (real) name. So I would deny his comparison. *Ulysses* – though perhaps a poor example of an 'average' novel – provides me with 1,000 citations, and Joyce, imitating a good lexicographer, certainly drew on every pertinent source, including a sixteenth-century canting glossary, but there the comparison ends. Look at the dictionary. It is not a narrative nor is it intended as such. It is a tool, an information kit. I read novels but for a purpose, which is, as ever, gutting them for citations, and mainly genre-based and in the way of the middle-aged and male I tend to prefer non-fiction for recreation anyway. If I do want a congratulatory quote, I go to Anthony Burgess, who understood and sympathised with my world and wrote about it to a more knowledgeable extent than perhaps anyone outside – and even inside – 'the business'. His own books are not exceptionally slangy and his uses number a quarter of those found in his hero Joyce, but Burgess had some training as a philologist and, while he largely borrowed from Russian, invented his own language, 'Nadsat', for *A Clockwork Orange*. He spoke of the lexicographers' 'energy' and 'doggedness', admired their 'clear brain' and suggested that 'the making of a dictionary is at least as heroic as the building of a bridge'. He also opined that we are 'a mixed and eccentric company' and that the craft can make its practitioners mad. We must take the bad reviews with the good (if, that is, we allow ourselves to acknowledge either) and anyway, who am I to argue?

Of course such angst is foolish, and the work has other values of which one may be proud, but the thing that eats most keenly into the soul is that making a dictionary will never be classed as creation. One is not creative. One's skills, as far as they may exist, cannot render one what is classified as 'a creator' (nor, mercifully, 'a creative'). I find this painful and frustrating and yet again hear that port-crusty don who sits on my shoulder intoning, 'Beta-double-plus, Mr Green. Quite good, quite good, but not, and probably never, quite good enough.'

Yet I think there is a form of creativity and that there is a story. It is not intentional, it is not conscious – if we are authors then this comes more from our work as constructors and authorities than as pure creators – and it happens coincidentally. It is a story that has a point and the themes to underline it. It is not fiction, although fiction's products are used to prove its point. It is a documentary, a docu-drama. The story of language, of the people who make and use it (the acknowledged 'creators') and of the societies which spawn it. Downmarket by default.

Tabloid television. If it does mimic fiction then it is in offering a cast of heroes and heroines, though in the taxonomy of stardom most would be relegated to the ranks – as villain or villainess or perhaps as good man 'gone to the bad' or 'fallen' woman – of 'best support'.

The lexicon is not *Finnegans Wake* but access comes only after effort. One must *use* a dictionary. Search it. Cross-reference. I am asked: why do people read your books? And answer, above all for pleasure. The pleasure of discovery, of learning, of having questions answered, information passed on, but also quite simply for pleasure. Of serendipitous revelation. The joy, to steal a phrase that has been noted elsewhere, of lex. All this will be easier as dictionaries, including my own, go online. The possibilities, if the software permits, are infinite. Few read the dictionary, as in A–Z, cover-to-cover, other than Ammon Shea who a few years ago read 21,730 pages of the printed *OED* and then created 232 more to memorialise his exploration. Few others, that is, than successor lexicographers who dare not offer a future without first scouring the past. For the craft is innately, inescapably plagiaristic. Not the sitting down to copy, word for word, entry for entry, the work of another lexicographer. But the absolute, inescapable need to look back.

I blame the raw material: the language. The intractable, implacable English language, prone to longevity, to reinvention, to faking its own death and then emerging, self-reincarnated with a new identity. Slang isn't separate. Just a new set of papers, a doctored photo: the nose lengthened, the lips thinned, the hair dyed, maybe a pair of glasses. We cannot skip. How does the reviewer most glibly prove themself – for very few dictionary reviewers have the first-hand experience of what their commission demands – but by shouting to their readers: he's missed a word. Yes, one replies, and what about the 125,000 that I haven't missed, few of which you have even dreamed of. Tough. This is no defence, it shouldn't be and who will listen? Size matters in lexicography. Mine's bigger than yours. If you say so. Who really believes that it's only how you use it? The language increases but it sheds its past reluctantly. We must look back.

Slang is not merely tenacious but repetitive. Setting aside the open-ended accretion of technology's new terms and the tracking of a steady flow of general neologisms, Standard English made most of its points long ago. To take a few of slang's primary themes, each of which continues to produce so many synonyms, Standard English had 'foolish' in place in 1300, 'ugly' in 1325, 'mad' in 1330, 'drunk' and 'violent' both in 1340, 'fat' in 1400 and so it went. Of course alternatives have developed, but the basics continue to do their job. Slang remains unsatisfied. For and of the young, like the world for the young it must be relearned in each generation, even in each successive teenage, and what went before is rarely good enough. Echoing those tribes who once slaughtered their leaders so as to water next year's crops with their blood, slang thrives on linguistic patricide. This lexis of synonymy continues to reproduce itself, but the themes are constant and the imagery stays the same. One attempts to keep up but, dare I admit, the fascination sometimes palls. Another word for fucking, for cannabis, for derision. The inventiveness, for slang has always boasted that, is always alluring but one yearns for something more. Occasionally, as in the emergence of MLE, which is perhaps destined for a longer life than most 'youth slang', that wish is granted and one amasses and dissects and gratefully takes one's pleasure. Too often, much as one loves, say, the unfettered creativity of those who contribute to *Roger's Profanisaurus* (and how I yearn to have myself guyed among its fake 'citations'), what we find is ultimately more of the same.

Looking back is easier. More satisfying. The chase more exciting, potentially more rewarding. Eric Partridge patently preferred the past to the present. I entered this world because I felt that he had failed on modernity, failed on teenage, failed on drugs and the rest of the so-called counter-culture. For him all drug users, no matter of what, were 'addicts'. A man of his era, he seemed to tolerate racism, not merely in the headwords but in his over-tolerant definitions of its vocabulary. He gazed with undisguised fascination at the miniskirt and shoehorned it into his dictionary accordingly. He was born in 1894. The gap between his consciousness – colonial New Zealand, two World Wars and between them the Depression – and mine – Brit baby boomer vintage 1948 – was vast. This time I was the reviewer, I was shouting. He had missed many words and failed to understand many more. Or so it seemed. So I signed on and remain enlisted. Now, at sixty-five, pretty much his age when the chronological Sixties began, I am drawn to his point of view. Slang stays forever young; I do not. I hope I still 'get' new slang, but how can I not be overlooking its subtleties, maybe even the obvious as well? The gulf between its coiners and myself, its codifier, grows larger every year. I should chuck it in. I do not. After all, I value the craft and I am loath to abandon it. I cannot happily turn my beloved lexis over to the foolish, relativistic crowd who post to Urban Dictionary website, a work in which the word itself, 'slang', is defined as 'the reason that Urban Dictionary exists'. Oh ferchrissake. To use its own gauge of assessment: 'thumb down' on that one. But Urban Dictionary may be the future, or at least a future, and I shall have more to say.

'Stay-at-home', 'lone wolf', 'mossy-back'. Slang is frustratingly short on such terms, though it manages nearly 200 for various permutations of 'coward'. I have said it before: I am a voyeur (not many terms for that either, a bit too subtle for slang and 'Peeping Tom' is Standard English; though the lexis musters 225 for gazing, staring and the like). Sitting at my desk, only venturing out through the screen or the printed sheet. This is what we do and perhaps Burgess is right: perhaps it drives us mad. Slang deals in excess, we restrain it. Ourselves too. Slang collectors have rarely been participants. Only the few whose wait for the gallows was rendered more palatable by composing their memoirs, which were made yet more commercial by a leavening of criminal words, had used the language in earnest. The dictionary-makers John Camden Hotten and, according to the folklorist Gershon Legman, John S. Farmer, were pornographers, but even so, Victorian porn is paradoxically free of obscenity. Flagellation, its mainstay, seems not to lend itself to genuinely violent language; in slang's world the whip is only brandished in judicial contexts. I too put in my time on the top shelf, but that was long before and never during. (Passing out assignments, one editor informed me, 'You've been to college, Jon, you can write the *history* of knickers.' I remember handstands and who could truly love a woman who opts only for quotidian lingerie.) Partridge, it is true, gained his first experience of slang on the Somme, and military usages were always his strongpoint, but there was no hands-on knowledge of the words that were included in his weighty *Dictionary of the Underworld*. It may be that Captain Francis Grose (who in 1785 had his flagellant, the 'flogging cully') was similarly intrigued by the language of the troops.

Need I add that I revel in it. If to some extent I have become, as the god-bothering and wilfully obtuse Mary Whitehouse used to claim of the consumers of pornography, corrupted in some way by my work, then it is not what she would have set down as 'moral' corruption. It is rather to have become coarsened beyond understanding, hardened against empathy, careless of the feelings of those more sensitive. I would prefer to think not. It is not a matter of being beyond shock but of expecting, and finding, the worst and whether this is a lifetime's cynicism or thirty years of researching words that pursue their existence in humanity's lower depths I cannot unequivocally say. Perhaps it is a closed and in every sense vicious circle.

The problem (if there is a problem) is that if one takes things seriously (and I take my job very seriously), one has no time for debate. For shifting the gaze from the central issue. Slang by its nature has no time for kindness. It lacks empathy. All price, no value. Cruel and heartless though it is, its role is to highlight what is, not what should be. It demands descriptive dictionaries that in turn demand that the user remembers that talking about it isn't an instruction to adopt it. Of course these words are repellent, vicious, hurtful. What else are they meant to be? That is not to say that slang's negatives, for example racial slurs, are to be celebrated. They remain vile, but, however we may deplore them, they are. The dictionary-maker is a witness, not a judge. Even if, like any of those who deal with law, *parti pris*.

One thing has changed of late. Ironically it is that same digitisation that has thrown my world off kilter that has also permitted me to forge ever backwards in pursuit of primary examples of what was once new-minted. The voyeur, as stereotyped, tends to the flash, in every sense. Enshrined in what smug and youthful commenters, seeing themselves as iconoclasts, like to term dead trees, there are many more sources than one might have imagined, but at least there was a sense, still in place as I worked, that one might actually look at the great majority of what was on offer.

Even if I wish otherwise, and how at times I wish it, that fantasy is over. Every day sees a new arrival online: some of it from sources that have been created through and for the Internet; but many – and these are more pertinent to my research with its focus on the past – bringing into easy access tens of thousands of ageing newspapers, magazines and journals. The material was there but effort was required and I am naturally lazy. I hate leaving home. I hate working where there is no decent coffee, no shelves of my own work books, my own desktop, the chance, free of fellow-toilers, to pick my nose or scratch my arse. Now I have the opportunity, even the lust, to gaze at the plethora of databases, offering up material, especially from the press, that had always existed but had also been so much harder to approach. These scanned editions let me cut to the chase and never shift that arse. In addition we have Google Book Search, which may be notoriously and even dangerously sloppy in its bibliography* – created by engineers, its importance is that, being feasible, it should exist at this moment rather than that it should be of real and lasting use – but with judicious assessment, an unprecedented tool for finding material by date. Morgan Le Fay's new enchantments are alluring, but the grail, the first use, informs the quest.

A quest that continues without ending but will have to go on without me. I shall not live long enough to assay even a small proportion of what is on offer. This is frustrating but it is undoubtedly true. And is there a successor? I do not know – the world long since turned upside down for reference works as for all else that once found shelter between two covers – and I do not speculate. If slang lexicography does not pass down the generations,

* Not to mention frustrating; the use of original publication dates for magazines has one slavering over what seems to be a remarkably early example . . . only to realise that no, 'nang' was not on offer in 1711, merely the first ever edition of the *Spectator*, which started using it, well after the pack, in 2012.

neither does it engage apprentices, though I would not wish to discredit those researchers who have helped in my own work. The terms of employment are, sadly, not over-alluring. It is not coincidence that we number so few.

I Theory: What is Slang?

He had strayed from conventional language into rough, truthful speech.

Anthony Trollope, *The Eustace Diamonds* (1871)

For those who would have answer to the perennial question, what is slang? there exist a variety of answers, both academic and popular.

Whether, as one observer suggests, it is the working man of language, doing the lexicon's 'dirty work', the language that as the grindingly populist poet Carl Sandburg suggested, 'rolls up its sleeves and goes to work', as John Moore suggests in *You English Words* (1961), it is 'the poor man's poetry' (refined in 2009 by the American academic Michael Adams as 'The People's Poetry') standing up for the disenfranchised, or, as its many critics still proclaim, it has nothing but the most deleterious effects on 'proper speech', slang remains a law unto itself.*

As a linguistic phenomenon it surely predates Christ. The mid-nineteenth-century slang lexicographer John Camden Hotten, as keen as any other Victorian scholar to find antecedents in the

* Nor does lexicographical lyricism reside in slang alone; writing in 1989 of the second edition of the *OED*, Anthony Burgess concludes his essay with the suggestion that the revised dictionary 'must be the longest poem ever written'.

classical and pre-classical worlds, offers the readers of his *Slang Dictionary* (1859) an alluring, if somewhat fantastical, picture of this 'universal and ancient' species of language. 'If we are to believe implicitly the saying of the *wise man*, that "there is nothing new under the sun" the "fast" men of buried Nineveh, with their knotty and door-matty looking beards, may have cracked Slang jokes on the steps of Sennacherib's palace; and the stones of Ancient Egypt, and the bricks of venerable and used up Babylon, may, for aught we know, be covered with slang hieroglyphics unknown to modern antiquarians . . .' And the Phoenicians, the Greeks and the Romans all, presumes Hotten, had their own slangy speech.

Greeks, Romans, yes. The rest, who knows? We must stick to proof (though proof, as one finds in pursuit of language, is always up for re-analysis). As a word in itself slang does not appear in the (printed) language before the mid-eighteenth century. The *OED* (its entry written in 1911), which included only that slang terminology which occurred in literature and in the 'cant' glossaries that appeared in the sixteenth and seventeenth centuries, defined the term as 'The special vocabulary used by any set of persons of a low or disreputable character; language of a low and vulgar type,' and adds, 'Language of a highly colloquial type, considered as below the level of standard educated speech, and consisting either of new words or of current words employed in some special sense.' (The tacit equation of two supposedly different registers – slang and colloquialism – shows how even the most informed of lexicographers come to grief at this particular border.)

Until an earlier instance is uncovered, we find the word's first use as a reference to language in William Toldervy's play *The History of Two Orphans* (1756): 'Thomas Throw had been upon the town, knew the slang well.' However the slang in question is somewhat vague. Was it language pure and simple or was it more metaphorical, a style of dress and/or manner that set young

Mr Throw among the fast-living men-about-town? Was he even a criminal? Because the line continues '. . . and understood every word in the scoundrel's dictionary.' Certainly by the turn of the century, when such young men were known as The Fancy (a term first used of pigeon fanciers but elevated to the prize ring and the turf), a knowledge of slang was a prerequisite of the type. Pierce Egan's bestseller, *Life in London* (1821), which first brought us that long-lived team 'Tom and Jerry', owed much of its success to its use of such terminology. And by the mid-nineteenth century 'slang' had also begun to be used as an alternative to jargon (itself most simply definable as 'professional or occupational slang') and such luminaries as Charles Kingsley (in a letter of 1857) and George Eliot (in *Middlemarch*, [1872]) referred quite naturally to the 'slang' of, respectively, artists and poets. In 1853 Dickens, through his mouthpiece George Augustus Sala, excoriated slang in *Household Words*, but seemed to mean verbal affectation, no matter what its source; his lists of 'real' slang are much too impressively knowledgeable to suggest a genuine disdain. Meanwhile the modern meaning of the word, if not its vocabulary, had been enlisted in Standard English by the mid-century and dignified by John Keble (in 1818), Thackeray (in *Vanity Fair* [1848]) and many other respectable users. In 1858 Trollope, in *Doctor Thorne*, speaks of 'fast, slang men, who were fast and slang and nothing else', a citation that points up both their language and their rakehell, buckish style. But Trollope, as noted above, also appreciated that slang, in more general terms, was 'rough, truthful speech'.

Set firmly amid respectable language within the *OED* – it is, after all, a Standard English term – 'slang' as a linguistic subset remains essentially unchanged as to its definitions and in its use, even if it continues to develop as a vocabulary. The philologists and lexicographers remain generally consistent in their opinions.

Since the *OED* laid down lexicographical law they may have replaced one simple definition by more complex explanations, but they differ only in the nuances.

Those nuances, however, can go further. The American critic H. L. Mencken, who more than anyone before him set out successfully to emphasise the substantial differences between 'American' and 'English' English, suggested: 'Slang originates in the efforts of ingenious individuals to make the language more pungent and picturesque – to increase the store of terse and striking words, to widen the boundaries of metaphor, and to provide a vocabulary for new shades of difference in meaning.' The late David W. Maurer, author of the current *Britannica* entry, states 'Slang consists basically of unconventional words or phrases that express either something new or something old in a new way. It is flippant, irreverent, indecorous; it may be indecent or obscene. Its colourful metaphors are generally directed at respectability, and it is this succinct, sometimes witty, frequently impertinent social criticism, that gives slang its characteristic flavour.' Such opinions underline an essential difference between British and American definitions. The English, class divisions aforethought, concentrate on slang's proletarian origins; Americans, flaunting their iconoclasm, see it as an instrument of glorious revolution.

Ultimately slang seems to be what you think it is. An empty vessel into which any and everyone can pour the filling of choice. Fittingly, it parallels that other notorious defier of simplicity, obscenity, which, as a number of otherwise baffled judges have declared, is something we know when we see it.

In the end, I'm with that old reprobate John Camden Hotten. His *Slang Dictionary* appeared in 1859 and ran to five editions before its author died in 1873. It remained the best available slang dictionary for the next twenty years and its author's comments on slang are still pertinent.

> SLANG represents that evanescent, vulgar language, ever changing with fashion and taste, . . . spoken by persons in every grade of life, rich and poor, honest and dishonest . . . Slang is indulged in from a desire to appear familiar with life, gaiety, town-humour and with the transient nick names and street jokes of the day. . . . slang is the language of street humour, of fast, high and low life . . . Slang is as old as speech and the congregating together of people in cities. It is the result of crowding, and excitement, and artificial life.

The general assumption is that slang is a language. More than one book has been titled 'slanguage' and the image is that of an established, if unconventional form of communication. Another question: is that assumption correct, is it really a language? or no more than an aggregation of words? A lexis? A vocabulary? If a language demands the fulfilment of certain rules: pronunciation, word order, grammar, then no, it is not. It is marginal, used by the marginal, expresses marginality. Those who use it may see it as a language, they may be wrong. That posited etymology, the 's' for 'secret' and 'lang' for 'language' suggests that the belief is deep. But that suggested etymology is wrong too. It may be, or rather may have been secret, but no matter: it still fails the tests that render it a fully fledged language. What it is, perhaps, is a lexis of synonymy. There are themes: topics it embraces, the philosophy of its use ('counter'/'subversive') but even if it demands dictionaries, it is not a language as such.

Yet with all that said, the diagram with which James Murray, its first editor, prefaced the *OED*, setting linguistic groupings around a central core, does equate slang with jargon/technical terms/dialect as equally valuable subsets of the overriding 'English language'. Even if Murray seems to mix the concepts of 'vocabulary' and 'language'.

I Theory: What is Slang?

The current *OED* (in its revised definition of March 2008) offers this under **language**:

> Definition 1.a. The system of spoken or written communication used by a particular country, people, community, etc., typically consisting of words used within a regular grammatical and syntactic structure.

In that case, no. It is not a system. Nor, even if Victor Hugo wrote, in *The Hunchback of Notre Dame*, of 'the kingdom of argot', and playwrights such as Thomas Dekker and Ben Jonson rendered visible a 'beggar's brotherhood', is it a country or a community. But let us look further:

> Definition 2.a. The form of words in which something is communicated; manner or style of expression.

Then yes, slang is certainly that. And here the *OED* even cross-references to 'slangism' and 'slanguage'.

There is a further qualification, used by some theorists: that language both represents and forms the world of a given community. A national, even supranational jargon, as it were. If that is the case then slang surely qualifies as such. Even if its world and worldview are *de facto* limited.

As such, it must come from somewhere. People demand that it should come from somewhere. It has creation myths. Like the Biblical original they are undoubtedly unsound. They involve a great leader and his community of criminal beggars and the establishment of codes both social and linguistic. In France it was *le Grand Coesre*, a word surely linked to Caesar, who gathers his followers and lays down the laws, including those of secret communication. In England it was one 'Cock Lorel', King of the Beggars, who performed the same office, bringing his people together at the pleasingly named Devil's Arse Peak in Derbyshire. But since 'cock lorel' means no more than what we would term a 'top villain', then, or so I hope, it was his successor, another pleasing name: Jenkins Cowdiddle.

But if as I say slang is hard-wired, then the creation myths are just that: myths. Nonetheless the need for secrecy was genuine. The French term *argot* denoted a people before it was a language (or rather jargon) and when it became a language, then it was for criminals only. In France, at least, this was probably true until the last world war: the *milieu* had its own lexis and it, as much as any street, delineated its boundaries. It was not the same as *l'argot commun*, the slang of civilian life. It is harder to see where cant, the criminal jargon of the underworld and the slang of the common user, draw their lines in the Anglophone world. Cant dictionaries abounded, albeit plagiarising relentlessly each from its predecessor, until the nineteenth century. But cant only had the stage to itself until the late seventeenth century. After that the dictionaries of non-standard language, even if 'slang' itself had yet to enter their titles, begin to include non-criminal words and phrases – 'civilian slang' as it were. Cant persisted in appearing – as did the criminals who spoke it – but year on year found itself overtaken by the growing vocabulary of the mainstream. Today we all speak ghetto, African-American, a by-product of rap's world-conquering proliferation.

II Practice: What is Slang?

A confession: I cannot define slang. This is not so much an expression of ignorance, but of a reluctance to force a hard-and-fast role on so fluid a phenomenon. A disinclination to tie it down after immersing myself so deeply in the subject. I can ponder it, think aloud about it – what else is this book? – put forward my opinions based on a professional lifetime 'in the trade', but claims of lexicographical authority aside I am lousy at laying down such law and slang is so resistant to having itself set in stone. There are definitions, dozens. There are also amateur pontifications, too often banal. Litterateurs have tossed in their tenpenn'orth, but their views tend to suit a more personal agenda. (Dickens, for instance, was a masterly user, but professed to scorn it; Balzac, who claimed to love it, rarely wrote of worlds in which it was used.)

Slang with its vulgarity, its crudity, its impudence, its irrepressible *loudness*, offers a vocabulary and a voice to all our negatives. Our inner realities: lusts, fears, hatreds, self-indulgences. It subscribes to nothing but itself – no belief systems, no true believers, no faith, no religion, no politics, no party. It is, for Freudians, the linguistic id. The id, as laid out in Freud's *New Introductory Lectures on Psychoanalysis* of 1933:

> is the dark, inaccessible part of our personality, [. . .] most of this is of a negative character [. . .]. We all approach the

> id with analogies: we call it a chaos, a cauldron full of seething excitations . . . It is filled with energy reaching it from the instincts, but it has no organization, produces no collective will, but only a striving to bring about the satisfaction of the instinctual needs subject to the observance of the pleasure principle.

Id. The German and before that Latin for 'it'. And 'it', as we know, stands in slang for sex.

Admirable stuff, and I have offered my own tenpenn'orth in my definition of slang as a 'counter-language', cut from the same contrarian cloth as the 'counter-culture' of the Sixties, though a good deal older. Maybe it's all these years, more than half of a professional lifetime spent in its ever more intimate company, but I find myself conceiving images that are far from conventionally linguistic. In its determinedly macho vocabulary, in the concentration of its major themes, slang reminds me of nothing so much as one of those pictograms that depict the male body as sensed by its inhabitant: the brain is tiny; the mouth and hands huge; the penis vast. It requires no great imagination to delineate what might be the features in an equivalent pictogram, again glimpsed through male eyes, of the female form.

If what James Murray termed 'common' English represents the entirety of a traditional newspaper then slang is the crime pages, the court report, the *faits divers*, the gossip column and in every sense the 'sports pages'. It is the *roman noir* of language, and when it essays wit, its farce. There are few if any happy endings and a good laugh is the encounter of pomposity and banana skin. Its pessimistic, deflatory vocabulary echoes the same dreams of loss and exclusion that underpin *noir* and give slang something to rail against. If slang were film it would be *noir* too, and if it were storytelling it would be pulp. This is reverse engineering, of course. My debt to the unsung authors of 1930s' pulp fiction and the dime novels of the 1950s is vast. They needed slang to underline their fiction's authenticity; I need their usage to testify to my lexicographical truths. Slang is the lexical reification of Lenny Bruce's dictum: 'Everybody wants what should be. But there is no what should be, there is only what is.' Slang, as Jonathan Meades has noted, is 'a depiction of the actual, of what we think rather than what we are enjoined to think'. Slang is even, dare I suggest, a sort of lexical WikiLeaks, revelatory of our own otherwise guarded opinions.

It is voyeuristic, amoral, libertarian and libertine. It is vicious. It is cruel. It is self-indulgent. It treats all theologies – secular as well as spiritual – with the contempt that they deserve. It is funny. It is fun.

Given its position on the margins one might see it as a means of self-affirmation: I denigrate/blaspheme/utter obscenities, therefore I am. Shouting dark words into the darkness of the world. Slang is aggressive, angry. It is frustrated by the way the world works, by the hypocrisy of the powerful. It is cynical but its cynicism is that of the failed romantic.

Like the tramp I see almost daily on my walks along a street near my flat in Paris, it lies cheerfully in the gutter. And, like him, it may be gazing at the stars but far more likely beneath the skirts of passing women.

And 'gutter' is the word, not 'ditch', because slang is the language of the city. For Jack-the-lad not Johnny hayseed.*

* Yet I have come to wonder. Researching the Internet's cornucopia of nineteenth-century local newspapers I have found a number of unsung 'slang lexicographers', far away from and even ignorant of the contemporary slang mainstream. These collectors, with a skill that Thomas Harman would recognise, have found and interviewed passing tramps and vagrants, and listed and explained their vocabularies in the local paper. The language is cant, criminal, and may well have originated in London, but its use has undeniably been carried beyond the pavement and along the lane.

Standard dictionary definitions of 'slang' make clear what it is that links the city and its language: the overriding suggestion is of speed, fluidity, movement. The descriptors that recur are 'casual', 'playful', 'ephemeral', 'racy', 'humorous', 'irreverent'. These are not the terminology of lengthy, measured consideration. Slang's words are twisted, turned, snapped off short, re-launched at a skewed angle. Some with their multiple, and often contrasting, definitions seem infinitely malleable, shape shifting: who knows what hides round their syllabic corners. It is not, I suggest, a language that works out of town; it requires the hustle and bustle, the rush, the lights, the excitement and even the muted (sometimes far from muted) sense of impending threat. To use slang confidently one needs that urban cockiness. It doesn't work behind a yoke of oxen, even athwart a tractor.

Then there are the value judgments: 'sub-standard', 'low', 'vulgar', 'unauthorised'. The word we are seeking is 'street'. Street as noun, more recently street as adjective. The vulgar tongue. The gutter language.

In a way slang is the true Esperanto – the real international language. And even if, because it is found in so many different languages, it cannot be a true Esperanto, it remains so in its overarching imagery and its role in communication and as a statement of self. My second language, if I dare thus dignify the ability to read Simenon, with his pared-down 2000-word vocabulary, and a selection of modern *romans noir* as such, for I have no articulate conversation, is French. I am constantly delighted by the parallels in the imagery that argot offers. A century or so ago John S. Farmer added a variety of synonyms – French, Italian, Spanish and German – to his late nineteenth-century *Slang and Its Analogues*. The same thing held.

There are few languages that have resisted slang. Perhaps they are spoken in the few countries that have no city, slang's necessary crucible. Languages, of course, are different: some vastly, some relatively slightly, but all are different. But in their slangs, as in the humans who speak them, *plus ça change*. The details differ, the big picture is much the same. Slang has a story, and that story has universal themes.

Slang's thematic range is not wide, though its synonymy runs very deep, and one can see the same ideas recurring from classical Greek and Latin onwards. The content changes, the form remains the same. It offers the narrowness of conceptual waterfronts but that very narrowness is the best testament to its utility. Stripped down, modernist, cutting edge – at whatever time, that is, that it has reflected the currently 'modern' and whatever edge has been at that moment 'cutting'.

Which proves to me at least that even if the individual terms that make up the vocabulary may be dismissed as 'ephemeral' – and that is a far from accurate dismissal – the persistence of these themes ensures that slang lasts. The imagery does not vanish; it is not short-term. It reflects the way that we think of certain topics. One might call it stereotyping since it is often in stereotypes that slang deals, but could a better synonym be psychological 'shorthand'?

So what do the similarities tell us? That the basic concerns remain consistent in slang as they do in much that is human: sex, money, intoxication, fear (of others), aggrandisement (of oneself). The preoccupations are all concrete. No abstracts. Caring, sharing, selflessness and compassion: sweet fuck all. If slang professes a philosophy then it has to be deduced from what it chooses to leave out. If slang can boast a single abstract concept, it is *doubt*, with which it mocks and undermines every vestige of true belief. With that in mind, let me offer some heresies:

It is surely ironic that the word slang itself defies all etymology. A language that prided itself on secrecy maintains this secret at its very core. Slang, said Eric Partridge in his history of the lexis, 'that prize-problem word'. Are there still 'prize problems'? Not that I've encountered, but I encounter slang daily and while in the sense Partridge meant, the mystery of slang's etymology, its linguistic root, there are no prizes, no ascertainable 'win', it is a problem.

Although the word *slang* has received definitions in every major dictionary since Webster's *American* in 1828, it remains a slippery customer. Unlike such peers as 'dialect' or 'technical' it defeats the linguists who seek to establish it in a specific register. Even the *OED* seems confused: its current definition runs thus: '*Language of a highly colloquial type, considered as below the level of standard educated speech, and consisting either of new words or of current words employed in some special sense.*' But slang is not colloquial; that's its point. Colloquialisms are not slang. Other dictionaries are equally baffled. Slang ducks and slang dives. We are forced to accept the answer of a lexicographer's essay of 1978, which asked 'Is slang a word for linguists?' And answered: 'No'.

There is a further question, far more perturbing. Attending a recent workshop on the craft, *le tout slang* – all twenty of us, and far from all of them dictionary-makers, in attendance – we turned, less than enthusiastically in my case, to abstracts. Linguistic stuff. We dealt with 'what is slang?' This took several hours and no real conclusion was found. That, if I may comfort myself, might be characterised as showing the innate egalitarianism that ought to go hand-in-hand with our work. No elitist diktats here. That, however, was not the perturbing question. This is: does slang exist?

You see? Not the sort of query that those of us who have spurned all other for thirty years want to ponder. Not hard. Nor indeed at all. I am no philosopher, and my only Wittgenstein quote is the usual one: 'Whereof one cannot speak, thereof one must be silent.' Clunky, archaistic 'whereof' aside, it does nag. So if you can't define it . . . In the event we side-stepped, taking refuge in practicalities. But they should be noted. Major dictionaries of Australian English refuse to label anything slang. Nor yet colloquial, though surely much such terminology is, and this seems to recall the *OED*'s original definition, which defines slang in term of colloquial language. A similar reticence is found in the Caribbean where one finds divisions into 'Formal', 'Informal' and 'Anti-Formal', but again no slang. Yet there exist, on and offline, many volumes entitled 'Australian Slang' and one can find similar publications devoted to the West Indies. Then there is Scotland. Are all those terms so laboriously mined from Irvine Welsh and, for that matter, Walter Scott merely nativisms or even dialect? Some would say just that. But in that case, as in the others, many would not. A large number of people believe that 'their' slang exists, even if the linguistic priesthood has serious doubts. As a lexicographer I have long since made my choice.

In any case, may I suggest that the official definitions of slang are ultimately a waste of time, intellectual marginalia for a supremely non- (but not anti-) intellectual code. And like pornography, conveniently defined as that which induces an erection in an otherwise elderly and impotent judge, we know it when we see it.

To me its greatest charm is that at its heart, even its most obscene and gutter-dwelling heart, it is subversive. This is not political subversion – slang is above politics – but a subversion of the English language itself. And by subverting English, it subverts the givens of the world that English informs. So many of its terms do no more than turn standard usages upside down. Appropriating them for reinterpretations that mock their lost respectability. Standing aside from the standard world, the slang user rejects standard language and substitutes a code within which he or she feels secure and which serves to define themselves. Of course no one exists purely in slang-world. It is feasible, perhaps, in a closed society such as a prison, but rarely elsewhere. One must discard slang to enter 'real life' just as many of us must still discard casual clothes to go to work.

And for all the cries of 'limited vocabulary', to use slang demands articulacy. Thus the city person creates and expresses it. The taciturn peasant – inarticulate through choice or verbal inadequacy – cannot rise to slang. And it offers articulacy to the otherwise inarticulate, or at least those who lack the mastery of standard usage. Like beauty, articulacy is wholly relative. I watch *The Wire*. Sixty episodes back to back. A five-minute scene with no script but the iteration of 'fuck', its compounds, its derivations and its phrasal verbs. Lines that tell us 'We got a decomp floater was John Doe for three weeks.' If these are not poetry then perhaps it is me that lacks articulacy.

Another question: does the etymology of the word 'slang' really matter? For most of the twentieth century the orthodox view was that it came from a variety of Scandinavian terms all meaning to sling, to throw. The Oxford panjandrums were divided but Eric Partridge, my predecessor, had no doubts. But Partridge is dead and Oxford still remains unimpressed, and pronounces 'etymology unknown'. Because it remains unknown. There are inevitable suggestions but they turn on populism and its wishful fantasies and we, in this case self-denyingly, must look for something more solid. Etymology unknown: let us leave it at that.

Slang is an evocation of (marginal/rebellious/contrary) self. The etymology of the term is unnecessary icing on the cake. Is it, to keep things culinary, over-egging the imagistic custard to suggest that like the great human givens that provide its vocabulary, slang too simply *is*. Perhaps I do it too much honour. Yet how can I not admire something that has reached so far beneath the moralising skin?

It is, of course, quite possible that I reject the linguistic aspects of slang because I lack the intellectual equipment to approach them. This is not false modesty, simply a necessary admission. If the succession of slang lexicographers, however hard they work, may be categorised as scholarly dilettantes or supremely dedicated amateurs it is because, having eluded formal training, we can go no further (and may have no wish to do so). Perhaps this suits the lexis, which by its nature concentrates on surfaces and stereotypes. It is even arguable that slang lexicographers – and we have all been very much of a type – have never been 'real' lexicographers, if that means considering the deeper roots of etymology or of honing our definitions to the demands of informational hierarchies used by standard dictionaries. What we do, for a large proportion of our headwords, is to run herd on an ever-expanding collection of synonyms based on well-established themes. We are, perhaps, cataloguers as much as lexicographers, and our more complex dictionaries resemble the art world's *catalogues raisonnés*, lists that have been augmented by descriptive expertise.

Linguists in turn steer clear of slang. Especially the theorists, who prefer the complexities of grammar to actual words and their meanings, and prefer to invent the examples with which they work than look at the messy cussedness of real-life usage. They demand rules, slang pooh-poohs them. What the computational lexicographer Patrick Hanks terms the 'imprecision and dynamism of language in use' is exactly what makes slang tick. Slang is constantly rebuffing those (lexicographers as well as linguists) who want to enclose it by rules. The refusal to submit to such rules indicates another of slang's underlying principles: doubt.

Rules demand its suspension and slang is not interested. Time and again it is seemingly wrestled to a standstill by one theorist or another and then with one bound it leaps free. It resolutely resists the linguistic norms. The great project of reverse engineering that is corpus-based lexicography and linguistics cannot risk slang, so determined is it to throw spanners into every aspect of the work. Is it even sampled in the great corpora, billions of words from thousands of texts, and if included does it provide material considered worthy of study?* My sense is no, since to deduce rules one must have consistency and the very essence of slang is that it is governed by subversion and cussedness: it will not submit. Or perhaps the image should be of the patient (or recalcitrant prisoner) fighting off the (punitive) strait-jacket. Like me slang is claustrophobic.

Yet I may be wrong to see it as something apart. If slang cannot be constrained by the lists of alleged common characteristics proposed by Eric Partridge and others (which lists I have always found ultimately arbitrary and even rather desperate), then perhaps it is – being as I am always keen to stress, just one more part of English – nonetheless as susceptible to the patterns that Professor Hanks sees in language use as any other part of the lexis. For him, though he does not specify, it falls into the rubric of *exploitations* – the antithesis of *norms* – defined as words that demonstrate creativity and inventive playfulness, those that 'show some abnormality, aberration, eccentricity or some other departure from the norm'. If that is not slang, what is? And exploitations, he assures us, have rules too.

* On the other hand there is simple practicality: a slang corpus would be impossible since we lack sufficient texts. Slang is simply found as and when, which is another proof, at least to me, of its role not as some alien, but as just one more aspect of the wider language.

I am fascinated by such possibilities, but as I work with slang, I have a different take, like so many of my beliefs based as much on emotion as on data. Rightly or otherwise, I see slang first and foremost less as a language phenomenon but as a psychological one: it seems visceral, hard-wired. A need.

Or do I flatter it, this mongrel outpouring of a greater social marginality? I celebrate it but there is another side. Slang is also the cry of desperation and want. The complaint of need and greed and jealousy and angered deprivation. The have-not poor who see the rich and hate them for their easy privilege. The ugly who see beauty and wish only to deform it.

Were slang an animal, what could it be but a rat? The gutter animal, symbolic of the gutter language. Quintessentially urban. (If cities, not to mention rats, could talk, wouldn't their language of choice be slang?) Intelligent, resourceful – and vilified. Rats are silent, but the word 'rat' is the source of a mini-lexicon of hatred and abuse. Like slang the rat is stereotyped, and always negatively. Even if, when one looks at the rat, and looks at slang, it is hard to see quite why. Slang has always been an easy form of shorthand for those who wish to condemn that which they fail to understand. Thus dismissed, slang words are as undifferentiated, and as worthless as a mass as those who create them. To justify mass murder we first remove humanity from the victim; to justify the condemnation of the way the mass choose to speak, we remove our toleration for their language.

Slang-dense speech acts as a linguistic carapace, a defensive wall giving the speaker a space for action. You can duck and dive within slang. You can Ali shuffle, you can jab and hook and uppercut and dance and bob and weave and no one can touch you. It is an aura. A diving suit for the lower social depths. A whip to crack at the social lions. A spacesuit. A fireproof uniform. A showplace for cheerful amorality. Slang does not exist to comfort the afflicted nor to make anyone feel 'better'. There is no feel-good factor (other, perhaps, than the masturbatory). Its role is to afflict the comfortable. It is a vote for the disenfranchised. Or possibly those who simply eschew the polls.

Slang refuses to take the whole game seriously: cynical and insolent (and who, pray, defines what is 'insolent'?), it deflates and disdains the pompous and the self-regarding. One can also see, again on the basis of its great themes, that slang operates as a vehicle for a side of the collective imagination: downmarket, of course, lacking 'taste' (and like 'insolence', what exactly is 'taste'?), but hugely energetic, and at its best devoid of artifice and affect. The novelist Peter Carey, discussing coal, anthracite and mineral oil, terms theirs to be 'practical smells'. To me slang has the same metaphorical 'smell': practical not ephemeral, the stench of reality.

This is not, I find, a position that many wish to accept. It is perhaps due punishment; since nothing stereotypes as enthusiastically as does slang, but the great fight for the lexicographer is to convince the uninitiated – who in one's bleakest hours seem even to include all too many who really should know better – that slang, and the dictionaries in which it is collected, are not *de facto* primarily foul and quasi-pornographic. To drum into stubborn heads the vast difference between the topics on which slang concentrates, and the subtleties and wit that the language itself is often capable of offering. And at the same time to make it clear that, while these same topics may be focused on the gutter, the scholarly effort that underpins its assembly in a dictionary requires the setting of sights a very great deal higher. Do I talk from experience? Is that the Holy Father I see sneaking away through the woods, bog-roll in hand . . . ? But – and you may judge as you wish – I am not (yet) an ageing saddo tapping out obscenities on a computer screen.

II Practice: What is Slang?

We are seduced by language. Like Oscar Wilde we embrace the primacy of the superficial, the external show. WYSIWYG. Or if not seduced, then repelled. The user of slang, that 'bad' language, is a bad person. The writer of pulp fiction, even more so of rap lyrics with their macho fantasies of guns, drugs and bitches and all-areas excess, is identified with their product and duly condemned.* Or, just as fallaciously, lauded. As cant slang existed to mask criminal conversations, it began on the wrong foot, even if, as I do, one believes that slang emerged from no more than non-standard speech, the people's speech, as such set out condemned as unworthy of the elite and thus, for centuries, of proper consideration. Merely exclusion. A linguistic ASBO.

Slang needs an underlying element of social immaturity, likewise sexual prudishness (or ignorance), for the synonyms to be both necessary and exciting. Slang is the language of the young. It is made by the young and is weary of the world from birth. Its pose is rebellious and so is theirs. It works best in the mouths of those who can still delude themselves that rebellion is possible, that utopia is just around the corner, that the new boss will not be just the old boss revisited. The old know better, or should do anyway. Form alters but substance does not and we shall see more of the same. Thus slang is the property of the young. The old may persist in using the language of their own youth – it forms, after all, a once-useful social dialect that they have learned and if they wish to persist with it well beyond the sell-by date, so be it. Slang has moved for them from the sexy novelty of adolescence

* There exists, at least in the London Met, an officer tasked with that very expertise: testifying as required that if one adds 'suspect young person to have self-penned rap lyrics' the answer is logically an arrest warrant. The concept, another proclaimed by Lenny Bruce, that information about syphilis is not an instruction to contract it seems not to have penetrated.

to the comfortable old pal of age – but they should never backtrack to embrace the fantasies of their inexperienced, unhardened successors. Slang knows this and does not attempt to transcend its established themes. To steal Nik Cohn's summation of the Bohemia of youth cults once again, generation to generation not much changes in slang.

A Word in Time

A question? Yes. Does it actually matter? This is all well and good, Mr G., as I was once asked, and of course you seem to do it well, but why do you do it? I understand the definitions, and there are times when we need to know these things, but this thing with the dates, the first uses. Why devote your life to finding out who first called liquor 'booze', a bribe a 'bung' or, for that matter, first screamed out 'motherfucker' in a fit of rage? Should we, frankly, give a fuck?

This was not, of course, quite how the charming lady at the festival put it but she had been belaboured for forty minutes with words that may or may not have been part of her daily round, and she hadn't noticeably flinched and she deserved her turn. Nor can I recall what I told her: some variation that starts 'I'm very glad you asked that question' and quickly moves on to an irrelevant, but rehearsed and thus more articulate answer. If I might, I shall try again.

This is not what the publicity department, let alone their targets in the media, wish to hear, but I must admit again that I do not, nor am I remotely sorry for the omission, care that much for the hot new slang. Because as I have been saying for longer than I can recall – certainly since I noted the fact when compiling a book called *Slang Down the Ages* – slang is about themes. The reason that there are so many slang terms for drunk, for mad, for ugly, for all those preoccupations that have failed so substantially to interest Standard English beyond the most rudimentary of terms, is that what we are delineating is a lexis of synonymy. It is not a language, with all the necessary rules of spelling and pronunciation and grammar that go to make such a thing (see *OED* 'language' def. 1), though it is a form of communication, which, looked at from another angle, is what many might term a language (see *OED* 'language' def. 2). Like successive verses of Leviticus or Deuteronomy, we are in the world of 'begat'. In the beginning there was the act of intercourse and it was required, perhaps from stimuli within the subconscious, or perhaps from man's natural inability to leave well alone and to coarsen that with which he tampered, that something short and sweet and pointed be coined and thus there were 'fuck' and 'swive' and 'jape' and 'sard', and John Florio placed them side by side as definitions for *fottuere* in his dictionary of 1598 which was not simply a bilingual listing of Italian to English, but the first use in a work of printed reference of many English terms, these four included. And he looked upon them and lo, he said, they were good. And fuck begat offspring to which it gave its own name and they were 'foutra' and 'futter' and 'futz', 'fuckle' and 'fulke' and 'fug', and 'fugh', 'fickey-fick' and 'fucky-fuck'. And unto these were born many, many more, including those that rhyme: 'Donald Duck', 'Friar Tuck', 'goose and duck' and 'trolley and truck'. And so it goes *in saecula saeculorum*. But I shall not labour my point.

And while sard fell by the wayside (but for the adjuration: 'go teach your grandmother to sard', which possibly afforded her more fun than merely sucking eggs), and jape was dragged away to the schoolroom to rub adolescent shoulders with 'yaroo!' and 'biznai' and other Billy Bunterisms and swive exists only in heavy-handed archaism, fuck and its underlining imagery – hitting, moving, playing, and those phrases compounded with 'do' and 'have' and 'get' – lives on.

There are, as noted, nearly 1,750 of them and there will be more and there may have been others that long ago slipped the net. Fine. No worries, as everyone appears to say. What gets me hot is not that Multicultural London English, slang's current 'new' incarnation, has thrown up another term that essentially means 'man hits woman' as such synonyms have been doing since the sixteenth-century's 'wap'*, or one for 'mad' that is drawn on an image of 'not all there' wherein rupees lack annas, picnics sandwiches and communions the requisite number of wafers, but just when such terms first hit print. Or, if coined in an era when print had to jostle with other media, then when it arrived in lyrics, scripts, cartoon captions, and beyond all those, the ink-free zone of pixels. What matters is not format, but first. As in use.

That is what matters. This is what thrills, excites, stirs, motivates. Pushes the buttons, pops the cork. The true, the blushful, bubbling and winking and brimming over. This to me is the central driving force of this office-bound variation on investigative journalism, purpose-built for risk-averse stay-at-homes who would never pick up a phone to demand the unpalatable from a stranger; for this species of travel writing that offers snapshots but has no finite destination other than the travel itself. The paradox that in finding

* The modern term, 'wok' or 'wuk', also suggests a figurative use of 'work' – which is itself an MLE/rap synonym for 'murder' or 'kill' – as in 'work one's body' and thus takes us on to the words that equate sex with 'dancing', a slang linkage that has existed since the early seventeenth century. It is also suggestive of 'whack', another word for kill.

out the key facts of this most modern of languages, we must beat on ceaselessly into the past.

There are other excitements. Let us not yet descend into monomania. The first use lacks the lustful allure of some confection of spike and strap, sinuously en-French-ed as *escarpin* (even if it does, disappointingly, come from Italian *scarpino*, a little shoe, rather than *escarpé*, steep, which would surely be more logical), spins my head upon its axis, leaving my body in mid-stride and reminding me that the Victorian appreciation of ankles was far from risible, but this vision also gives me pause, and thought too. My kind of lex is infinitely regressive, pushing ever backwards against the tide of synonyms and ever renewed evidence, replacing one proof of existence almost as fast as I have unearthed the one that came before, or to be more precise, can now be ranked as coming after. The ante-date that is now nothing but a post-date and disdained as such. Let the new marker strut its stuff. For as long as it may.

It is a game – all my work is a game, were it work I could not and never would enjoy it so much – but it is serious. I've got X. What have Oxford got. Bingo! Fuck you, even. I am a consultant for the great work, but they love me only for my citations and these they will not have. Not at least until I have published them and, distrusting the abilities even of one whom they claim to respect, the legions of Little Clarendon Street have re-researched my efforts and displayed them online as if their own. Meanwhile let them delude their poor public, offering alleged 'first uses' that fall far short of what I have disinterred. Hah! I do but jest – it is, as I say, a game. As I also say, serious, since who, in the guise of authority, wishes to be found purveying inaccuracy. At least, of course, Oxford can purvey. Improving on the printed dictionary is easy: one simply keeps researching. But for me, making it visible is more problematic. I may have found substantial new material – whether new slang or earlier examples of that which I already have – but they remain my secret hoard. Not by volition, but as of writing, you couldn't give 'em away. Or perhaps I could but even for the ostensibly disinterested scholar there are limits.

This is the crux. The core, the pith, the marrow. The *medulla*: a word by which prototype dictionaries were once known, specifically the early fifteenth-century *Medulla grammatice*, the 'marrow of grammar'. The marrow: the inner region of an organ or tissue, whether fauna or flora, animal or vegetable. The essential or central matter of a subject. The 'guts' as we put it down the linguistic market. This is why I do it. Why I have bent to the keyboard and stared at the screen for thirty years. Why I could do no better than render up my same unchanging answer to those who for seventeen of those years would ask, 'What are you up to now?' and would look – was it surprised, embarrassed, disappointed? – when yet again I gave no more novel response than one that had been offered up so many times before: 'I'm working on the slang dictionary.' And why, in 2011, when the book had come out and garnered its remarkably kind reviews (kind? no, enough of the falsity: to deny that they were better than good would be to deny those who genuinely were kind in their writing but then I never doubted that they should be. I have simple beliefs and one, most foolish of all, is that we should occasionally be rewarded for our efforts.), I spent the best part of the twelve months that followed in tears and self-evisceration. This was odd and unexpected and – at least in a professional context – had never happened before. On finishing an earlier dictionary, a dozen years before and a mere five years in the making, I had spent an evening in my darkened office lost in some panic that also engendered tears, but that was a one-off and the demands of continuing work soon indicated the path back to what passed for sanity. This was quite different and the ground, having opened beneath me, refused for some long time to reaffirm itself as solid and remains prone to after-shocks.

This is not unique. One hears of it from all sorts. Post-creative depression, although I refer you again to my caveats as regards the 'creativity' of dictionary-making. Though I for one did not come to hate the work. Merely realise, as research continued, that what had been so well-remarked was already out of date and more so with each passing day. Now that, that might justify despair.

It did not start that way, the first efforts were in every sense juvenilia, but we live and, at least in matters professional, we learn. I want, you cannot begin to imagine the extent to which I want, to get this across. And I circle it and play with it and pick it over and find myself at a loss. It seems to me – I speak for none other – that outside the practical – making entries for a lexicon that I wish to be the best of its type – I do it out of terror; terror of the unknown. I am indeed Shakespeare's coward, dying a hundred times without ever nearing a real threat of death. I have mentioned closed doors and the fear of big top explosions. I have to know. I dare not ignore, which literally is 'to not know'. It may be that all such self-analysis is bullshit. Gilding a less than beauteous lily. Eggs, custard; cooks, broth. It's research. Right. Research. Millions do it even if scant hundreds pursue your craft and as regards your own particular workbench you cannot claim even a handful of peers. I call it the odd job, and concentrate on the adjective, but perhaps it is merely one more job. Certainly it lacks glamour, and success in its achievement fails to bring material prizes, glittering or otherwise. Respect. Yes, respect, that much-valued currency within the 'hood, but I'm far too old for gang-banging at anything but second hand

and my dreams are made of other fantasies. And words, however congratulatory, remain cheap. I should know. This, of course, is the ego's fault, not that of the job. The evangelist has no satisfaction in preaching only to the converted, even if that, generally, is the majority of the audience. Still, one preaches on because what is more fun than extolling the craft, endorphins surging, mouth in motion (brain trying to keep up), preaching, quite literally, the Word.

Yet the inescapable, slippery untrustworthiness of dates, the stubborn, provocative refusal to stay put, means that I cannot know. Not unarguably so. Not for sure. Not for long. All is nebulous, temporary, on approval, and if I gain a small comfort from some leap backwards in time I am immediately wondering how much further, in this case, I might go. I crack the whip. I dig again. No, this is not remotely masochistic. Just ego again. With the honourable by-product of improving the stock of knowledge, however marginal my shelf may be.

In any case, a dictionary is never finished. You cannot simply put on the brakes, turn off the ignition and abandon the car. What happens is that the car stops, and you break down.

I do not know, madam, whether this answers your question. That this endless pursuit matters to me should be plain. But to a larger world? Perhaps I am trapped in the obsessive's dilemma. As Louis Armstrong responded to someone demanding 'what's jazz about?', if you need me to explain it, then you'll never know.

That of course, is why it matters to me. If it matters to you then it matters because dictionaries seem also to have mattered in the way that we have come to accept that anything that we need to supply us with information matters. Dictionaries differ, not merely as to bulk (perhaps there should be a mean measurement: the 'table', based on how many piled volumes of dictionary X might be required to balance a wobbling item of furniture. My work is a 'coffee table'; the *OED* a 'dining table', etc.). The bottom line is that they tell us things that we want to find out about language.

Why Do I Do It?

A parenthesis. What has gone before is, concerning myself and others, the 'who'. What follows, and taken from my own working experiences, is the 'how'. What you have here, in the paragraphs that come next, is the 'why'. It is the big question but it is my question – though others have always posed it – and if my answers seem solipsistic*, I can only apologise. As I have suggested, I've never written a book (excepting, perhaps, the pseudonymous *Diary of a Masseuse*) that hasn't looked to answer a question. None more so than this. I am looking at the guts of my life and for once eviscerating not text but myself. Forgive me if, in so doing, the scalpel occasionally grates and the viscera are a little ripe.

No one asked my predecessors. If they had, Robert Copland would have said to make money, Thomas Harman to warn the respectable, Francis Grose to show that no true-born Briton (unlike the servile French) tolerates any form of fetter upon the freedom of his speech, Pierce Egan to show London's glorious versatility of language, and John Camden Hotten perhaps to balance his reputation as a pornographer. John S. Farmer must have hoped for money

* *Solipsistic*: self-obsessed and from the Latin *sol-us*, alone. Being who I am I wonder as to a link to Latin's other *sol*, the sun, and thus want to pun on this as my very own *Chasing the Sun*, my history of lexicography. Sadly, I am assured that this is quite beyond any etymological question.

too, but never received it. Eric Partridge made some, but it was always difficult and, as Anthony Burgess suggested, what drove him first and foremost was logophilia: a literal 'love of words'.

They ask me. A man – pink-cheeked, rosebud-lipped, something in the City – approaches. What do you do? I tell him. He finds it 'fascinating'. I doubt it – everyone finds it 'fascinating' and they doubtless mean well but I do not believe them either – but I do not demur other than to joke about income. So what's your favourite word? There are 125,000, they cover five continents, five centuries; how can one have a 'favourite'? He is unshakeable. What's the best country, the best period, the best . . . I escape, but I have not answered and I cannot answer. Who could? You could throw them some bullshit but I care about this stuff and, fuck it, I won't.

Why single him out? Everyone asks. Is it so bizarre? After all, dictionaries in one form or another have been around in English since 1604; in Latin, for translation into the vernaculars of Europe long before that, and in various forms for much longer still: there were attempts to define what words meant as far back as the third millennium BCE, when the invading Akkadians 'translated' Sumerian terms on pieces of pot. I doubt that the world's population of lexicographers, irrespective of language, is that substantial, but we are there, we have been there for centuries, even if it seems that the first 'team' did not emerge until the French *Académie* published their *Dictionnaire* in 1694.

I ask myself, and at the same time I don't. There are those introspective moments – what happened to the last thirty years? – when one does wonder quite how one came to devote one's life to searching out these marginal and much-reviled terms. That's a whole life question, and the detail, which happens to be lexicography, is almost irrelevant. My predecessors were surely never troubled in this way, but we moderns are cursed with self-psychologising. We register Sophocles' strictures on the worthlessness of the unexamined life and ponder accordingly.

Two things to note: This is, quite literally, all my own work. I would not and could not speak for my fellow dictionary-makers. I read the stories of the great dictionaries such as the *OED* and appreciate that mine is a far simpler task. So what I write here is, like me, grossly solipsistic. I speak only for myself and trust that others will forgive me. Perhaps there are things in common. Thirty years of lexicography may mean that some of my suggestions may strike chords. What comes out over 65 years of life is strictly my problem.

The second point is that while I talk of work and of life for a long time, now they have become the same thing. I can no longer remember when life and work were still easily distinguishable. When, to render it in as simple a way as possible, I didn't work or aim to work 7/7/365. When I didn't live in terror of the abyss of inactivity. Of 'relaxing', of the 'day off'. I find no joy in the list of popular gap-fillers – popular culture, hobbies, travel. It all, ultimately, bores. I want only to be excavating, anatomising. I want to work. Or to be more precise, I want to do this work. I want to 'do' slang.

So, slang, how and why do I love thee? Let me count the ways.

I'm a workaholic

So are many. If, as am I, one is lucky enough to find that one's work is also one's delight, then of course it is no longer work, with all the negative freight that term carries unless it is extended to 'work of art' or 'life's work'. Or, particularly for the lexicographer, since no dictionary is ever 'finished', 'work in progress'.* My life's

* Slang research is perfect for one who is eternally dissatisfied, who never has

work, at least as reviewers have categorised it, is my most recent dictionary, a solid tome of three volumes containing more than ten million words of text, but that has never been how I have seen it. It is a way station, a temporary halt, a pause to take on fuel – a new look at what has been done so far, the assessment of new sources of material, taking new stimulus from what have been largely positive reviews – before travelling on. Language has been described as a long freight train. The lexicographer is an inspector, climbing aboard, checking each wagon's contents, climbing down again to compile and circularise a list. (The climbing on and off might also suggest a hobo, but the hobo has no interest in a wagon's contents, merely that the wagon exists and the way in which it is most easily accessible. Perhaps the hobo is the linguist?) The train meanwhile rolls on, and by the time the inspector next catches it it will have picked up more trucks, and the original ones may have taken on new freight or at least rearranged what was already there, and the task of inspection starts again. The inspectors grow old and retire, the train just grows. I have yet to retire (that word, as I joke, is not one that is included in any dictionary of mine) and I have every intention of climbing back on board. But I cannot go on for ever: the steps are too high, the train goes too fast, the freight is too plentiful and comes in too many new varieties. I have a sell-by date, even if it is too blurred to read. Unlike language, and its subset slang, which will continue as long as there are human mouths to speak.

What does it really mean: 'my work has become my life'? Or vice versa? A statement of abdication or one of unreserved

---

what he wants but finds it immediately disappointing and boring and yearns again for the unattainable. Research never exhausts the potential sources, dictionaries are never finished; there is no concept of 'The End'.

commitment? On either count it seems to peel away that necessary layer that one requires when dealing with those who feel otherwise. I have been fortunate in my reviews but I still read them – doesn't everyone similarly positioned other than the magnificently confident or perhaps unassailably popular? – with trepidation. Disinterest, unfortunately, foolishly, is beyond me. This definition is weak, this etymology misguided, this word ineligible as slang? It is me, not merely the text, that is weak, misguided, ineligible. Of all works the dictionary is supposed to be neutral, monochrome, devoid of personal input. Was it ever true? Even for the teams of experts who produce the standard works? There is no such thing as 'impersonal'. Sarah Ogilvie, writing on the *OED*'s feted, heroic James Murray notes that even he – benignity, snowy patriarchal beard and academicals notwithstanding – could be 'territorial, competitive, and even a little paranoid.'* Now there, if nowhere else, I can stand alongside Sir James.

I am a voyeur

I am a voyeur. A peeper. A watcher. Reading and marking so that others may learn. I watch. I gaze. I pipe. I cop a hinge. At prostitutes, at junkies, at jailbirds, at violent men and promiscuous women. And vice versa. At the beautiful but more often the ugly. At the smart but mainly the dumb. At blacks, at Jews, at immigrants of every tone and persuasion. And at the young. Especially the young.

I listen at keyholes. Peek through bedroom windows. Eavesdrop on intimacies. I gaze into the darkness. The shadowed sides of streets I would never dare walk. Shuttered rooms. Blind alleys. The shooting galleries, the drug corners. The bars, the nightclubs, the backs of stages, the no-tell motel, the solitary cells, the whore's

* Sarah Ogilvie, *Words of the World* (CUP 2013) p. 129

parlour, the schoolrooms and the college dorms, the mansion and the slum. I do not acknowledge the word private.

How else can the desk-bound slang lexicographer represent himself? For all of us, usually male, middle-aged, middle-class, it is the great escape. Sex and drugs and rock 'n' roll and never leave your desk. Even easier with the Internet. Peeping through the curtain, huddled behind a tree in Lovers' Lane, eavesdropping in the villains' pub, covering the war from well behind the lines.

I am a resurrection man. Opening warm bodies to deliver cold information. I am a vivisector. Gutting my squirming victims to assuage my own insatiable lusts. An anatomist of the underbelly cutting not into ripe cadavers but into riper language. We are Dr Frankensteins sewing together our monster dictionaries and setting them free to wander in the name of our study-bound, data-dominated lives. Do our victims scream? Do they feel pain? Do I care? The greater my bounty the greater my satisfaction. I cannot even hear their cries, let alone acknowledge them. The scalpel is not an equal opportunity employer.

We are voyeurs of other people's dramas. *Flâneurs*, or at least aimless, anonymous wanderers, in the thronging streets – some lit brightly, some less so – of slang's vocabulary. Fantasist, dreamer, parasite. Even if the truth is that like all voyeurs we can know only superficiality; the content remains closed. The novelist has a voyeuristic side but uses it to mint novelty. What we see we simply use.

Nor are we merely voyeurs upon the sensational. Like Henry Higgins (who was at least part-modelled on the Oxford phonetician Henry Sweet) in Shaw's *Pygmalion* we view our subjects as ciphers ripe for exploitation. Disinterested, unmoved, we are heartless; we have no human interest. Nor human interest stories. Just words, words, words. The beggar is whipped, the whore has a backstory, the junkie dies. We do not care, unless if frustratingly, impudently, they remain mute. We neither prescribe nor proscribe. We describe. The guilty appeasement of political correctness holds no sway. We do not check our privilege. We lay out the stall. It is up to the buyer to assess what they desire. We do not suggest, we do not advise.

The other truth of voyeurism – my truth, the lexicographer's truth rather than the novelist's – is that I know nothing. Just the superficialities. As it is for everyone on the wrong side of the windowpane, the closed worlds remain impenetrable beyond the upper surface. Unless, before it is too late, I finally force upon myself some unfound degree of bravery. Meanwhile my only bravery has been deception and that is nothing.

I do not do fieldwork. Aside from any other problems one's interviewees do not talk in citations and if asked, 'Please give me your slang' are likely to disavow any knowledge thereof or to dismiss the questioner with one of slang's briefer exclamations. Some have done it, but who knows whether their targets invariably told them the truth. I prefer the bookshelf and the screen, the reinforcement of repetition that implies proof of existence. Nor do I have much in the way of correspondence. Eric Partridge gives the impression of an endlessly bulging postbag as his readers rushed to offer their own additions to his lists. Those days seem to have vanished. Technology has changed, but for all the tweeting, blogging and the rest, I receive very little directly. Questions, perhaps, but not suggestions.

I am a soloist

I am not a team player. Such seems to have been the characteristic of those who amass slang. We are all solo artistes. No patrons, no gangs of researchers,* no academic tenure. Some might label this reluctance to take part, this desire to follow one's self-determined road as cowardice, some might call it courage, but either way I am a volunteer-out, far too much influenced by what the author Duncan Fallowell, writing of the real-life original of Waugh's Sebastian Flyte, terms 'The failures of nerve in the face of life's demands and opportunities'. A therapist would call it masturbatory. An ironist, punning, self-abuse. I hide behind my three gross volumes as once I hid behind my multi-volumed *Children's Encyclopedia*. I am bad at games, real and figurative. Having discovered that I could never win, never impose my own rules, I abandoned them. This is known in the UK as 'bad sportsmanship'. I have also regarded it, thus disturbing another British shibboleth, as intelligence. Which also tells me that the nature of 'the game' is extensive. There are so many things that one cannot win. I choose the one at which I can, even if that is only because so few others wish to play.

Even so, words are my way in. My password to so many areas of life that might otherwise remain locked away. To assume, as an outsider, the task of defining and explaining these words may be considered as supreme arrogance or at least an example of power wielded by the conventionally powerless. Diktats for the failed tyrant. It could also be seen as a task that the outsider is best placed to perform.

So I do not participate. Too cynical or simply too scared of life to join in. Flinching from the chaotic worlds to which slang gives a vocabulary. 'Some people say life is the thing, but I prefer reading,' Logan Pearsall Smith, rich American in London *c.*1920, a

* This is not to impugn those who have indeed worked with me and to whom I remain hugely grateful; but the ultimate responsibility, the name on the cover, remains my own.

self-conscious aphorist who gave Cyril Connolly his first job. I have this on a postcard and it provokes no argument from me. Life suggests a soccer terrace in the days before seating – an 'end' – and is it coincidence that 'end', once sports-bound, has expanded in slang to mean whole city sections? Tossed helplessly amid vast shifting crowds, while its true believers, screaming fanaticisms fuelled by ideological dedication, roll up their programmes and piss down your leg. No, I am not misanthropic: I have friends, I have given many parties. And attended them. But I prefer the former: the word 'host' may equate with sociability but the pertinent synonym is 'control'.

Solitude equals control. Slang represents chaos and placing it between covers allows one to crack the whip of conformity, forming up the inchoate into regimented columns. The 'organisation of base matter', as Anthony Burgess put it in one definition of art, although he qualified the organisation as 'an illusory image of universal order'. Like slang, I find it difficult to take too seriously. The moral panics, the crises, the world-shattering, new-paradigm events. I am too old to believe in them. What there is now has been before and will come again and we seem to learn nothing, other than the creation of new technology. We will have to deal with it again and when we do it will be in the same old way. Slang fits the pattern: it has its abiding themes and they return, over and over again. Nothing lasts, says slang, or at least nothing changes, least of all humanity. As for events: shit happens.

What I do take seriously is the job. The craft. The work. Spotting an instance of 'fuck' at fifty characters? No. Rather rendering the nuances of a parallel language that sets out quite consciously to make itself obfuscatory and in so doing is condemned as 'gutter'. So I take it seriously. Perhaps more seriously than it deserves. This derided, marginal subset. Moving from fascination to obsession and thence self-obsession, self-indulgence, and – where else – self 'abuse'. At the same time I wholly distrust abstractions: faith, zeal. But if one does not take it seriously, then why do it at all? It is, dare I suggest, a duty.

There is nothing so bad about solitude. As A. J. Liebling put it of his youthful days in Paris: 'I was often alone but never lonely.' Half of America's literary superstars were just across the Seine but Liebling chose to keep his own company and explore the city in which he found himself just as, in time, he would explore New York. Might the job also have something to do with being an only child? The ability, through necessity, to be alone. The fact that, lacking siblings, one grows up closer to adults, but – still being a child – has a need to work them out. Language included. What Liebling celebrated in his great chronicles of city life also points to my own preoccupations. His biographer explained that 'low life, rant, dedication to an art of low social prestige in a déclassé setting, and the presence of a demonic creative person, usually someone unknown to the public [. . .] these are the themes that attracted [him].' He also terms the author as 'the artist as old codger'. I wonder.

The greatest (or is it safest?) satisfactions – and yes I know exactly what response such admissions elicit – have been those of solitude. Or they have for this only child. That said, the most gregarious person I know is an only child too. There are no rules (or none that work).

There is, in any case, an out. Books, they say (well, Jonathan Franzen does or maybe David Foster Wallace), exist to make us feel less lonely, so consciously or otherwise I've found the perfect companions. The treatment I give them in return is less generous: the scalpel to eviscerate their parts followed by the blender to purée my specimens, then spread them out as evidence. Their physical integrity dies so that the dictionary's figurative version may live.

I am not a democrat

The lexicographer's virtues betray his vices. The monocular focus on the task implies inflexibility, solipsism. The creation of definitions, stating as best one can what is correct, leads to dictatorship. A willingness to embrace every word, however vile, makes one forgetful of other sensibilities (and even as I write this I am thinking: tough! slang does not bend to 'taste' or 'politeness'). I do not turn the other cheek, I prefer to pluck out the eye that offends me. But, being cowardly, must do all that by proxy.

Lexicography is a passport to non-participation. Standing on the sidelines, and definitely not cheering. Getting as far away as possible from the messiness of the world but at the same time arrogantly setting oneself up as one of its arbiters. It dictates, it does not debate. Power without responsibility set between a pair of covers. If you are a drudge (and did ever a man shove his tongue further into his cheek than Johnson when he wrote that definition?) as the years of accumulation pass, then surely when the book comes out you are reincarnated as a deity, however tinpot and clay-footed. Your commandments are heeded. I hate arguing when the answer is so fucking obvious. No, 'niggardly' does not excoriate African-Americans. Nor 'nitty gritty'. Do we need to discuss this? But people say on the net . . . QED. I couldn't have put it better myself.

No user, seeking for information, answers the dictionary back. None debates with it. In print it is monolithic; there are no links, no access to the writer. Perhaps when the database goes online I shall admit the opinions, or at least suggestions, of others. But I suspect the crowd. The crowd are too easily led and their destination is too often the castle, on which they advance with flaming brands and sharpened pitchforks, all the better to compensate for their fearful ignorance. The crowd are running towards gates that tell them *Arbeit macht Frei*.

My work is trusted and I am naturally pleased, but that worries me at times. I know too much of what goes on backstage. I am at the same moment the omni-competent and wholly unreliable narrator. As slang lexicographers we are making a vast and complex structure with no choice but to settle its foundations on sand – sometimes well-packed sand, sand that, at its best, can be moulded into a prize-winning castle that wows the beach, but otherwise shifting sand, at worst even quicksand with all its treacheries. This is not to demean our efforts, but to acknowledge the properties of the material with which we work. Slang's speakers are traditionally marginal, they aim for deliberate obscurity; at least at the start its records were patchy. We can only work with what is available, and what is available may tell only a part of the story. The other fallible material is ourselves: humans. Dictionaries do not come from on high: they are made by humans, Need one elaborate?

I am an escapologist

I no more admit to favourite books than to favourite words but I have a pantheon which includes Neil Gaiman's *Neverwhere*, masterly in its evocation of language and its games, of the city and specifically of London, and, overarching both, of escape. It also has rats, a species that I love and with which I identify. It is the escape that counts and I feel the tears pricking every time I reach the book's final pages, where the hero, failed by the 'real' life he has been believing he should embrace, steps out of it for ever. The tears are not for his departure, but for Gaiman's teasing us with the possibility that he might stay. How could there be anything I desire more? The problem being that real escape only exists in death and that, which I do not (always) desire, will come soon enough. Instead one works and makes that a substitute escape.

Why do we escape: why do we twitch our hand from the flame? I see no charm in pain. I would prefer pleasure but there are limits and merely to avoid pain may be as much as is available. What is important is not to think. 'Getting out of it' in every sense. This can be attained in various ways. Heroin, until, inevitably, it demands more than it gives, performs as stated on the box; the infantilist comforts of adultery can work; most forms of self-delusion can offer possibilities. Perhaps it is the supposed morality of work – and I own to little morality, merely cowardice in the face of social norms in which I have no especial faith – but the pursuit of slang, for me, remains best. If it takes me away, if it facilitates escape, how can I not be grateful. Of all things, this is one that I will not betray and to date it has repaid in kind.

I fail the 'cool' test

'Cool' has been among slang's usual suspects for more than a century, but slang itself is the antithesis of cool. Requiring verbal articulacy, it cannot exist in the wilful silence that gives power to those who mask their stupidity in silent posing. If I sound jealous then perhaps I am. I was never cool. I always blamed it on ill-delineated cheekbones but I fooled no one. Like slang I am unsubtle, too brash, too eager, too fast to respond. 'Let me finish' shout my justifiably irritated friends. I am too little thinking, too keen to jerk the knee, too poorly capable of reflection. Still shouting 'Please, miss!' and 'Please, sir!' desperate to be top. Or at least noticed. And proud, of course, of all these faults and too many more and seek to justify them, looking for another link to work, as an overpowering need to inform. A heart on my sleeve, or in the centre of my forehead. Too vulgar. Perfect for the vulgar tongue. This is not to smear my peers. Lack of restraint is not a qualification for the job. Those I know in slang-world are not like this. Quite the opposite now I think about it.

I am a Jew

I have, I am aware, made this adequately clear but let me offer one last perspective. For which I can best quote Art Spiegelman, he of *Maus*: 'For me the romantic image of the Jew is not the khaki-shorts Sabra conqueror planting trees in the desert with the rifle on his shoulder, but the pale marginal, cosmopolitan, alienated, half-assimilated, international stateless outsider Jew, existentially poised for flight with no place to run, eager for social justice since that might make the world a safer place for him to live, with nothing but his culture to hang on to.'* Thanks to, history I know nothing of my lineage. I assume it must have included the obligatory rabbi or at least Talmudic scholar, and thus what I do seems to me to be a suitable job. I lack the pallor but most of Spiegelman's other adjectives fit and if the desert must bloom, let others do the planting. The desire of a Jew, the urban made flesh, to become a peasant continues to astound me. At the same time, my true lineage isn't blood but books, and I trace that 'family' – of which I know much – back from one slang collector to the next.

I love to read

I love the words, I love the sensual, almost tangible beauty of letters inked onto a page. Wilfully deserted by too many of its own publishers – both terrified at missing the next new thing and as unaware as the rest of us quite what it may turn out to be – the physical book may vanish. For reference this is no problem: the Internet suits it and will in time improve it, but for the book as an object to vanish is surely tragedy.

* 'Looney Tunes: Zionism and the Jewish Question', *Village Voice*, 6 June 1989

I have always read, always loved books; to have written them is the icing on my cake. The job demands that reading takes on a new purpose: assimilating and anatomising information. Quite simply, looking for examples. One reads differently: plot, for instance, is irrelevant though character is often underlined by speech and rough people speak the rough language. But alongside that there is always pleasure. Slang research has taken me to so many places that I would otherwise never have experienced. At second hand – how else – but the chase after vocabulary is quite personal.

How can one resist the language? The magistrate-cum-cant collector Thomas Harman in 1565: 'There was a proud Patrico and a nosegent, he tooke his jockam in his famble, and a wapping he went.' London pamphleteer 'The Hon. F. L. G.' in 1846: 'They took their tightener – viz., a bag of brown lap, a brace of pickled deserters, a dab of smeerums, a nob o'pannum, a wedge of beeswax, and a go of blue.' 'Dirty South' rappers UGK in 2007: 'For the girls popping pussy, and the boys with the blow / Cadillac'ers and flat-backers, I'm out here repping for it hoe.' Perhaps you can. Not me. None of these – the sixteenth century priest on the razzle, the bill of fare in the nineteenth century thieves' kitchen, the avowals of contemporary Texan crack dealers – are my worlds, but taken as a whole all this and much more is exactly my world, which is slang. I am besotted and I chase accordingly.

I wonder also whether I have not grown up. That to gain such pleasure from slang – lexicography's equivalent of *Viz*, at which comic I am still unable to resist laughing – one must remain deeply immature. That the subjects of my research – so often focused on hard-boiled thrillers, pulp magazines, dime novels, ghetto melodramas, villains' memoirs and the rest – represent boys' fantasies and the language that of mouthy adolescents. It is a measly excuse, but I am too fond of it all to care. These are the means I need to reach my end.

'Our cities become our families', says Jonathan Lethem. If that is the case then for me the city's language is my collection of family language: nicknames, teases, insults, bickering and shared jokes.

I believe in what I do

My whole rationale: slang matters and must be seen to matter (and, taken to an extreme, acknowledged by the world as mattering to the same extent as it does to me). Lacking an iota of poetry or spirituality, self-protectively superficial, wholly narcissistic, I am slang's dream bedfellow. I am perfect for my job, which in turn is perfect for me. Are we born to do X or Y? Only insofar as that is what we find ourselves doing. Especially if, as it has for me, the 'work' has become co-terminous with the 'life'.

I am also a missionary, though I trust that in proselytising I destroy no other culture. Outside what I term the 'slang-world' – that is, the handful of working professionals – slang suffers from simplistic mis-identification. In popular terms it comes in just two flavours: the rhyming variety and the so-called 'dirty words'. It is, in its entirety and in every sense, 'bad' language. I shall be fair: the popular view is half right. Slang is not 'bad' but it *is* language. It is language as much as Standard English is, as much as jargon is, as much as technicality is, as much as dialect is. As much as any one of the variant registers that make up English is. But I am not an old man writing obscenities on a computer screen or wandering the city with my loudhailer and portable stepladder. I simply have a job to do. It is my intent, in every dictionary, in every talk and in every article or post, to refute the concept of slang as pariah. It is my pleasure to do so.

I cannot sidestep the demands of ego. I want slang and its collection to be considered intellectually worthwhile, and at the same time I fear that it is not and I am not and that is what the world – as far as it notices – believe of it and thus me. I want publisher/salesperson/critic/public to discern the difference between the content and the work that has been put into it. The one is, of necessity, downmarket, the other, by choice, scholarly and ideally, as far as possible, authoritative. I rail against the lazy, thought-free denigration or sniggering that greets the subject of my work, and, because I make no distinction, the life that focuses on it.

I am not in it for the money

Make no mistake, were that possible, I would be. But lexicography, almost wilfully, avoids the road to riches. Any tale of dictionary-making is threaded with money problems, even that of the *OED*. Scholarship – requiring space and time – is badly attuned to the bottom line – which demands cut corners and deadlines. The largest royalties I ever received were for a book on which I was loath to place my name, though I managed a signed introduction that made it clear that the underpinning database and thus the authorship were mine. Nor did I cavil at the cheques that followed. I received a generous advance for the major dictionary but divide that by seventeen years and the numbers, if not the generosity, thin out. I was saved, as in the final chapter of a three-decker novel, by a legacy, equally generous, wholly unexpected and, by my standards, substantial, which plugged every hole and more. It thrust me temporarily into the lost category of 'private gentleman of means' and conferred the vast luxury of pursuing my obsession, a task that for my predecessors had always been private, though less usually accompanied by much in the way of means. Of course what goes around . . . and another legacy, that once I might have expected, was stolen away by what slang terms 'ambidexters' greedy to ensnare an old, demented woman. Another Victorian plot: I recommend *Bleak House*. Not for nothing does the pub sign 'The Honest Lawyer' depict a headless body: no head, no lying mouth. I work on regardless. Just as I continue to breathe.

I love this job

I want to find out, discover, uncover, recover. And pass on those findings to a wider world. The job is my very own charitable project: collecting, protecting, nurturing, promoting. In French I am *un lexicographe*, which sounds like a machine for dictionary-making. The concept delights me. Something out of Lang's *Metropolis*. Or Orwell's Pornosec.

At university I read history, or rather failed to do so. Now I revel in research's by-product, which evokes lost worlds that are simultaneously so like our own and so different. I rarely travel and in any case slang takes me to places I would never have considered.

I revel in slang's pragmatism. The dictionary that reduces the aesthetic to the linguistic, the vibe to the verb. This is not to say that slang doesn't appreciate the simile, typically when dealing with drunkenness or insanity, or some negative assessment of a passing female. Not to mention Australia where the need to define adjective A in terms of phrase B – 'dry as a dead dingo's donger', 'cold as a nun's nasty' – has surely transcended self-parody. Beyond such flourishes slang's world view, like the themes with which it deals and the language it uses to illuminate them, veers to the concrete. To bluntness. Its etymology may not, as once believed, lie in sling, to throw, but slang is definitely 'in yer face'. The lexis is short on abstracts, on emotions other than the extreme, and these are usually used to describe others rather than express a personal experience. Slang, so obsessed with sex, does not offer its users a word for love.

Slang opts out of possibilities. Or moralising, except the overriding suggestion that 'the other' – gender, mindset, race – is never to be trusted. Chary of abstracts, the only one slang embraces is doubt. In the battle between faith's exclamation point and doubt's question mark, slang lines up alongside the latter. Everything, everyone, simply 'is'. The 'what should be' is not on offer. Like a dictionary definition. Like, too, a self-obsessed ego which brooks no contradiction. Because one could label that pragmatism as nothing but a creation of adolescent cynics and tough boys taking refuge in tough language and denying it depth, because they lack the capacity either to appreciate or create it in themselves. I too lack the depth for revelations, and am presumptuous even to assume that there is anything to reveal. Never a novelist, barely, at least in the confines of a dictionary's print, a monologist. The pleasure is in the manipulation of the words for manipulation's sake – playing, punning, turning inside out and round about and always has been since my teens. But I cannot plot. I like to sketch the puppets – I cannot then pull their strings to make them dance. Lexicography, which names its *dramatis personae* but takes them no further, does not demand that I do.

Conclusion: Why do I do it?

I could be pious and suggest the motive is the passing on of information, and that is true. I have no desire for my researches to exist in a private vacuum. Technology has done for Johnson's rule that no one but fools write other than for money, but everyone writes with publication in mind. Otherwise we are merely compiling journals. Or in my case, trainspotters' notebooks.

But that is not quite what my question asks. The focus is on the *I* rather than the *it*. And my answers? I do it for the same reason that most of those who offer their work for public consumption – even on the margins of creativity that I occupy – do it: for self-expression (however skewed is my definition of that phrase), and so that perhaps my name may be spoken for at least a while after my death and thus in that metaphorical way keep me alive a little longer. Even if no one any longer knows to whom that name belonged and the medium that offered the original work has been consigned to the archives.

I do it to make my dreams come true. Or true by proxy. Slang throws the bombs, carries out the killings, fucks, dopes, insults, mocks class, wealth and power. All the things I dare not. My fantasy self. Aggressive, confident, witty, promiscuous, sexy, fearless, amoral, mocking of liberal pieties and of PC. Maybe even, who knows, racist and anti-Semitic.

I do it in an attempt to make everything fit together, to provide an answer to my own life and to the world which so stubbornly refuses to offer itself for filing. Having failed to put the world in order – as much as I ever tried – I try instead to put the words in order. And admit to the knowledge that however hard I try I shall invariably lack the intellectual apparatus (or is it rigour? perseverance?) to say properly what I am struggling to express. That sense that, however hard one tries, there is always something left unsaid, some connection unmade. And if I cannot attain intellectual honesty, then dictionary-making is my replacement. Linguistic analysis as a substitute for personal analysis. Tearing words apart, not myself. Doing the former seriously while the latter – for me – is carefully immersed in superficiality.

I cannot escape my own life: in thought, in deed and in profession. If my life is a failure then it is a perfect representation of the character and personality of the individual who has cursed themself to live it. If slang is superficial, then who better to catalogue it? The words are so much cleverer than I am.

I am no Johnson. I do not, as he complained, dream as a poet only to wake still a lexicographer. I am satisfied on that score at least. Still, were I, as a prose person, to seek poetry for a change, I might put it thus. Life/work, Work/life. Quite indissoluble. So let us reduce life to a lemma. We are all our own headword. Our experiences, as much as we understand them, our etymology, our desires and self-image, our definition. And our justifications and rationale our citations. Too neat? If nothing else it underlines the depths of my dedication. Or perhaps delusion.

Let me stick to prose. Why do I do it? Because of many things. And one above all: those days when, books dragged from shelves, websites loaded, a tricky term under the microscope, it all comes together.* And I say, even out loud: this, this beyond all else, is what you should be doing.

* A phrase, I realise, that tips the hat to my sons' favourite '80s television show: *The A-Team*. Fair's fair, the scripts yielded 155 citations, and first uses for 'cracker-box' and 'nutburger', both madmen, the pejoratives 'scumball', 'scuzzball' and 'swamp-breath' and 'zip it', as in shut up! I pay my dues.

Tools of the Trade

If I look at my shelves, on which, between London and Paris, there stands the best part of 5,000 books, what is there to see?

A good thousand are tools of my trade. First among them the dictionaries. From the facsimile versions of the earliest sixteenth-century glossaries of criminal 'cant', to lovingly collected first editions of the eighteenth century and beyond, through to my own latest effort. (The rest of my publications are in boxes or cupboards.) There are some titles produced by the friends who, like me, are 'in the business'. Alongside all these, several dozen more that, for me, exist only via the Xerox machines of the British Library or its New York Public equivalent behind the lions on 42nd Street (and how long before they too, in tune with the rest of that once wonderful street, are replaced by Disney's wretched geldings).

And alongside dictionaries? Books on words, books of words, books specifically of slang, books from which slang comes, books on cities where slang is bred, books on prisons and on crime, the worlds in which it is most regularly used. Shelves of background reference books left over from a world before Wikipedia and its more focused online peers. Twelve volumes of the 1933 *OED* plus its supplement, plus the four successors that appeared after 1972, plus the three of 'annotations' that followed them. My computer held the CD version, now I crank up the online one. I also contribute to it. Neither the *OED* nor I are likely to see the hard copy again.

They are not in perfect condition. I treasure the first editions, and try to keep them from harm, but first and foremost I use them. I don't do 'reading editions', that weaselly book trade evasion for 'worthless'. To me they are all of worth and I revel in the history that each may have accrued. And some, especially the modern ones that, in a pinch, could even be replaced, are as beaten and weathered and scarred as a craftsman's tools. And just as valuable to their user.

Then, since it would be very foolish to overlook this most central of contemporary tools, there is my computer. Scorning cars and kindred big boys' toys I am a sucker for this end of tech. I buy new but my heart is in the '80s: the smaller, the matter and blacker the better, the Azzedine Alaias of Turing machines. The first machine arrived on my desk in late 1983. The earliest IBM PC. It ran at 4.77 megaherz, sported a 14″ monochrome screen and gloried in the fearsomely expensive bonus of an external 20 megabyte hard disk. Otherwise it had slots for 5.25 floppies, that strange word that we had no sooner accustomed ourselves to throwing off with glorious insouciance before it vanished, almost overnight. Replaced by the 'hard-bodied' 3.5-inch disk, then the CD ROMs that host most of today's software – or at least that which has not, as is now almost invariable, been downloaded from the net. And storage has moved on to terabytes. Total cost, £7,000. It took me five years to repay my father the loan that funded most of it. Seven grand: I could barely find enough kit to spend even one on today.

Still, I recall its arrival with much affection, though for the first three months I dared move nothing, not even the keyboard, from the place where it had been placed. Until I realised that the box-shifter who sold it to me knew barely more than I did. And him I did know well: of the three component parts it seemed that while any pair would couple in happy partnership, a threesome was out of the question and there were many fruitless visits. But it truly did change my life and I said goodbye to the drawers of file cards with the same lack of sentimentality as that with which I ditched my last typewriter. The idea, now, of trying, with stubby fingers, to extract some information out of what would be perhaps one million such cards makes me shudder.

Its successors have been legion, reflecting the development of the computing world. First the box-shifter, than a start-up retailer in Kentish Town, then a man who built them for me, pausing in his mysteries only to puff his joint or indulge in incomprehensible but apparently antagonistic conversations in Greek with his mother back in Cyprus; and now back off the peg, back with IBM, rebranded as Lenovo and made not in Scotland, IBM's old home, but, like everything else, in China.

Beyond my office? I am not a great user of libraries. Not, that is, to work in. My partner spent ten years – day upon day – truffling through the British Library, but I yearned for, and still maintain, my solitude. Now she too has turned to the riches of the Internet, conveniently available at home. I hate the lack of privacy, even if, having exhausted the potential of the shelves that surround me, I bemoan the lack of material. Now the web, especially Google Book Search, salves that conscience. Only the London Library calls for my allegiance. Thomas Carlyle, who founded it, was a notorious antagonist of Jews, and the new wing is named for T. S. Eliot, another such, but the shelves are unrestrainedly catholic. It offers many things, not least the terrible *mementi mori* of the lines of shelves, literally thick with dust, upon which reside, untouched, the rows of three-volume volumes – hell, those Victorians were so prolific – each representing a best-seller who might, for all that we register them today, never have been. M. E. Braddon, Henry Kingsley, George Whyte-Melville or Hawley Smart all gone and quite frankly forgotten. Except by me, who has found their tales so useful as sources.

Once I used the *Children's Encyclopedia* to build fantasy bastions, now my 5,000 books fulfil the same role. Books, as Anthony Powell noted, do furnish a room. With all available walls covered floor-to-ceiling with shelves there is, anyway, no room for alternative decoration. Just four pictures: one of apples, one of pears (both watercolours painted by my partner who, unlike me, is multi-talented), two featuring the word 'fuck' (one an illustration for a magazine piece, the other a photograph). My joke: 'Apples and Pears' and 'Fucking': the totality of slang as perceived.

Although in the broadest sense – 'any occupation by which a person regularly earns a living' – lexicography is a *profession*, it would not have been such according to the way in which the term was once defined: the Law or the Church, an establishment duopoly that could be extended to the army. Nor, in my case and I believe that of all my predecessors, can it qualify as an occupation 'that involves prolonged training and a formal qualification'. There are university courses in dictionary-making, but I am not sure how many of their graduates are now employed as professionals. The original *OED* team, under James Murray, assumed that they were bound to teach new recruits what to do from scratch, although they capitalised where possible on the novices' experience, for instance Murray's own philological skills. The main qualification thus seems to be practice. It may not make perfect – perfection is not available to a dictionary – but one does improve with age. I tell myself on occasion that I could have done what I do now at twenty-five, or at least thirty-five, rather than my current sixty-five (and since such occasions tend to the self-lacerative, ask why in hell, if that were the case, I hadn't done so and moved on to something more useful or at least lucrative), but experience shows me otherwise. The effort of my late thirties, my first essay at a slang dictionary, was a very limited thing. I can tell myself I simply didn't work hard enough, but in fairness, I don't think I had much of an idea what to do.

I have used the term 'tools of the trade' to categorise the reference books and sources from which I work, as well as the computer holding the database, but I don't see lexicography as a *trade*. (Even if 'the trade' was once shorthand for the world of publishers and booksellers.) Like 'profession', 'trade' offers a wide definition based around earning any form of living. That can allow for lexicography too, but trade implies some form of trading, of buying and selling and lexicographers do not do either. If Murray and co. were sometimes disdained by the high mucky-mucks of contemporary Oxford, it was not because of some alleged class inferiority in their activities, but rather because the academics firmly believed that they could perform such tasks better, not to mention quicker. Of course there was a distinct hierarchy within the ranks of dictionary workers. Charlotte Brewer has shown how the grandees of the OUP, although perhaps not the dictionary-makers themselves, looked at the 'little people', the lower echelons of their employees, from *haut* to very much *en bas*. This was played out on a larger scale. The ever-stormy relationship between the Press and the *Dictionary* displays a depressing condescension on behalf of the former towards the latter, even though, come publication day, it was keen to bask in the glories of an achievement that, as publishers whose eyes were focused more on budgets than scholarship, they had done so much to hinder.

Which leaves what? The vote seems to go to 'craftsman'. Or 'craftswoman'. But not, I think, craftsperson, an objection I proffer not as a curmudgeon, but because the word, so typical of anything where ideology brandishes its self-aggrandisement over style, is so very ugly. There is something modernist in lexicography's focus on reduction: I cannot speak for others but at the heart of what I do there is a vital element of cutting off/paring down/stripping away. It is this reductionism that makes me see myself as, above all, a craftsman.

Craftsman: a maker, an artificer, inventor or contriver. Obsolete, states the *OED* in its unrevised 1989 version, but surely not. Because that is what one does. One writes a dictionary, thus the direct translation of 'lexicographer', but one also makes it. The word is also synonymous with *artist*, when artist implies a general sense of being skilled. Hence, no doubt, Eric Partridge's 1963 work; *The Gentle Art of Lexicography*. I am one who has no physical skills, for whom the term cack-handed might well have been invented (our sons have luckily inherited my partner's abilities). I can cook with enthusiasm and some amateur skill, but the plastic arts defeat me. I have never driven, I indulge in no sport, and if I were to take exercise it would be in running as fast as possible from the tiniest suggestion that I might involve myself in any activity that might fit under the rubric of 'DIY'. I am word man, not action man. Yet, and this is doubtless overly romantic, but as I work on the dictionary, I see invisible tools, not just books, as extensions of my hands. A scalpel, to slice out extraneous matter, pliers to tug a mispositioned citation and set it down in its proper place, files and planes to smooth the definitions, sandpaper to put on the finishing touches. The perfect lemma – the entirety of a single headword and all that pertains to it – should display the same elegance as a perfect item of furniture. I would not dare suggest that all my efforts are so successful, but sometimes, especially with a 'big' word that offers a multiplicity of definitions, of sub-definitions, of derivations, compounds and phrases, there is a sense of having made something not just of words, but in some way a physical, tangible and, above all, usable object.

Ins and Outs

Love is the only word that slang finds taboo. Unspeakably so. Slang has no word for love. Instead it offers 1,700 for making love – which is of course not a euphemism slang uses. And 1,200 each for the giblets we use to do so. Plus 1,400 for the paid versions and those who facilitate them. And 200 for VD. But for love – the most storied and mythologised four-letter word of all – nothing but silence.

I see this as logical: slang's take on love surely springs from long, cruel and unchangeable disappointment. Spurned, jilted, rejected, those cuckold's horns ever prominent, the jeers of the successful (the happy? the satisfied? the deluded?) and the jealousy slang shows them in return. Poor old loveless, lovelorn slang. Daren't take the risk for fear that the dice will, to use the sixteenth century's term, be 'cheaters' – aren't they always? It has wiped love from the lexicon, opted for bitter, self-protective (self-justifying?) mockery and all the other empty strategies that offer no panacea, just the illusory, short-lived sublimation of pain. As for me, slang's lover, this is a lexis to be trusted – even for one who trusts virtually nothing and no one. In this I have overcome the fear that delineates each day and I have given my trust to slang and given a great part of my life to it. I shall not betray it nor it me.

The lexis is not the lexicographer and the collector can admit emotions denied to the collection. You must, they say, love language.

It is true: among my job descriptions is 'philologist' which means literally a 'lover of words'. Thus Anthony Burgess described my predecessor Eric Partridge and I am happy to follow suit. Loving them, I have no wish to leave them locked away but wish to parade with them on my arm, or least in the pages of my dictionaries. But is that simply what I tell them to seduce them into my database? After all, I don't want to fuck them but fuck with them. Lay them out, manipulate them. Research as foreplay. Consummation in a lemma. To do no more than love words is to subordinate what they mean, where they came from and how they are made to what they sound like. Those sappy lists that almost invariably include the self-congratulatory 'euphonious' but never 'turd', which, for my purposes, is so much more interesting. Lexicography, which permits no such pleasures, is perhaps an atonement for such self-indulgence.

What passes for the truth, that endlessly frustrating grey area, is that I don't know. And honestly, do I particularly care? 'Loving words': it isn't a topic that I really think about: any more than I pause to consider that I am still breathing. I assess slang therefore I am. (It sounds smarter in French: *Je lexicographe, donc je suis*, though I imagine that first verb would fall foul of the Académie Française.) I talk a lot, too much even, which means that I keep words busy, but whether that comes from affection or merely exploitation, I cannot say. Keeping the words at work so they don't challenge my skills with some sort of smart-ass theorising. It might be no more than an attempt to dominate (which some would say best defines any sort of love). But that's conversation not collection, which is all about meaning, fancy or as otherwise the dictionary demands.

Oh, I suppose there's some kind of passion, necessarily blind. I fail the test for much of culture, restricting myself to reading, which, like much else for which I opt, means control. I want to paint my own pictures, I do not want yours. I don't deny your having them, and being not without some cultural aspirations am happy to gaze at them, I just don't need them. Not in the way that I need words. I have this job, this trade, this craft, which is based on doing what I like. Good for me. But not for the wider world. I understand, I really do.

You must, they say, be so good at – [insert word game of choice]. Oh no I'm not. In speech, in writing, I tend to play with the words: bending, twisting, turning upside down and inside out and chasing connections that I suspect only I can ever see. This is not love. Nor does it denote any special ability – since I have none – to play word games. Acronyms remain jumbled, cryptic crosswords baffle, I can perhaps manage those themed grids of letters whence one extracts pertinent terms by reading in one or another direction, but I make no promises. None interest, none have a deeper meaning; designed as amusements none amuse.

They are occupations of the hand, not the mind, or certainly not the dictionary-making mind. I acknowledge my comparison of lexicography to craft; I stand by it, but virtuosity at word games doesn't count, at least to me, as displaying linguistic skill. If we equate 'craft' with joinery, then these seem more like some form of carpentry, even DIY. Yes, the common material is language, but there is more to words than an arrangement of individual letters.*

So no, I do not seek diversion in Scrabble, create acronyms, do crosswords. I play no word games, simply games with words. With

* To collect slang is not to live it. Nor is this a game. Even a word game. The critic Jonathan Meades once proposed that Andrew Payne, then writer of *Minder*, and myself should join him for a game of slang-only Scrabble. It was disaster – an insufficiency of 'F's? – and the *Tatler*, for which it was earmarked, looked elsewhere that month.

names. Captain Grose was, look at the portraits, gross. So what is Mr Green? Jealous, naive (like Cuthbert Bede's fictional Oxonian freshman 'Mr Verdant Green'), a dollar bill, marijuana? A 'greenhorn', which was what they called those of my people who came fresh off the boat in New York, but not a 'green nigger' which meant Irish. Counterfeit, as in 'green goods', fucked, as in 'green gown'? Farmer. Partridge. Myself. Are we really country boys with country names seeking to unravel the big bad city? *Do you see any green in our eyes?*

Yes, I love words but only as print on the page (or in whatever medium from which I extract them). As Terry Pratchett suggests in *The Truth*, his pastiche of journalism, words do what they're told. At least at the stage of writing them down. Even if once read and out in the world they are subject to change and interpretation. Of course I do not write fiction, nor have I ever cherished the fantasy of expressing that novel that we are all supposed to have 'inside' us. We do not, even if the Internet, perhaps its greatest sin, has permitted so many to transfer their failings from green ink and lined paper to the Amazon bookstore, and thus unleashed what Leslie Fiedler, writing, I think, of Hemingway, termed the garrulousness of the inarticulate.

I tell a lie: I did manage one work of fiction, my purported 'diary of a masseuse'. I am ashamed of it now; not for its content, but for its execrably unexciting prose, though the friend who was then expiating his dope-dealing at Her Majesty's pleasure said that it was well received inside. But that was back in a very distant day, and definitely under another name. I was not further tempted (for all that I have occasional rigorously suppressed hankerings towards *noir*, and a hero called 'Lex Argot') and as for quality literature, the stuff of Booker prizes, the nearest my working self comes to that is passing it by on my way to more usefully eviscerable pulp.

Ins and Outs

Loving language is not enough. Immersing oneself in words is not enough. Delighting in invention, playfulness, pertinence, even in the glories of unalloyed vulgarity and coarseness is not enough. It is not that 'Nebuchadnezzar' once meant penis because that ill-fated king ate grass and grass is green and to the Victorians 'greens' meant sexual intercourse. You have to put the words in order. And before that to make a choice: which words will they be?

To steal from H. L. Mencken, who was talking of women, a love of language is to cherish the illusion that one word differs from another. Break them down and, to countermand what I just declared, it is a variety of game: the biggest game of Scrabble on offer. An infinite acronymic variation on a theme of twenty-six. Who was it described a masterpiece as no more than a dictionary out of order? (Jean Cocteau, it appears; suggesting that Victor Hugo, if honest, would have done better to offer readers simply the most recent *Larousse* than his latest work.) Not so fast. Infinite? That's what the *OED* must struggle to delineate and I deal only in slang and the turf, mercifully, is more constrained. I need to cut out my herd from the stampede. The problem is the branding.

If these musings have a theme apart from professional self-exploration then I would suggest it is the fundamental question: what, in purely practical terms, is slang? That there are a number of answers should have become evident and they vary according to the current angle of the question. I am not, in this context, thinking of the definitions of linguists, lexicographers or more or less informed amateurs. I am thinking of qualification: what goes in a dictionary with a title page labelled 'of slang' and what does not.

The answer is not made easier by the reluctance of the word itself to appear in print for some time after a good number of those to which it refers were coined. It is true that many of these antiquarian coinages must strictly be prefaced by the adjective 'criminal' and properly described as 'cant', which is still the proper label for such material. For my own taxonomy I prefer 'Und.' as in 'Underworld', even if, on consideration, it has a certain vintage air, redolent of master-criminals and Fabian of the Yard.

Nor is the lack of a concrete definition for 'slang' much help. I might sidestep the issue but we cannot overlook the ambivalence. It produces its own problem, best seen in comparing one dictionary, in my case of slang, to another.* I am constantly coming up against the question: if this, why not that? Were the definition of 'slang' to be concrete, then all, presumably would be identical. But it ain't so. These value terms like 'pungent', 'colourful' or 'unconventional' really ask more questions than they answer. I mean, who is to say what is 'pungent' and so on? A recent news story had an aggrieved sports commentator complaining that he was called 'the second worst word you can use on the BBC'. The word was 'cunt'. I didn't know the BBC had a list, but there you are. The old BBC Green Book, with its strictures against mocking royals, politicians and the utterance of such nudge-nudgery as 'winter draws on' would never even have considered such a thing. The short-lived Broadcasting Standards Commission, a piece of BBC self-defence from the 1990s, had 'motherfucker' at no. 1, but I assume cunt was in there somewhere. The lexicographer doesn't think 'pungent' and the rest; there is even a problem with 'vulgar', though the *OED*

* For instance, one of my reviewers noted that '*Green's Dictionary of Slang* (but not the *New Partridge*) has crowbar ("penis") and crowbar brigade, crowbar hotel, crowd-pleaser (US term for police-officer's gun), Croydon facelift, etc; *New Partridge* (but not *Green's Dictionary of Slang*) has crowded cabin (a poker term), crowbar palace, crowie ("an old woman")'; my response is that the poker term is jargon, and neither 'crowbar palace' nor 'crowie' have ever appeared in my researches, nor are they given cites in the *New Partridge*. Beyond that? We make our own choices.

was presumably thinking 'popular' rather than 'poor taste' even if slang would epitomise the latter in many minds.

James Murray had no problem with slang, at least including it in the diagram he drew up for the introduction to the original *OED*.

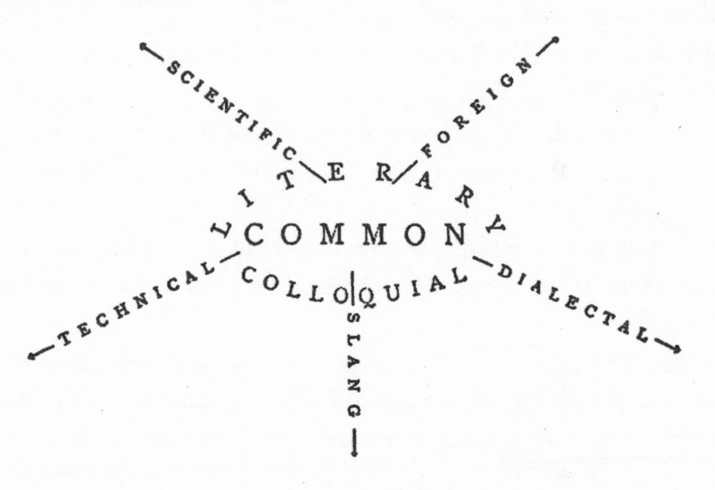

Slang is a subset of *Colloquial*, itself a branch of *Common*, in other words the current entirety of the English language. I suspect that linguists have long since torn Murray's simple formulation to pieces, and I doubt somehow that it will be reproduced, other than for historical purposes, when the great revision that will create the dictionary's Third Edition comes if not to a halt then to a necessary pause for breath, before moving on, I assume, to the Fourth. No matter. I find this satisfying and reassuring and it remains my line of last defence when facing those who would claim, shrill, condemnatory and ultimately ignorant, that slang is in some way alien to the greater whole. Good enough for James Murray? Exactly. That it is positioned above an arrow pointing towards the lower depths is merely a bonus.

Murray, while undaunted by slang as theory, did have a problem with it in practice. It was accepted from day one that the literary quality of the *OED*'s sources would be irrelevant* – all that mattered was that an example of use was provided – but the nature of the terms unearthed was problematic. That Victorian morality was all that restrained the inclusion of material prepared for 'fuck' and 'cunt' is a myth: they were neither researched nor printed prior to the supplements of the 1970s and 1980s. All Murray could do was encourage John S. Farmer, who sent him his proofs, and who put everything he could into *Slang and Its Analogues*. There was no way that contemporary Oxford could even ponder such excesses. Like Farmer I am unhobbled. The netherworld beckons and I jump in.

Having entered, there is, unfortunately, a degree of abandoning hope. The further one retreats into one's researches, the more the problems appear. What, for instance, about the sort of words that one finds in, say, Chaucer who is credited with the first recorded use of forty-five terms, over half from *The Miller's* or *Reeve's Tales*. Among them are 'swive' (to have sexual intercourse), 'prick' (to enter a woman), 'quaint' and 'quoniam' (the vagina and as such playing on cunt. He also offers the euphemistic *belle-chose*, 'beautiful thing' and as such a rare piece of congratulatory description for anything female), 'fire' ('of Saint Anthony', a venereal disease), 'hot' (sexually aroused and/or available), 'arse' and 'tail' (the anus or buttocks), 'hole' (the anus), 'fart' and 'piss' (both found as nouns and verbs). All of which are unassailably candidates for one's dictionary, but can hardly qualify as 'slang' more than

* This was true for the lexicographers; their academic and literary critics, bound to the canon, were less forgiving. Murray did not back down, noting, *inter alia*, the importance of newspapers as a source of language as a practical, rather than purely literary phenomenon.

three-and-a-half centuries prior to the concept's existence. Or further back, to Abbot Aelfric, a proto-lexicographer working in 1000 CE whose work translates terms from Latin into Anglo-Saxon. Which offers *ars* as his translation of *podex*, and *beallucas* as that of *testiculi*. Arse and bollocks: it is irresistible, but it is not yet slang.

The word itself does not appear, entering as part of the counter-linguistic lexis, until the early eighteenth century.* Over the next century or so it comes to mean, variously, verbal nonsense, a line of work, criminal jargon, illiterate, 'low' language, banter and teasing, the criminal fraternity, a travelling show, a set of counterfeit scales, counterfeit weights and measures, a legal warrant, a hawker's licence, and the speech given by a salesman or showman to attract customers. There are certain links between some of these definitions – an underlying sense of crookedness – but nothing points at indisputable origins and the etymology remains unknown. The most recent incarnation, based on an extended use of 'sling', to throw, and as such one of language-slang's once-popular but now rejected etymologies, is the verb to 'slang', to sell drugs.

This all takes time. We have no choice but to wait. The store of words that fall outside elite speech, which includes that 'slang' found in Chaucer, gradually expands, although we are still only looking at hundreds of examples. The sixteenth century, for instance, provides 'belly-ache', 'better half', 'the clap', 'cuckoo' (as a fool), 'every mother's son', 'the grape' (for wine), 'kaffir', 'ninny-hammer', 'play' (as in sex) and so on. Shakespeare alone, whose slang lexis runs to 500 terms, is the first to record nearly 300 terms. Among them 'it's all Greek to me', 'guts' (a fat man), 'pickers and

* The term 'Standard English' is not found until 1836, although the reference looks back to the appearance of 'Southern or standard English', and sets its appearance in the fourteenth century.

stealers' (the hands), 'sponge' (a drunkard), 'Tom Dick and Harry' (albeit as Tom, Dick and Francis) and 'what the dickens!'

In all – and excluding glossaries – I have found 900 terms for the sixteenth century. (The fifteenth is barren, a mere twenty-eight, the fourteenth, Chaucer excluded, a mere eighteen.) If there were others – and I continue to believe that there were – they were probably not recorded since the source material is relatively limited. Criminal slang, which in turn almost certainly existed earlier, is noticed and recorded in the 1530s (and earlier outside England). Such glossaries and dictionaries as would appear refer to the speech of the 'canting crew', criminals, and to cant. In 1785 Francis Grose looks somewhat further afield with his dictionary of 'the vulgar tongue', wherein 'vulgar' equals popular. He includes the word 'slang', defined as 'fetters', but in linguistic terms merely as a synonym for cant. Only in 1859, styling himself 'An Antiquary', does the bookseller-pornographer John Camden Hotten make himself the first collector to label his lexicon a 'slang dictionary' and, seeming to exhibit uncharacteristic *pudeur*, chooses to mask his authorship under a pseudonym. Hotten, unlike any predecessor, also offers a lengthy introduction, giving the history of his topic. Although an earlier work, published *c.*1698 and as such the first to extend its lexis beyond the tried and tested vocabulary of cant, is now considered to be 'the first slang dictionary', and Grose followed in that tradition with his listing of the 'vulgar tongue', Hotten is arguably the first true 'modern'. The language he offers is very much that of the thriving, expanding, powerful London of his era. Since Hotten all major slang dictionaries have announced themselves as such.

So the name is established. There remains the content. What goes in? What does not? The first edition of my *Cassell Dictionary of Slang* in 1998 offered around 87,500 terms. So too did the second in 2005, but at least 15,000 of them were different. More research, based on my new project, the fully-cited *GDoS*, had unearthed more material. Binding and costs being what they are, I couldn't simply pile on pages. In any case, I could see that there were plenty of the original headwords that, on second thoughts, should never have qualified. This, however, was a personal assessment. As ever, I could see the flaws. Others, or those whose voices I heard, did not. Critics might dispute etymologies and even definitions, and offer the usual triumphant references to material I had overlooked, but no one stood up to declare 'That isn't slang.' The power, presumably, of that mystical generic 'the dictionary'. It works for Standard English, it also works, it would appear, for slang. If the lexicographer says it's slang, then so be it.

The professionals are less tolerant. Nits are picked, even axes ground. And useful criticisms offered, entries pored over, held up to the harsh light of professional and academic amour-propre. Such and such is merely standard use, another, however garlanded with impeccable examples, is no more than occupational jargon, a third is some playful author's nonce-use and should have been left unfiled. Less tolerant, but also more expert. Errors are noted, changes must be made. Unfettered by academic affiliation, I have no career to build, no need to promote my own omniscience on the ruins of others' supposed inadequacy, but of course, granted space to review another, I am no better. I too am an expert and desire to display the fact. My rationale is commonality, mutual aid: how, my friend, can I let you display so painful an error? Oh, how this hurts me more than it does you. Whack, whack, whack.

The reality is that the borders are porous. I can seal my lexis off from dialect and technology, and from the occupation-specific slang that I would corral as 'jargon' (the sort that intensifies insider identification and outsider exclusion rather than that which embellishes establishment or institutional obfuscation). But the line between slang and colloquialism? Not so simple. Eric Partridge sidestepped the problem by expanding his self-declared remit. His dictionary is not only of slang but of a nebulous concept called 'unconventional English'. Its subtitle includes 'Colloquialisms and Catch Phrases, Fossilised Jokes and Puns, General Nicknames, Vulgarisms and such Americanisms as have been naturalised'. Is there anything left? The online Urban Dictionary claims that the slang lexis expands by some 2,000 terms every day. Its own lists certainly grow without end. My only response is: 'prove it'. And not merely by listing some nonce-term online. I lack the time and energy to check for examples, but while slang is fecund I cannot believe such seemingly endless invention. Then again, this is a dictionary of 'urban' language. Urban (which has entered the revised *OED* as a synonym for 'black' and thus black-inspired culture) is still not a synonym for slang. And the Urban Dictionary, though unbidden by me, has removed the 'slang' from its self-description.

There are, it is true, a number of sets of rules, whereby slang can supposedly be judged. One expert posits twenty qualifications, another seventeen, another four. I have never joined that party. It is perhaps another aspect of my encompassing cowardice, my reluctance to stand up and be counted, but I cannot see slang as so susceptible to such linguistic shoe-horning. Slang prefers the kitchen – draining bottles, doing a line – to attempting that particular dance.

Critics, seeking an image from nature, equate me with a bird. A magpie for one, a bowerbird for another. The presumption of indiscriminate hoarding. Though not yet – even if it is surely the traditional avian link with larceny – the jackdaw (plus verbosity here: rhyming slang for 'jaw'). Nor indeed the jay, of the genus *Garrulus* and, in slang, a chatterer, a whore and a rustic (hence 'jay-walking'). Magpie is good, outstandingly intelligent and I like the monochrome colour scheme. No more twitcher than trainspotter

I had to look up bowerbird: a sleek black creature that collects brightly coloured objects to attract females. Not so far as I've noticed. It is not just from my identification of the creature with my language of obsession that I see a rat: hoarding, but discriminate, like a beloved companion who, tolerating human foibles, takes what one offers, but assesses it in private then – since unlike the cliché she is, like all her kind, fastidiously clean – piles up the remainder to be removed from her cage.

So much is down to discrimination, in its original sense of informed choice rather than racism. Dictionaries can be large but the aim is not to make them all-encompassing. Not their job, mister. Even if the early examples did aim for encyclopaedic coverage and the great *Calepine* of 1585, a multi-columned building block,* offered each headword in eleven separate languages with fonts and typography to match. The name became a generic word for dictionary, lasting until the mid-seventeenth century. Figurative uses could be found in French, in the phrase '*Cela n'est pas dans son calepin*': 'that is beyond his understanding', and in English, in 'to bring to one's Calepin': 'to bring one to the utmost limits of their information'. Times change, Calepine survives only as *une calépine*, French for 'a notebook'. Such items are by their nature small and of course empty of text. Derive such symbolism as you wish.

Given the boundless infinity of online one is tempted to toss out restraint and return to the *omnium gatherum* fantasies of medieval schoolmen who believed – mistaken even back then – that all knowledge could be displayed in a single tome, but we must

* First published as *Dictionarium ex optimis quibusquam authoribus studiose collectum et recentius auctum et recognitum* in 1502 and the life's work of Ambrogio Calepino (1435–1511) who went blind in the attempt.

resist.* If a dictionary is to be useful then putting it together is as much a work of exclusion as inclusion. What is out matters as much as what is in. What qualifies; in this case as 'slang'. I do this word puzzle – the only one I want to tackle – every day and I find it hard at times. I am not alone. Look in dictionary A and the word is slang, in B and it is colloquial, and C, wherein the author has decided not to risk their neck, there is no label, or something ambiguous such as 'informal' or, for more aggressive representations of the non-standard, 'anti-formal'. Some Australians, who seem at times to have built a whole language out of slang and whose first dictionary of any sort was one of criminal cant, deny that there is anything of the kind.

I retain my list of 15,000 deletions, from 'aagey-wala', an Anglo-Indian term for the penis, to 'Zulu golf', a racist one for pool. Why did they qualify for the chop? The first proviso, dully practical, was space. Online it will not matter, in print it still did. Then 2,500 failed to come up with a citation, good reason in a dictionary that, like mine, depends on such examples to kick them free. This too is no longer set in stone: a few random casts into the Internet's pool changes that, at least for a proportion of these terms, and some of the keep-net's contents might find themselves returned to the pond. Another job to do. Though 'Adamize', to have sex, remains something that only John S. Farmer and W.E. Henley seem to have caught, and there are many equivalents, usually drawn from one glossary or another. Still, some of the exiles are going to be allowed home. Others, such as 'according to Cocker' and 'to Gunter', those mathematical experts, were never slang and here, as overly often in those early days, I have made too eager a bow to Eric Partridge.

* Or must we? Like the reference to 'binding and costs', the digital possibilities make such restraint seem archaic and unnecessary. If a link is possible, why not include it?

Thus such colloquialisms as 'alive and kicking', 'all bets are off', 'as all get-out', 'at sixes and sevens' and 'at a loose end' have also gone. (The *OED* tells me the last is not even colloquial, what in hell was it doing there?) Some, such as 'act like dead lice are falling off' or 'agree like cat and dog', find their roots in proverbs and, while they could do with a second glance, may very well stay gone. I removed over 500 terms for masturbation – 'accost the Oscar Meyer', 'address Congress', 'adjust the bowl of fruit' . . . These again were mainly glossarial but there was also a sense that most of such terms were so artificial – sometimes it seems that any combination of verb plus noun can serve the purpose – that the list was ripe for culling.* Sometimes one simply made bad choices: I found no room for the Malapropism 'asparagus', as in 'cast asparagus' (aspersions), but 'cast nasturtiums' is in so surely it must be both or neither.

When, I ask myself, did I first start to discern this thing called 'slang'? The honest answer is fuck knows, but I would like to and the personal canon that I have listed suggests prep school, meaning ages ten to thirteen and acquaintance with the fundamentals of obscenity. Today I realise that *Oliver Twist*, which I read early – and largely uncomprehendingly – is stuffed with criminal slang. Dickens had done his research. Sapper and Wodehouse too, among a growing list of candidates. But at the time if there was absorption it was pretty much unconscious.

There had also, around that time, been a *Swallows and Amazons* character – none, of course of the titular sextet who, while never exactly prissy, were invariably polite – who possessed the marvellous attribute of swearing for thirty seconds or even minutes, without repetition. I have always placed him in *Peter Duck* and research suggests I may be right. A member, presumably of Black Jake's gang:

* Those who will not be deterred can consult my purpose-built *Big Book of Filth*. There they all are, and more.

'Simeon Boon just out from two years hard, Mogandy the negro, George (a brother of Black Jake, who is wanted by the police), and a man with a scarred face who was chucker-out or bruiser at the Ketch as Ketch Can.' Sounds about right. I was to meet their type again. I was not aware, however, that at least some of this was 'slang' (and the swearing was, sadly, unspecified). No label appeared, although the suggestion was that such language possessed slang's fundamental ability to call down disapproval and to intrigue. To a child all words have equal weight, though some must be guessed from context. But 'two years hard' means nothing if one has no knowledge of the missing 'labour' or 'time'. 'Chucker-out' or 'bruiser' were not part of one's daily discourse. I cannot imagine that I knew of Jack Ketch, the generic of all hangmen, in whose Newgate 'kitchen' the heads of freshly executed traitors were boiled prior to being exposed at the Surrey end of London Bridge. Arthur Ransome didn't offer footnotes. Interest is not mandatory, but I must have had it. And noted that the interesting words – I was less intrigued by the young sailors' own vocabulary, far too often allied to some kind of vessel – went with the more interesting people. The baddies, it is acknowledged, are easier to draw than the goodies, not least because, having set aside the best tunes, the devil also enjoys the superior lexis.

Which remains, for me, a signpost. The pantheon of middlebrow crowd-pleasers who regularly delight the literary festival-going classes tend not to produce those who fall into the category. Warring media types, 'chicks', lit. or otherwise, adulterers of various hues and backdrops, metropolitan stereotypes dancing out their crises on the head of a Hampstead- or, nowadays, Hoxton-based pin. These are not my people. They are dull, colourless. They angst – at length – but I fail to feel their pain. They lack the language after which I chase. It is possible that they say fuck, but so does everyone else. And with far more feeling.

There was an element of contrariness, even of rebellion, in

pronouncing this new, exciting vocabulary which dealt with things that, just like those who spoke it, were interesting. Sex. Drugs. Villainy. I yearned but, fearing rejection above all things, still lacked the self-confidence even for mildly explorative sex; drugs were for a little while longer something one only read about, and villainy remained the staple of the sort of books where, to complete the circle, one found slang in the first place. The adoption of slang would have been an easy option – perhaps remains so – for that other perennial: the school rebel. Do they still exist? Amidst the great relativism is there anything against which to rebel? It was my role, though I didn't appreciate quite how clichéd a quid pro quo such posturing had been until all was finished. I appreciated this non-standard subset of the language, more and more of it associated with America whence came such pleasures as Bob Dylan and Lenny Bruce, but I had yet to place a single term on file. I undoubtedly used such slang as I knew – and much that I did not wholly understand, but fortunately nor did anyone around me – but I doubt that I saw it as such. Today I am, I have come to realise, far more foul-mouthed – though I eschew such judgment – than most of my peers. It is, after all, my professional duty. Back then, perhaps not. We effed and indeed blinded, but barely so. Schools impose their own vocabularies, and while they may be harsh, they are not especially obscene. I recall the use of 'shag', but not in the usual sense of copulation, but merely cleaning up the tables. Did we even ponder such things? I do not, today, attempt fieldwork. Laziness? Probably. Fear of life out there in the high-rise, high-digit postcodes? Perhaps.*

* I tell a lie. I did try, once. A friend obtained a group of teenagers. Schoolgirls. We were doing quite well, until one came up with the term 'shiner'. This reduced the speaker and her pals to hysterics. They did not recover. The term means 'blow job' and is not, I suppose, something one explains to one who qualifies as an uncle, maybe even a grandfather, theoretical or otherwise.

The knowledge that those who allowed me conversation would not think to single out their 'slang' since these words were simply what they use? That, undoubtedly. Again I come back to 'interesting'. That's what these words were. That's what these words remain.

I think I know why I do it now, but why did I start? If I liked books and their words so much, why did all that childhood reading lead to codifying, analysis and clarification and not to creative mimicry, fiction? Or, to go in from the other angle and keen to join the pantheon of those drudges morphing into deities, why did I choose slang rather than 'straight' lexicography? There comes a focal point when you call yourself a 'lexicographer' and ever more shall be so. In my case it was after writing my history of lexicography, *Chasing the Sun*. Ah, so this is what I do. And what I must be. But what gets you there? When do you set out on the path whereby you meet your self-description? Your very own definition.

Interest was there at the start and has remained. But is interest enough not just to sustain a long career, but to make a dictionary that is both utile and authoritative? It seems so mild a justification. Passion, surely, would be better, but that would have to be an after-thought. I didn't feel it when I started. One must start somewhere and I did, believing that Eric Partridge's age excluded him from a proper understanding of the young and their preoccupations, notably drugs. (He was in his mid-fifties when 'teenager' was coined in 1947 and fell foul, as one must, of that inescapable gap that keeps widening between the ever-ageing collector and the ever-youthful coiners. I am a decade older, and certainly not immune.) The market had a niche and I set out to occupy it. My very first dictionary, published in 1984 and containing a mere 11,500 entries – supposedly the slang lexis as used since 1945 – is best hidden behind the excuse: juvenilia. Or, kinder, my very own take on teach-yourself. At the time its reviews were positive – the appreciation of novelty, as I had worked out – and I wonder whether I would have gone on if they hadn't been and I, never one to dare disdain the negative opinion of others, had been discouraged. I look at the book now and see only gropings and a terrible lack of skill and, worse, of knowledge. The text would fit, with room to swing a sizeable cat, within the letter 'S' of *GDoS*. No surprise that the 'bibliography' ran to less than 250 titles. (I didn't even know enough to cannibalise my predecessors.) There were, much against my wishes, illustrations. But one is always learning and, if fortunate, improving.

Why grandmotherly skills should be represented by the ability to suck eggs I cannot say (and as a noun 'suck-egg' is a young, not an elderly person); I know only that one is adjured to resist teaching it to her. In my world that warning against the obvious means that no, in putting together a word-list you don't start at A and end at Z. The lexicologist Einar Haugen versified the profession: 'At the dictionary's letter A / Mr Brandt is young and gay. / But when at last he reaches Zed, / He's in his wheelchair, nearly dead.' Neat, but we don't do it like that. That this is not as obvious as it seems is borne out by Anthony Burgess. The novelist and polymath, commissioned by Penguin to write a slang dictionary, appears to have decided on a sequential treatment. Noting correctly that B and S were the largest letters, and dismissing the latter since from a linguistic point of view it was properly divisible into words that began with the 'ss-' sound and those that begin with 'sh-', he opted to test his own abilities with B (as well as the far smaller A and minuscule Z). The day came when he was just about to settle down to a celebratory drink – B as far as he could see being done and dusted – when someone mentioned another b– word: 'bovver boots'. He had missed it. (Interesting: Burgess was working in 1967, the *OED*'s first instance of 'bovver boots' is dated 1969; I would like to get my hands on

Burgess' example.) This was disheartening, and could all too likely happen again. He passed the job back to Penguin and kept future slang researches to conversations with his friend Eric Partridge.

You can see why Penguin might have envisaged Burgess as a slang collector, but his creativity far outweighed the demands of codification. In linguistic terms he is of course best known for Nadsat, the language he created for *Clockwork Orange* and its gang of psychotic droogs. This is not, in the end, a 'real' slang but an argot – a private language or jargon – confected primarily of Russian, which he adapted through both literal and ludic, usually punning, translations. The name Nadsat is typical, playing on the suffix used for the numbers thirteen to nineteen, but used in context to mean 'teen' as in teenager. Beyond Nadsat Burgess' slang was generally conservative. Like Partridge he sidestepped America, and stuck with what he knew, often gleaned from Army service. He also made up for *Enderby Outside*, in which his quasi-alter ego encounters the ex-pat hippie world of Sixties' Morocco, a sort of cod-Australian: 'donk' for genuine, 'passy' for passport, 'bulgy' for a beer glass, 'feel like a sack of tabbies', to feel good, and so on. None, even the alluring 'dunnygasper', a latrine-cleaner, had the slightest substance.

It is only at the various proof stages that one takes the alphabet as it comes, with 'A' representing a relatively undemanding saunter, followed quickly by the sheer rockface that is the ascent of 'B', the gradual descent through 'C' (though in Standard English 'C' outscores 'B') to 'D', at which point, if the dictionary is in English you will have completed 25 per cent of your journey, and on through the other twenty-two, with climbs of various heights at 'F', 'G', 'H', 'M' and 'P', and the one final, heart-sapping challenge which is 'S', though a sight of 'W' proves that the final descent to 'Z' is not entirely without effort.

But amassing the entries is quite different. Not exactly serendipitous, but definitely a matter of tossing a stone into the pond and seeing where the ripples go. The lexis I have compiled has, as I say, gone through changes and continues to do so. The 87,500 entries included in the *Cassell Dictionary of Slang* in 1998 were not – for some 15 per cent of their number – those that would appear in its successor of 2005. These in turn, though there were also major changes to the word-list, notably in making it 'nested' (essentially taking all those phrasal verbs that start typically with 'do' or 'have', 'get', 'put' or 'take', and placing them at the appropriate noun; the same goes for a proportion of derivatives and compounds) changed once more in the Chambers version, published in 2008. *GDoS*, the full-on, multi-volume dictionary of 2010 was different again, but much of that depended on the corrections and emendations (coming from another two years' research) that I was able to include. The current database, another three years on, is different again, though this is mainly a matter of adding new terms, and improving many of those that already existed by finding earlier first uses. The welcoming, boundless Internet will, of course, bring an end to problems of space.

There is one constant. Slang, drawn from so wide a variety of chronology and sources, constantly underlines the ephemerality of what is touted as 'important'. Nothing lasts, says slang. Shit happens. Or at least nothing changes, least of all human beings.

Etymology: Story Time

If the headword is the dog, with its homonyms, spellings, definitions and citations as the legs (the derivations and the rest serving as a tail), the controlling hand on its leash must be the etymology. It is the etymology that sets the headword in its place, separates it from other, seemingly similar terms (homonyms), guides the reader to the correct definition (chasing off the rogue pack of popular misconceptions), and may even nudge the researcher towards the best source of citations.

I do not like closed doors. I like to have a room of course, better for work than anything open-plan, but if I work alone, I rarely isolate myself completely. Sometimes one has no option – I am not among those who inflict on others their lavatorial strains and stinks – but the closed door is exclusion. It shuts out, it bars the way, it threatens.

As I have noted, my parents, when they rowed, sealed themselves off from me to trade embittered accusations. Not that often but it was so. The only child grows up nearer to adults and such exclusion, even for one's own good, or so it was suggested, is painful. And what is 'your own good' – that 'because I say so' by a more emollient name – but the speaker's convenience or their guilt? My lexicography, abhorring deception, focusing on revelation, prefers its doors left open.

Not all doors begin as open, and lexicography is the great picklock: the 'dub', the 'betty', the 'gilk' to use crime's own terms. It rebels against the sealed, the padlocked, the off-limits. Like love, it mocks the locksmith. It prefers to unravel than to cut; language's Gordian knots respond badly to violence: you cannot slice open 'jazz', 'posh', 'up to the nines' or 'the whole nine yards' and others of slang's persistent insolubles. In any case, where's the fun in shortcuts? Lexicography prefers to don the mask, the striped sweater, the bag marked 'swag' and tweak and twitch and tease the tumblers until they fall as needed. It is perhaps my focus on slang that conjures up such an image. I note that others – the etymologists Walter Whiter in 1800, Anatoly Liberman in 2005 – working with standard words, prefer the word 'art'. *The art of etymology*. Perhaps, but I must admit to a degree of scepticism and a preference for Professor Liberman's dictum, as offered in his book *Word Origins* (2005): 'As a general rule a good etymology is simple (only finding it is hard).' Dragging out the etymologies of slang, which seem so often resistant to discovery, is less like art and more reminiscent of hard labour. If I want an image I think of the name of Nelson Algren's fictional bar in *The Man with the Golden Arm*: 'The Tug and Maul'.

Etymology makes visible what lies at the heart of the word. To offer its own origins, it comes from Greek ἔτυμον (itself the neuter form of ἔτυμος, true) and means, as set down in the *OED*, '(1) the 'true' literal sense of a word according to its origin; (2) its 'true' or original form; (3) hence, in post-classical grammatical writings, the root or primary word from which a derivative is formed.' Truth is a tricky concept at the best of times. Slang presupposes some degree of secrecy and its base position is the smokescreen and the misdirection. It is less amenable to truths, even if its aggressive vocabulary tends more than any other to calling spades spades. None of which will let it hide: it demands exposition.

In dictionaries of Standard English this can often require taking a root back to classical Greek or Latin or even further, to Sanskrit, the fountainhead of what are known as Indo-European languages, another term for those that are spoken in most of Europe and of course India. The travellers' language Romani, which crops up consistently in slang (though not perhaps as regularly as certain theorists like to claim) is a perfect example: its speakers gradually made their way westwards from India (even if their popular, and slightly derogatory name 'Gypsy' is based on the mistaken assumption that their place of origin was Egypt). One looks to Romance languages such as French or Italian; Teutonic ones, which extend into Scandinavia, or any other of the languages, Indo-European or not, that have been used to make 'English'. It necessitates comparisons between several languages, pointing out the valid links, dismissing those that are not. Some etymologies are anecdotal. Some are unknown.* The word or phrase appears to have sprung from nowhere but that cannot be true; it can still defeat research. Slang etymologies tend to dig less deep. The housebreaker's 'dub', the picklock, is traced to dialect 'dup', to open, and beyond that to the thirteenth- or fourteenth-century sense of Standard English 'do up' as to put up, to raise, to open. But we do not push back further and inquire about 'do' or 'up'.

What one might call 'deep etymology', taken to its limits, goes further back and travels further down. The slang

* And must be acknowledged as such, however reluctantly: '"Origin unknown" a resigned acquiescence in inevitable ignorance, as Jespersen put it in a Micawberian way.' Anatoly Liberman, *Word Origins* (2005) p. 166.

lexicographer, who tends to work alone and must demonstrate a number of skills rather than enjoying the luxury of focusing on one, has to call a halt. It is a matter of digging, and the lexicographer, who, unlike the full-time etymologist, is a generalist, needs other tools. Prosaically, there has also been the matter of space on the page, though that recedes as everything turns digital. The ideal tool would be polymathy, or at least a proper grounding in a variety of root languages. Both of which I lack and blunder accordingly.

It helps, or allows some rationalisation, that slang's overriding nature is to play with Standard English, perhaps 20 per cent of the lexis works in that way and the etymology is marked 'SE' accordingly. To offer the standard root is thus redundant and we don't bother, leaving the reader to check elsewhere. (There are also several thousand that offer no etymology, typically verbal phrases such as 'let go', where the Standard English root is obvious and only the slang definition need be spelt out.) In addition come the 3,000 odd examples of rhyming slang, almost as many abbreviations, 1,500 puns and plays on words, the borrowing of nearly 900 words that began their life as dialect, of 370 proper names and 90 brand-names, and of 250 onomatopoeic recreations, matching the sound of the word to that of the action. Some are self-evident and one can only state the superficial obvious: 'betty', for a small crowbar used to force doors, works like that. At best it seems to be part of a group ('jenny', 'billy', 'jemmy', 'jimmy') all of which refer to a prying tool. The most recent is the 'slim jim'. In the end we are simply looking at nicknames, based on Elizabeth, William or James. There is no innate 'pryingness' that can be traced to any of them. There are roots that link to the proper names, but unless there was a specific Betty or Jemmy who had some characteristic that first joined their name to the tool, then the slang follower doesn't need those. Another group of crowbars: the 'citizen', 'gentleman', 'alderman' and 'lord mayor', are nicknames too, but the hierarchy is consciously nodding to the ascending size of the tool. Again, slang etymology – having noted this – does not need to dig deeper.

Compared with those words claiming Standard English origins, slang's 'foreign' input, including Scottish, Irish and Welsh – some 550 roots between them – is relatively limited, although it is a mongrel tongue (as of course is the Standard English on which it draws). Latin has a role, as do Yiddish ('cocum', 'mazuma', 'shicker'), French ('boocoo', 'dishabilly', 'mack'), German ('bladder', 'farshtinkener', 'schicer'), Italian ('camesa', 'deener', 'mulenyam'), Spanish ('cojones', 'loco', 'pot'), Romani ('chav', 'mash', 'rozzer'), Hindi ('Blighty', 'ganja', 'pukka'), and others. Different countries add their localisms: tribal languages in Australasia and South Africa; island terms from the Caribbean.

There are also just under 1,000, (out of 120,000) terms that, shame-facedly, I have had to label 'etymology (or origin) unknown'. The *OED* does this much more frequently, such is its rigour – and perhaps its self-confidence – that it is considered more judicious to concede defeat than promote a specious and ill-directed guess. The slang lexicographer is reluctant to follow suit. One third of my 'unknowns' also offer a possible etymology but one that I will not print without an admonitory question mark, to indicate 'perhaps'. Perhaps even that is mistaken. Eric Partridge believed firmly that something was always better than nothing. This was a mistake and he was savaged for it, notably by Gershon Legman who in 1951 tore apart Partridge's latest dictionary as 'The Cant of Lexicography'. Much spluttering ensued, but sadly, Legman was right. To paraphrase Anatoly

Liberman, no etymology is better than bad etymology and, along with the near-invariable dictum that when considering the longevity of words 'everything is older than you think', this important advice should be inscribed on all our desktops.

As regards the temptations of unproven, but alluring etymologies, I have, I believe, disciplined myself reasonably well, but it is hard not to think out loud. Another mistake: that way lies the mirage of popular etymology, that way lies 'fuck' rooted in 'fornicate under the command of the king'; of 'nitty-gritty' as the detritus of a slave-ship hold; that way lies 'OK' as a variation on 'och aye'; that way lies populist bollocks and the glaring downside of the Internet, the grotesqueries of the crowded cloud. I dream of hellfire: a purging storm to blow such dross away and lightning to illuminate the facts.

How come people actually bother with these confections? These elaborate stories are often magnificently dismissive of historical, let alone linguistic data. Don't they simply feel wrong? Is the need for comfort so great that it overrides all questioning? If slang can be reduced to a single function, it is to present doubt in linguistic form. Doubt of givens, of directives and of zealotry. That doubt should be extended to its etymologies. Fairytales are fun, fairytales – at least sometimes – are comforting, but fairytales are fantasy. Not every frog becomes a prince and it is sometimes more useful to smash the glass slipper rather than blindly force it onto an unsuitable foot.

Why does it matter so much that every word should have a root? Can't we just take them as they are and accept, just as slang is neither 'good' nor 'bad' language but just *is*, that some words just *are*? I deceive myself, if no one else. Because it does matter. I know it for myself. Back to that shut door, with the mysteries behind it and the desperate need to throw it open. I don't even have to look that far for my frustration: the word 'slang' itself – like France's semi-synonymous *argot** but not Germany's *Rotwelsch*: rogue-speak, or Spain's *germania*: brotherhood (words) – still resists a provable, cast-iron etymology. This is intolerable: it has to come from somewhere. 'Cant', the proper name for criminal jargon, is more accessible; it comes from Latin *cantare*, to sing, used of priests who mumbled their way through a mass and was thence transferred to the mutterings of con men who played at beggars seeking alms. But slang repels a simple solution.

So lexicographers, who already find it hard enough to define the word's meaning, set themselves to pondering and come up with the clinking of prison fetters (no, although that '*slang*', which comes from German *Schlange*, a watch-chain, or Dutch *slang*, a snake, has meant chains whether of metal or of sausages), the elision of *s*ecret and *lang*uage (the popular option, but irrelevant); an archaic field measurement (and if so, where's the

* *Argot* is perhaps even more elusive than slang. Suggestions include *zingaro*, the Italian word for gypsy, or Latin *argutus*, pointed and subtle, and finally, most feasible, the French word *ergot* (also spelled *argot*), the spur of a cockerel. This last conjures up the image of the *argotiers* (beggars) raking in their loot like a cock rummaging his dunghill with his ergots or spurs. Not everyone agrees: it is suggested that the shape of the spur does not resemble the hook with which, like England's contemporary 'angler', thieves lifted items from stalls and windows. In addition the original *argotiers* were beggars, albeit criminal ones, rather than thieves. Further theories include a link to *harigoter*, to rip or shatter, which is, in turn rooted in dialect *haricote*, to argue or swindle, and *haricotier*, an impoverished merchant. However the dialect is not recorded until the nineteenth century. And while it has been suggested that the rue d'Argoud, in what was once the heart of Paris' underworld, might not only be linked linguistically but might also have hosted the Cour des Miracles, the city's semi-mythical equivalent to London's criminal sanctuary Alsatia, there is no proof.

connection?), and the twentieth century's best guess: a link to 'sling', to toss (plus various Scandinavian antecedents) and thus the image of speech as a means of aggression. Eric Partridge and some Oxford etymologists were in favour; others were dubious and they have won. The root in 'sling' has gone, only surviving as the origin of drug-dealers' 'slinging' and 'slanging', selling the product. We too are susceptible and the search is not over. Does one really want to dedicate a lifetime to words of which the most important remains a mystery? Origin unknown. Why not? One can always fall back on the symbolism. Fine. But we remain unsatisfied: the only proviso being that we do not pour our fantasies into print or cyberspace, masquerading as reliable information.

It is possible that the reliance on Standard English will disappoint many users of slang dictionaries. Not to mention the list of unknowns, whether or not some more or less valid guesswork has been appended. Because in a slang dictionary it is etymology, the 'story behind the word', that counts. After all, of the various parts that make up a lemma – the headword and all its constituents – spelling, often an important part of the information provided by a standard dictionary, and pronunciation, ditto, play little or no role. As for the latter, who knows how the villains of seventeenth-century London or nineteenth-century New York actually spoke the language that they used. The occasional slang lexicographer has offered pronunciation, but it's hard to believe they had much real clue. As for spelling: slang starts off spoken, as does most language, and stays there for a while before – and this doesn't include every example, and some must vanish unrecorded – appearing on the page (or other accessible media equivalent) and thence within the dictionary. In which place it is not so much spelt out, but transliterated. Do users, in any case, look to slang collections for the spelling? I would doubt it, or certainly not as the first port of call. 'Monniker' which means a name and first turns up in mid-nineteenth-century London, can be found as 'monacher', 'monack', 'monacker', 'monacre', 'monaker', 'monarch', 'monekeer', 'moneker', 'monekur', 'monica', 'monicher', 'monick', 'monicker', 'monika', 'moniker', 'monikey', 'monker', 'monnick', 'monniker', 'monoger', 'nomaker'. The odds are that this list is not complete.

I have no problem with elitism, which, after all, comes from nothing more complex than a word that means 'the best', and I continue to be confused as to why people should volunteer to accept the second rate, let alone the downright nonsensical. I sympathise with the need for popular etymology, but still despise it, which perhaps I should not given that I specialise in popular language. I am unrepentant. It is shoddy, simplistic, lazy and, most important, it tells lies in the guise of circularising truth. The Internet, in its role as leveller, has intensified the problem – though it might be hoped that proper use of it could also make it easier for all of us to access what is in fact correct. That, of course, requires effort.

Pitted against some intractable term the lexicographer – standard or slang – makes a great deal of effort. There are researchers who have devoted years to the pursuit of a single word, in many cases those that suggest an origin in a specific name or incident. Those of us who are committed to making whole dictionaries don't have that luxury, though the temptation is there, and we draw gratefully on the efforts of those who do. That it is perhaps less luxury and more necessity, and that regarding it as the former may and does lead to error must also be acknowledged. Yet there remain, and I speak only for my own lists, those 600 terms that won't surrender, even to a possibility of source. All the investigation, all the teasing out, all the effort that can be made hits a blank wall. Why, for instance, does 'grote' mean an informer? Why did 'modock' once stand for one who became an aviator for social prestige or publicity? What made a 'weejee' into a chimney pot and why exactly does 'zebbled', at least at British schools, mean uncircumcised? (And what was wrong with 'cavalier'?) Sometimes the terms seem consciously artificial. The London printer John Duncombe, responsible for a good deal of mid-nineteenth-century porn, issued a slang dictionary around 1850. It has such entries as 'caddock', the stomach, to 'elk', to give a loan, 'ravellavern', a person who steals luggage from travelling coaches and 'swap-perchop-brammums', a bank. There is a group that uses the preface 'abb-', all referring to prison: 'abb-clouts' – prison dress; 'abb-discipline' – whipping in the prison court-yard, either publicly or without witness; 'abb-gammonry' – a condemned sermon; 'abb-tanger' – the passing bell at execution; and 'abb-whack' – gaol allowance. Why 'abb' (which turns up as 'abs' in another set) should mean prison (the nearest equivalent is the Latin 'ab': from, by, since and of) does not, as they say, compute. The sole possibility is 'abbot', meaning prison warden, but this appears only in Duncombe, and in Kent's canting dictionary of 1835, and Kent makes no reference to 'abbs' in any form. There is also a whole set of numbers listed as 'the Cracksman's new mode of counting' and running 1: Yunibec, 2: Twibecs, 3: Tribecs, 4: Katrambecs, 5: Knimtrambecs, 6: Hexambecs, 7: Septzambecs, 8: Octzambecs, 9: Nouxambecs, 10: Dyams, and goes on to 500. None of these terms have survived, other than in subsequent dictionaries. None of them, over and above the Latinate prefixes of the counting system, are subject to an etymology. We can still admire Duncombe's inventiveness. Isn't this, in its way, an example of perfect slang? Absolutely incomprehensible other than to its users. The only problem is that as regards hard evidence, there doesn't appear to have been any.

Etymology, that story which demands, even if it fails always to obtain, a happy ending, that Ripley's Believe It or Not of language, remains the slang dictionary's primary appeal. Aside from the endless pursuit of first uses, it also provides the lexicographer with a sense of genuine discovery. The assembling of headwords, the long hours reading for citations, only to find that one source has come up with nothing that one has not already pinned down in others, can perhaps be drudgery. It is part and necessary parcel and we do it. But the teasing out of meaning and of origins, the wrestling with possibilities, that is, there is no other word, fun.

Let us take the phrase 'happy as Larry'. Meaning? Simple: very happy. First recorded use: 1881 in J. F. Keane's travelogue *Six Months in the Hejaz*, wherein the infidel explorer dragged up as a pilgrim to enter various Islamic shrines. There are many similes for such cheeriness and among others Larry equates with 'a box of birds', 'a clam' (at high water), 'a cricket', 'a horned toad', 'a sandbag', 'a dog with two dicks', 'a pig in shit' and 'a nun weeding asparagus'. ('A bastard on father's day' and 'a boxing kangaroo in fog time', while allegedly 'happy' too, actually represent the antonym.) Many are from Australia, that unstoppable creator of simile. And most, within what passes for slang's version of reason, are logical enough. But Larry? Why Larry, the only proper name among them? The popular assumption is the Aussie boxer Larry Foley (1849–1917), one time leader of Sydney's all-Catholic larrikin gang known as the Greens and, latterly, as champion against all-comers irrespective of weight, the 'Father of Australian Boxing'. So far so good. But was Mr Foley especially jolly? No such mention in the *Australian Dictionary of Biography* where, tellingly, there is no mention of any eponymic coinages either. However, although the very first is not, all the early cites are indeed Australian: a vote for Mr Foley. One is not enough, we must look further.

Which reveals that 'larry', deprived of its capital letter, means other things, in Australia and elsewhere. In Ireland, for instance, it means a fool. The word borrows Irish *learaire*, a lounger, an idler. Irish, of course, is central to Australian, coming over with the tens of thousands of unfortunate 'Emeralders' who made the involuntary passage on His and later Her Majesty's ships. Lounger, idler, fool . . . witless, grinning idiot. Mr Keane, he of the seeming first use, would seem to be Irish, although I have no proof. But I'm shoving my money down: that's the 'larry' for me. Larry Foley's fans may of course argue.

If popular etymology calls up anecdotes as 'proof', slang is more reticent. The late eighteenth-century's dictionary-maker Francis Grose may have offered this for '"Cauliflower" [. . .] the private parts of a woman; the reason for this appelation is given in the following story. A woman, who was giving evidence in a case wherein it was necessary to express those parts, made use of the term cauliflower, for which the judge on the bench, a peevish old fellow, reproved her, saying she might as well call it an artichoke. Not so, my lord, replied she, for an artichoke has a bottom, but a **** and a cauliflower have none.' Modern lexicographers are less likely to echo him, conserving their discussions for the fine points of linguistic linkage rather than anecdote. It is not always the case: the *Dictionary of South African English* has 'gentoo', a prostitute, and explains it as 'named for the *Gentoo*, a ship which arrived at Cape Town in the mid-nineteenth century with a group of women passengers who became prostitutes; the countries of origin of the women and the ship, and the circumstances of their arrival at the Cape are obscure and in dispute.' Other terms that seem to demand a story prove dead ends. We have 'Billy Harran's dog', 'Joe Heath's mare' and 'Paddy Ward's pig'; 'Dolan's ass' and 'Tom Bray's bilk'; 'Jerry Lynch', 'Jack Smithers' and 'Tommy Dodd'; 'drunk as Cooter Brown'; and

Australia's term for that outcast who in the land of the 'shout' dares to drink alone, a 'Jimmy Woodser', but if these were ever well-known people rather than mysterious generics, their fame has vanished.

The great repository of proper names is in rhyming slang, the pearly kings and queens of language and slang's equivalent of the black taxi and the Routemaster bus, and anchored around the same time in history. It continues to innovate, but does not evolve. It began in the 1830s and while it was allegedly invented with secrecy in mind, holds but a single gimmick: the rhyme is unspoken. Hence 'apples' (stairs) have no pears, the 'flounder' (taxicab) no dab and 'barnet' (hair) no fair. The listener, therefore, might be wholly unaware that there was a rhyme – the clue, as it were – involved. Such attenuation can have other effects. Take 'berk'. A fine old term; it means a fool. It is also rhyming slang. An abbreviation, it so happens, of an abbreviation. Berk stands for 'Berkshire', though some say 'Berkeley'. Coming originally via Cockney lips both are pronounced 'burk', and not 'bark'. And the missing word? 'Hunt'. And hunt's rhyme? The figurative use of slang's second favourite monosyllable. The word is 'cunt'. The vagina. The fool.

Proper names of once celebrated figures make up 530 of rhyming slang's 3,000 entries. They keep coming – especially footballers, pop stars and other members of the D-list – and there is a sense that a short-term inclusion in slang's lexicon is a gong that comes with a brief celebrity. Rhyming slang also embraces most appearances of brand names in slang, though not all. The US prison term 'maytag', a weak male prisoner who is abused by other inmates, forced to do their menial chores and possibly raped, is not a rhyme, but tips the hat to the country's well-known brand of white goods.

My own feelings towards rhyming slang are ambivalent, and, as regards its modern version, dismissive. In purely linguistic terms, even if it has gained a foothold in Australia (which has terms that never appear in London) and, thanks to visiting British seamen, enjoyed a short life in San Francisco and other US ports before World War II, it is not in fact slang. Had it emerged in, say, Liverpool or Birmingham it would have been dismissed as a dialect. A regional usage. In this case the region is the East End of London, but in a small island London rules in counter-language as in standard, and rhyming slang duly benefits. There was a point to rhyming slang once, and for a while only the London costermongers who seemed, if not to have coined it, then to have adopted it most enthusiastically, were alone in 'getting' the new creation, but there is little point now and it is a vapid, empty form. The internal wit that might be acknowledged for 'trouble and strife' for wife or 'saucepan lids' for kids, is absent from slang's fawning embrace of celebrity culture in such equations as 'Posh and Becks' with sex or 'Britney Spears' with beer. The complexities of 'arris' for posterior, with its path through 'arris' = an abbreviation of 'Aristotle' = 'bottle' (and glass) = 'arse' = rear end will not return. The reality is that rhyming slang, at best 2 per cent of the lexis, has come via the lazy shorthand of brief attention spans to stand for the whole. Only the obscenities, the so-called 'dirty words' – of which there are but an official dozen, at least as laid down by America's Federal Communications Commission, and which find themselves slang as much by default as design – have come so powerfully to be identified by the same shorthand. Gresham's law wins again, the bad drives out the good and rhyming slang remains.

Does the etymologising of slang really count as 'etymology'? I am loath to call it 'shallow' etymology but that is what much of it has to be in the face of the deep excavations that come with the investigation of Standard English words. In a discipline that demands full disclosure, is the halfway house at which so many of my entries pause sufficient? Some entries do get their due, typically the obscenities, which one might suggest – and everyone else does – are slang's 'own' words. Though that's not so: the core terms for sex and defecation, those most human of preoccupations, were once standard, even if their nature made their acceptance short-lived, and they arrived in slang's domain only after being rejected by more respectable hosts. But those terms that have no etymology, since their link to Standard English is so plain, or those that, perhaps redundantly, explain that such and such is a 'figurative use' of Standard English, do they represent a kind of linguistic cock-teasing? So far, but no further?

I think not. It is interesting to peruse the 1,000 plus learned words with which the *OED* debates the etymology of Standard English 'dog' (and comes to the conclusion that there is no established root; 'cat' doesn't offer one either, nor 'pig', though 'cow' does), but not for slang's purposes. What we need to assess are the meanings of slang's thirteen discrete noun uses of 'dog' (plus two forms of 'the dog'), the eight verbs and the one each of adjective, adverb and exclamation. On top of those are well over a hundred compound and phrasal uses that develop from them and the various senses that each offers. The variations on a single word – spelt the same but listed separately – are known as homonyms: words that sound and spell alike but have different meanings; this is not the same as the different senses that can be found within the same word. Slang is big on homonyms: there are, for instance, twenty-one separate 'jack' nouns plus 'the jack' and six verbs. Drawing lines between them is based on their deeper meaning whether in Standard English or in slang.

Thus 'jack' n.5, a sailor, comes from 'jack tar', but 'jack' n.12, the anus, comes from 'jacksie'. Senses are grouped at a single homonym, thus 'jack' n.4 has three senses: a farthing, a generic for money in general, and in the Australian game of two-up, in which one bets on how a pair of tossed coins fall, a double-headed coin.

Deep etymologists look to what are called linguistic 'cognates', defined by the *OED* as 'descended from the same original language; of the same linguistic family. Of words: coming naturally from the same root, or representing the same original word, with differences due to subsequent separate phonetic development'. Slang looks at cognates too, but of a different variety: the relationship is not so much semantic but thematic. It is about the links between repeating imagery rather than the search for linguistic roots. The ways in which the essential playing with different Standard English words is linked not by the words themselves, but to their original meaning. For instance, the various stereotypes of 'dog' that lie behind the uses of the basic word. Or what I term the 'DIY group' of terms that all mean sexual intercourse, e.g. 'grind', 'screw', 'nail', 'plank', 'hammer', 'drill', 'bore', 'scrape', 'rasp', 'shaft' and simplest of all, 'bang'. (And never forget the 'carpenter's dream': flat as a board and easy to screw.) These in turn belong to that larger group of terms for intercourse that can best be described as 'man hits woman', which image may underpin 'fuck' as well. All simple enough, you might suggest, or at least simple in context. But what about 'sharge'. We are not helped by the sole example of this, in a dictionary, but it is defined as 'to copulate'. Why? Because, it appears, 'sharge' is also dialect and the dialect meant to grind and to 'grind' . . .

All words, or all words that fail to identify themselves at once, are subjected to this thematic filter. Slang is as much a collection of synonyms as anything. Terms that mean 'mad' or 'eccentric' often suggest that the subject is 'not all there', terms that deal with drunkenness suggest physical instability. Many are self-evident, others can be subject to reverse engineering. The endurance of this synonymity (what some would decry as over-lexicalisation – too many words for the same thing – but then that's what happens when you let linguists opinionate) and its fundamental role within slang offers rival interpretations. On the one hand one can see it as a means of avoiding the real world (as represented by Standard English) by conjuring up an infinity of parallel terms. On the other it suggests a better means, by offering up so many possible descriptions, of burrowing deeper inside it. Either way, there it is. Ask any slang dictionary.

If tasks such as defining are usually simple when compared with the challenges faced by the range of abstracts or technicalities that a standard dictionary has to assess, etymology is as near cleverness as I can approach. Even when it transpires that my 'cleverness' is wrong. Because perhaps in no other subsection of the entry is life as a soloist less useful. Working alone is perhaps necessary – if there were a joke about slang lexicographers and lightbulbs my sense is that the punchline would be 'not enough of them' – but it is restricting. Especially in the narration of a word's origins. Sins of omission and commission. For the first I know that there is a constant, unsatisfied, sense of failure. Failure (could it be simple laziness?) to push the connection that little bit further, to worry more determinedly at the meaning. To reach for and achieve that final necessary step: the one that makes the obvious interesting. As for the second, even if popular fallacies can be rejected, sirens still beckon and sometimes one embraces them. I have my excuses, but they do not obviate my shame. Omission

– times change, technology advances, new words are coined, older material is newly released, one's skills improve – is bearable. Commission hurts. Print is so painfully permanent. My lust to get the whole thing online isn't only propelled by a desire to provide better searches, a faster uptake of new words, a flow of user-generated material, though all these would be assets. It is also to wield the rubber, to wipe out and amend the errors, in short, to spare my blushes.

Definitions: The Meaning of the Words

> Lexicographers are masters of the unsubstantiated assertion. Definitions in current dictionaries are hypotheses, which owe more to art than science.
>
> Patrick Hanks, *Lexical Analysis* (2013)

The lexicographer, said Richard Chenevix Trench, whose 1857 lecture 'On Some Deficiencies in Our English Dictionaries' set what would become the *OED* in motion, is a historian and not a law-maker, but there is no easily discernible boundary. It is the supposed division between describe and proscribe, but is there really so simple a division? The emphases shift, one gets from the dictionary what one wishes and the lexicographer always plays a double game.

We are guided, as so often, by etymology. To *define* comes from Latin *definire* to end, terminate, bound, which itself depends on *finire* to end. The image is of setting a boundary and drawing a conclusion. The dictionary uses of *define* and *definition* emerge in the mid-sixteenth century though the ever-contrary Samuel Johnson still refused to acknowledge the latter two centuries later.

It is about describing in its sense of drawing lines, of establishing boundaries, of the literal sense of define which means bringing to a close. Of declaring limits. It is an art in the way that cooking is an art, perhaps the nearest that the lexicographical craftsman approaches it. The art, like that of chef and sauce, is reduction. Blending the ingredients to produce something simple.

Citations are there but not as quotes – even if the word's French origin means just that – but merely as decontextualised proof. Individual citations may be plucked from longer narratives but if we are telling a story then it is one of use, and it must be inferred. Like evidence when compared with the jury's verdict, the citations that suggest a background and thus proof may be ornate but the definition is always austere. The perfect lemma is devotedly modernist: a room without mouldings, ornate chimney-pieces and other fripperies. The best definitions represent a conscious starvation amid the linguistic plenty that is displayed when the word in question is used as part of a writer's creativity or a speaker's declarations. As with etymology, the premise is finding out and passing on, but where etymology can be complex it is mandatory that definitions are otherwise. Etymology can be prolix; it can also allow questions and theories. Frustrating reader and writer, it can confess to ignorance. The definition has to spurn the apologies of conditionals – I suggest, I think, I believe, in my opinion. No either, nor or. Just is. Definitions have only one task: to be . . . definitive.

There is also alchemy: turning the base, messy metals of the worlds we explore into the dictionary's shiny, unadorned gold. (Alchemy, as we know, was an unachieved fantasy; let us play safe and say we do what we can.) The antithesis of obfuscation, making life bearable. (I am unable to resist the pun on 'bear' meaning carry, and thus to note the portability of the life-enclosing dictionary.) Putting it down, labelling it, making it concrete, accessible. However vile the source the definition is to be unfrightening; there are to be no ambushes. Just that neutral, fact-based agglomeration of vowels and consonants. Even the most repellent of racism's projectiles which, like the dog crap plucked from Victorian streets and employed in tanning, can be neutralised and rendered useful.

Defining slang is usually simple. Words are words, you say what they mean. Almost like Standard English but with a fundamental difference. Not simply that there are fewer slang terms (125,000 as against the 600,000 currently offered by the online *OED*) but there is so much more repetition. Slang being at its heart a lexis of synonymy rather than a language extending to every aspect of life, certain themes predominate and with them certain definitions. Slang is insatiable in its search for reinvention, even if what it invents is as often as not more of the same. Its waterfront is narrow but very deep. *Noir*, naturally. Oil-stained, garbage-clotted water (is that bobbing shape a body?) lapping against rotten pilings, abandoned rusting boats, seaweed-encrusted stairs, and retreating backwards beyond easy recognisance, mounds of cargo, some forgotten, others recently offloaded, windowless bar-rooms, flitting figures, stumbling drunks, ageing whores, uniformed 'harness bulls' and 'private operators', wharf rats, real rats. The *OED* offers 382 terms for drunk, of these almost exactly half (188) are slang. Slang offers well over 2,000. Like the greater slang lexis, the terms for drunk fall into themes. These represent an image of being subjected to violence: 'basted', 'battered', 'belted', 'biffed', 'bitten by a barn-mouse' or 'by the tavern bitch', 'blasted', 'blitzed', 'blown up', 'boiled', 'bombed', 'brained', 'buckled', 'caned', 'clobbered', 'conked', 'crocked', 'crocko', 'cut' (over the head), 'dagged', 'damaged', 'done over', 'electrified', 'floored', 'fractured', 'fried', 'hammered', 'hit on the head by the tavern bitch' or 'under the wing', 'jug-bitten', 'lashed', 'nailed up', 'scammered', 'shattered', 'shellacked', 'shredded', 'slugged', 'smashed', 'snockered', 'smiflicated', 'spiflicated', 'squashed', 'swacked', 'swattled', 'thrashed', 'thumped over the head with Samson's jawbone', 'trashed' and 'twisted'. There will be more, and as ever – through ignorance or choice – I have not included every one that already exists.

I have written the two words 'the penis' 1,351 times (from 'aaron's rod' to 'zubrick'); 'the vagina' 1,180 ('a.b.c'. to 'zum-zum') and 'sexual intercourse', by which I mean the heterosexual variety, 1,740 ('action' to 'zot'). I allow for detail as it is necessary to be precise: sometimes it is a large penis, sometimes a small one, sometimes flaccid, sometimes erect. Sometimes a penis is just a penis. The same, with local variations, goes for the vagina and for intercourse. Oral and anal sex are sufficiently well represented to make a substantial showing. I have added such occupational or geographical labels as 'Und.' for 'Underworld' or 'Aus.' for 'Australia' even more frequently.

'The chief stimuli of slang,' J. Y. P. Greig wrote in the *Edinburgh Review* in 1938, 'are sex, money and intoxicating liquor.' Factor in drugs, just one more intoxicant, even if they have drawn the short straw as regards legality, and very little has changed. Greig of whom I know nothing other than that he edited the letters of the philosopher David Hume, was right. An outline taxonomy (from Greek: 'the arrangement of distribution') of the slang lexicon, which runs to approximately 125,000 words and phrases over a period of five hundred years and covering all English-language slang, offers the following (rough) statistics:

Crime and Criminals 5,012; Drink, Drinks, Drinking and Drunks 4,589; Drugs 3,976; Money 3,342; Women (almost invariably considered negatively or at best sexually) 2,968; Fools and Foolish 2,403; Men (of various descriptions, not invariably, but often self-aggrandising) 2,183; Sexual Intercourse 1,740; Penis: 1,351; Homosexuals/-ity 1,238; Prostitute/-ion 1,185; Vagina 1,180; Policeman/Policing 1,034; Masturbate/-ion 945; Die, Death, Dead 831; Beat or Hit 728; Mad 776; Anus or Buttocks 634; Terms of Racial or National abuse: 570 (and derivations = *c.*1,000);

Defecate/-ion & Urinate/-ion 540; Kill or Murder 521; Promiscuous/Promiscuity 347; Unattractive 279; Nonsense 271; Fat 247; Oral Sex 240; Vomiting 219; Anal Sex 180.

This does not add up to 125,000, and it's broad-brush searching, but what you see is what I get. Respect has not been due. Mother, a supposedly positive figure, receives just eighty entries and I fear one of those is only an abbreviation of the Oedipal polysyllable and several are synonymous with bawd. Women, girls and females are ranked as slang's fourth most popular topic, and that excludes the thousand plus 'working girls'. Not all are current, but, despite the popular idea that so much is ephemeral, slang is in fact remarkably long-lived and a substantial proportion of what we hear is far from freshly minted. Just to take a random year's coinage, 1600, in which ninety-seven new slang terms entered the records, 'biddy', a woman, 'chew the cud', to talk something over, 'chicken', a coward, 'fag-end', a remnant, 'fiddle', to take sexual liberties, 'jig-a-jig', sexual intercourse, 'old boy', as a term of address, 'old dog', as a man, 'poke' and 'ram', to have sex, 'soused', drunk, 'tub-thumper', a vehement preacher, and the exclamation 'what the dickens!' have all lasted the course. As for personal use, we tend to get stuck in the groove we achieved before thirty, maybe even earlier. This is fine: we do not want geriatrics aping their juniors. Myself least of all.

I have written a slang thesaurus but I had no need to look for many of Roget's original categories. More the ones you find from Roger, he of the *Profanisaurus*. Please do not search for caring, sharing, compassion or other positive virtues. If they do appear, as in 'soft-roed', kind-hearted, the implication is of weakness. Their omission is not an oversight. Slang is not interested. There are few abstracts. Many definitions are terse, to the point: here is an object, this is what it is. And that does not require much explanation. I do not have to define 'art' or 'love', I do not have to define the arcana of particle physics or neuroscience. Slang doesn't go there and I am grateful. Nor must I, even if one substitutes email for its snail-born antecedent, do this:

> 'I write to the Director of the Royal Botanic Gardens at Kew about the first record of the name of an exotic plant; to a quay-side merchant at Newcastle about the *Keels* on the Tyne; to a Jesuit father on a point of Roman Catholic Divinity; to the Secretary of the Astronomical Society about the *primum-mobile* or the solar constant; to the Editor of *The Times* for the context of a quotation from *The Times* of thirty years ago; to the India Office about a letter of the year 1620 containing the first mention of *Punch* [the beverage]; to a Wesleyan minister about the *itineracy*; to Lord Tennyson to ask where he got the word *balm-cricket* and what he meant by it; to the *Sporting News* about a term in horse-racing, or pugilism; or the inventor of the word *hooligan* in June 1898; to the Librarian of Cambridge University Library for the reading of the first edition of a rare book; to the Deputy Keeper of the Rolls for the exact reading of a historical M.S. which we have reason to suspect has been inaccurately quoted by Mr Froude; to a cotton manufacturer for a definition of *Jaconet*, or a technical term of cotton printing; to George Meredith to ask what is the meaning of a line of one of his poems; to Thomas Hardy to ask what is the meaning of a word *terminatory* in one of his novels; to the Editor of the New York *Nation* for the history of an American political term; to the administrator of the Andaman Islands for the exact reference to an early quotation which he has sent for the word Jute, or the history of *Talapoin*; to the Mayor of Yarmouth about the word *bloater* in the herring fishery; to the chief Rabbi for the latest views upon the Hebrew *Jubilee*; to a celebrated collector of popular songs for the authorship

of 'We don't want to fight, But by Jingo if we do', which gave his name to the political *Jingo*.'

James Murray, lecturing 'On Dictionaries' in 1910.

I am shamed. When necessary I naturally move beyond my own reference shelves, and of course consult the Internet, but on the whole slang's repetitions mean that it's what you know rather than who.* Context, thematics, patterns. That narrow waterfront makes exploration if not simpler, then more focused: the new species tends, on inspection, to be a development of the old. What was still the *New English Dictionary* (*NED*) had its share of synonyms, but Murray had to range much further. Though I wonder if even he invariably received answers. My immediate thought is: if Sir James doesn't know, who in hell will? But in these contexts presumably he didn't.

I don't know whether this was a day's work, perhaps not, but there is no doubt that such correspondence was continual. Many of his queries, one can see, were on technical terms, another area slang can sidestep other perhaps than amid the niceties of sexual preference. It is also another example of how hard it is to decide what goes in and what does not and there might be a suggestion that providing this sort of information is a hangover from the days when dictionaries and encyclopedias were as yet undifferentiated.†

* I have of late taken to consulting via Twitter. Nothing cut and dried has been offered as to such queries as 'Hang up, Algernon' as a comment, *c.*1905, to a passing and obvious gay man, or 'murty', which implies 'grubby' as in 'a murty yarn', but I live in hope. Perhaps I have fallen in with the wrong crowd.

† Those days, it seems are coming back. One reason that the two currents of reference split was lack of space. The Internet, as with so much else, has removed that problem and both editors and consumers are well aware of the potential.

I do not, merciful heaven, have to deal as he did with the verb 'set', one of those terms that required a statement of the 'general arrangement of senses' which fall into a dozen groups, totalling forty-three definitions, and exclude compounds that have a dedicated lemma.* Slang has its moments – 'hot', in nine major sense groups, offers thirty-nine definitions plus a multitude of compounds, phrasal uses and exclamations, and 'fuck', good for thirty-eight columns in my work, has elsewhere been granted an entire book – but the overriding story is less complex.

As with slang's etymologies, I do not need to go deep. Much of slang plays with Standard English but if I define those terms in the slang context then I assume that readers know the underlying meaning. This appears an acceptable method, although in certain areas, notably the names of certain drugs, it may not always be the case. In Standard English it is acknowledged that some of the easiest words make for the most difficult definitions, but on the whole slang allows me greater freedom. Thus I have no need, when considering 'down' or 'in' or 'up' nor indeed 'apples' or 'pears' and 'cats' and 'dogs', to go beyond slang's borrowed uses.

That does not exclude nuance. Slang may be restricted in its themes, but the very nature – the whole *raison d'être* is, after all, informality – can make it hard to know just what the user means. It is loose talk in its most literal sense: it cavorts, plays, stumbles about. It does not, at times, make sense. This is not a vocabulary thing, but a way of speech. I may cavil at what I see as a lack of

* Writing in March 2011 the *OED's* then editor John Simpson notes that the revised entry for 'run' has outstripped 'set', offering some 645 senses to the 579 of set. Given the modern developments of the two words, 'My feeling is that "set" hasn't developed as much as "run" in the twentieth and twenty-first centuries and so, when revised, it will be touch-and-go whether it hauls itself back into the largest-entry position it held in the first and second editions of the dictionary.'

useful authority in the multiple and often contradictory definitions that come with entries in the online Urban Dictionary but its only commandment is 'define your world' and thus people do. There are no laws against inconsistency. This might suggest that I include each of the Urban Dictionary's differing definitions in my own work. I do not; what I am looking for is more substantial proof of use. I find it where I can, primarily in print but I am not choosy. I find, where possible, original sources, or, to be clearer, do my own research. It is not, however, always possible.

All of which, I must note, is to assume the immutability of definitions and of the senses within them. If we agree with Patrick Hanks' opinion, which serves as this chapter's epigraph, then that edifice of belief shakes, if not collapses. Rather than being set in stone, the definition is no more than 'an increasingly delicate hierarchy of generalizations'. For Hanks a definition carries only 'meaning potential'; and the example (not a citation but the pertinent lines from the electronic corpus with which he works – its texts offering the chance to analyse the use of a billion and a half words) a 'meaning event'. In other words, if I read him correctly, it is only in use – slang's ever-important context – that a word gains a meaning. The lay users of the Urban Dictionary, ignorant of linguistics and acting on layman's principles, seem to do this instinctively: words are what the user makes of them. Nothing means anything until a particular speaker empowers it.

It is not only the political that is personal. So too is the lexicographical. I have no problem with this, finding it almost wholly impossible to embrace the idea of disinterest, even if, as I must, I strive for it in my work. Sometimes the person is another, which in professional terms means a predecessor, even a contemporary; sometimes oneself, in which case we are looking at bias if not egocentricity; and finally the person is idealised, at which point we are grasping at something for which the shorthand term is 'truth' and which, of course, is quite unattainable. These four sideshows might be termed Plagiarism, Personality, Prescription and Perfection and I shall consider them below.

1. Plagiarism

Why lie? It is an act of theft. Being the people's poetry, which definition I don't wholly believe but which serves me now, we can gussie it up as folklore and append the larcenist's eternal excuse: Robin Hood. Robbing those rich in words to explicate for those less well endowed. Or, since there is an element of scholarship, go classical: Prometheus, stealing not fire but language; his liver-ripping eagle, the knowledge that no dictionary can ever permit itself a genuine conclusion. Enough: yonder lies Pseud's Corner, even if in my experience 'pseud' was always an epithet hurled by those, with Molesworth's Grabber ma. as their role model, who were pig-shit stupid and proud to boast of the fact.

It is, I repeat, an act of theft. Theft of creativity, of language, of individual words. It starts with someone else: an author who has already written. Something else: a book that has been published, a script, a lyric, a blog, whatever. Native creativity doesn't enter the picture, even though the end product requires that one makes something new from all these borrowings, and that requires at least an arsey-versey variety of creation.

Let us be kinder, lexicography, or a proportion thereof, has no choice but to be plagiaristic. We intone the mantra 'To steal from one book is plagiarism, to steal from many is research' and dictionary-making, at least of my sort, is 'many books' plagiarism and thus research. That the quote, while multi-attributed, seems to rest up with the wonderfully amoral Wilson Mizner (who also provided that fine slang rationale: 'I respect faith but doubt is what gives you an education') merely adds to one's self-justification.

I am not, however, talking of the citations themselves. They are evidence of slang 'live' and even if I include, say, 1,045 quotations from the works of Damon Runyon, or 1,269 from those of Irvine Welsh – which means those works help inform the same numbers of discrete headwords – I cannot imagine anyone using this as a basis for recreating the books 'for free', and in any case they represent only a tiny fraction of the citations on offer. The plagiarism, the 'research', to which I refer is that inclusion, like it or not of one's predecessors. And that, inevitably, presents problems.

'When I use a word,' said Lewis Carroll's Mad Hatter, 'it means exactly what I want it to mean; nothing more, nothing less.' The Hatter, who is never called mad, is nonetheless portrayed as being so. 'Mad as a hatter', predating the book by thirty-six years, is first noted in 1829, in America. As for *Alice*, the popular assumption is that Carroll was referring to mercury poisoning, an occupational hazard although not, despite the general belief, a shortcut to insanity. According to Anthony Burgess, for whom 'The study of language may beget madness', it threatens lexicographers too. I do not know whether Burgess was punning when he noted that their tutelary deity was the 'rogue-god Mercury'. (Nor, given the role of institutionalised plagiarism, in making reference to Mercury's other identification: with thieves.)

Dictionary-makers, sane or otherwise, subscribe to tougher rules. Words – at least in dictionary format – have static meanings; such meanings do not go away. There are nuances, there are variations, there are additions, but as the prison slang puts it, definitions run not 'wild' but 'bow-legged'. Concurrent, not consecutive. There is no choice but to live with the meanings we have, and slang tends to simple ones. The problem is – what do you do when you're not the first? Nothing new here. In 1656 Thomas Blount, author of *Glossographia*, was worried:

> Of all works a Dictionary is most exposed to the charge of plagiarism, and is therefore the work against which such a charge should least be credited upon a surmise or allegation only. How shall I contrive not to define a word in the same manner, as some certain writer has done before me? Or am I under any such obligation? If he has defined it well, am I obliged to define it ill? Every dictionary-maker, great or small, will of necessity place other dictionaries before him, when he sits down to work, and will take his definition from one or other of them, when he finds that they have done it so, that he cannot mend it [do it any better].

Is this the voice of conscience? Blount was an appalling plagiarist himself. He names the classics – authors and dictionaries – from whom he 'borrowed' but conveniently omits mention of his immediate predecessors, whom he had gutted shamelessly. In time, still shameless, he would pursue another lexicographer, Edward Phillips, for literary theft (an unresolved and perhaps publicity-seeking quarrel that lasted until Blount's death). Yet he was right. I've been there. In 1998 I wrote a dictionary for Publisher A. My editor moved; now at Publisher B he requested a reprise. Publisher A saw no problems. The book would not be identical – the chronology and format were to be different – but still, it remained a book of slang. My mistake. Still, off I go. Do some work, submit some text. A summons: meet the lawyers. I was ill, flu, but no matter. We were talking definitions: the similarity thereof. The legal eagle, sensing lucrative debates before His Lordship, was adamant: what if Publisher A, noticing that a word was defined elsewhere as it had been for them, chose to sue? The law is a parallel universe. That 'fuck', depending on part of speech, cannot in its primary definitions mean anything but the act of sexual intercourse or to indulge therein seemed beyond them. I asked for alternatives, they were silent. I may have become ill-tempered, I hope not, but surely somewhat hysterical. We laugh that we should not cry. My editor looked embarrassed. The meeting ended. I went back to bed. The book was canned.

There really is no way out of this. We have to include what has gone before. Language is not reborn every time a new dictionary is to be researched. This is true for Standard English (or standard French, Hindi, Russian, whatever) and it is true for slang. Slang is wonderfully re-inventive, even if its underlying themes remain the same, but for any dictionary that pretends, as does mine, to 'start at the beginning' then one has no choice to look at what was on offer back in that day. Earlier sources are fragmented and one has to accept what we have noted above: that words that end up in slang dictionaries when used by such as Chaucer were not yet strictly 'slang' since the concept – even in its broadest sense – was a century and a half from existence. Of the sixteenth-century's 'slang' vocabulary, the majority of words exist only in one glossary or another. So back I go, walking the same roads as Robert Copland, John Awdeley, Thomas Harman and the rest of our earliest forefathers.

There will be new words, new meanings – why else the new dictionary? – but what there was remains. 'Fuck' has not suddenly experienced a rebirth as meaning 'change a tyre' or 'shoot a movie'. One might be able to tweak the definition of 'fuckwit', say, from 'fool' to 'idiot', but that root term remains inviolate and there is no way out. The professionals, if not the company lawyers, seem to accept this. There have been cases of plagiarism brought against dictionaries, but they are rare and more likely commenced by publishers, jealous of their profits, than lexicographers, who take so small a share in them. We know, remember, how it is done, how it has to be done. Johnson worked with his recent predecessor Nathan Bailey's dictionary open on a lectern; the *OED* refers back to dozens of lexicons; there was no way that, wishing to ensure that alongside my own forays into the contemporary I missed as little as possible of the past, I would not have deputed a researcher to check through Eric Partridge. And Partridge himself had turned to John S. Farmer and W. E. Henley and they in their time had looked at John Camden Hotten who had absorbed Francis Grose who ate up B.E. and so it has to go. A form of linguistic Pacman, munch, munch, munch. Each takes on the past and then blends in the present. However many original citations we may garner, and however much the use of other dictionaries represents frustration and surrender, we still have no choice. It is the dictionary-maker's dilemma and no wonder the tendency of successive volumes runs to bloat.

What fun to have been the first. Thomas Harman, the first genuine example of my persuasion – there had been predecessors and he used them but they had offered so very little and had different agendas – claimed to have done it all through field research, swapping money or food for sixteenth-century criminal slang. He listed his informants: the one who drivelled, the octogenarian who could chew through nails. Strange stuff, long vanished except in the pages of successor dictionaries: 'pannum' for bread, 'lap' for milk, 'dummerer' for a fake mute, 'dell' for a whore and 'chats' for gallows, which last Harman presents as 'So we may happen to the harmans and cly the jerk, or to the queer-ken and scour queer cramp-rings and so to trining on the chats.' This he translates as 'So we may chance to be set in the stocks to be whipped or go to prison and be shackled or to the gallows to be hanged.' We also find 'mort wapace', a sexually enthusiastic girl – 'apace' being both a literal and figurative use of 'fast'. Only 'bouse' soldiers on as 'booze'. At the same time, academe, always keen to carp – for careers are to be sustained and controversy, faked or otherwise, is a useful engine – claims that he made it up to bolster establishment scare-mongering (slang as corrupter, not for the last time and one continues to admire its power); that, phallocentric and patriarchal, he paid female beggars to 'talk dirty', that it was all fantasy, no more than a joke-book. You cannot win.

At which point one has the right to ask: is the whole edifice, these monuments to linguistic authority, no more than an aggregation of 'swag', tumbling from the back of hijacked lorries, piled up in some linguistic equivalent of the backstreet lockup, the 'slaughter' as the boys have it (abbreviating 'slaughterhouse'; violence is not mandatory and the image is of gullible buyers who, handing over money, are 'slaughtered'). I'm very glad you asked that question. Because the answer is no. You have an alternative suggestion? I didn't think so. It's not, naturally, what one might choose. Comes with the job. Fair cop, guv, I'll put my hands up: there is an excess of Eric Partridge in the first version of my *Cassell Dictionary of Slang*. Not text, but headwords. And why was that? Fear. Inexperience. Even respect. Partridge claims it's slang, OK, who am I to argue? Insufficiently knowledgeable of the ropes – still, yes, after five years of manipulating them – to risk cutting through the knots. Have you ever thought of writing a slang dictionary, said that editor in 1993 and I thought, 'well, I've actually published one', but I didn't fool myself into believing that if he didn't already know it the failure was anyone's but mine. Juvenilia's my excuse. Exploration. Discovery. Ignorance. One learns as one goes, but not quite enough and rarely in time. Subsequent editions have been more brutal. Sons know what must be done with fathers. Cutting Partridge headwords became automatic, almost mandatory. Not before time. And not, of course, all. Far from all, because, as I say, the language does not reinvent itself. But if the *OED*, looking to encompass the language, had to decide what qualified and what did not, so too did I, on my miniaturised level.

We have no choice but to plagiarise, but if so then we must

also hope to improve. Thomas Harman's treatment of 'booze', which he spelled 'bouse', does no more than define it: 'drinke'. *GDoS* offers derivatives ('booze-fest'), compounds ('booze-artist', '–factory', '–runner'), phrases ('hit the booze', 'sling the booze'), plus verbal and adjectival uses, and a variety of developments such as 'boozer', 'boozing', 'boozorium' and 'boozy'. In all, citations of course included, there are ten columns. I do not claim superiority to Harman – and he was not the first, since 'bous' could already be found in Middle English* – but there is undoubtedly an advance in information.

2. Personality

Johnson's definitions, or at least those for 'oats', 'patron', 'Grub street' and 'excise' (which last nearly landed him in jail for defamation), are to be found in every dictionary of quotations. The most famous is his description of his own task, but it stings less if one acknowledges its entirety: one who 'busies himself in tracing the original, and detailing the signification of words'. They are enjoyable – even if they are not, notably 'oats', especially original – and, if nothing else, transcend the Christmas cracker truisms of too many 'great lines'. They also represent another side of dictionary-making that hasn't survived modernity. Perhaps not actual humour, but at least a degree of wit. Compared with many predecessors, Johnson was impressively disciplined, but compared with modern dictionaries, his is positively jokey. And dictionary definitions – other than his – are no longer feted by their quotable cousins. Eric Partridge was equally opinionated, and never afraid to interject an opinion if he felt the need. But Partridge was, of course, dealing

* *c.*1325 *Mon in þe mone* ['The Man in the Moon'] (Hrl 2253) 29: 'Drynke to hym deorly of fol god bous [. . .] When þat he is dronke ase a dreynt mous.'

in slang. So do I, but I have imposed, slightly unwillingly but definitely necessarily, a far greater self-discipline on myself. The temptation is there – every drudge demands his day – but for once I advocate resistance. God resists smart cracks, or is at least supposed to. There are no jokes in the Ten Commandments (the coveting of asses notwithstanding). In any case, slang can make its own jokes. Spelling them out, other than the necessary explanation of ancient, creaking puns, is to over-egg a perfectly tasty custard.

3. Prescriptive/Descriptive

So here is our lexicographer, not just drudge but deity too. Or at least priest ministering to the linguistic Holy of Holies. If I go back there it is not from ego. A lapsed Jew, I espouse atheism, and 'God', invariably found in slang as a gateway to blasphemy, is merely a way-station between 'gock', a sticky substance, and 'go down', a drink. For many – and it seems to be the case in America more than anywhere else (though the Académie Française had enshrined prescriptivism in the *Dictionnaire* of 1694) – this is a role that we've been given. Whether Johnson and Webster muttered, most literally, 'That'll larn 'em' as they set down one thundering commandment after another, I cannot say. Their agendas are too easily revealed for there not to have been a degree of conscious didacticism. It is not how I go about it. Of course telling the world that the 'bald-headed-custard-chucker' is the penis or that the promiscuous female has had 'more pricks than a second-hand dart-board' and her male equivalent 'more arse than a toilet seat' fails, I will not argue, to equate with lofty statements as regards 'freedom' or 'faith'. As I say, a very tinpot deity.*

* Those who know his photos will note that James Murray, of course, has all the traditional attributes: old man with long, snowy beard, although no belief system, unless one seriously stretches Hinduism's juggernaut, appears to include his tricycle.

What I do not do, although some see it as the very essence of the lexicographer's task, is to pronounce on usage. This is a wholly unalloyed blessing. The 'Language Wars' (Henry Hitchings in his eponymous overview of 2011) or 'Usage Wars' (David Foster Wallace in a 1999 essay 'Authority and American Usage' that some felt revealed him paradoxically in favour of rules; he does the same thing in 'Twenty-four Word Notes' in 2004) are just that. Bloody, sometimes frighteningly personal, and in the end unresolved. I have no wish to gird my loins and get stuck in. In any case, usage rules as regards the employment of slang are simple: don't. The study and collection of slang, perhaps because its lexis offers little else, lacks the *Sturm und Drang* of what David Foster Wallace called 'the seamy underbelly of . . . lexicography'. Our controversies tend not to definition but to etymology and even there it is all very measured and the end result is to pass on information to those who appear sadly to have ignored it, rather than to damn a rival. We are drudge-deities not angels, and we have no desire to dance on pins.

In slang's limited, one-eyed (one-handed) world this is hardly a great sacrifice. There are labels, but they are very rarely based on social position – far more usually indicating geographical origins or sexual or professional orientation. Slang is simple: the lexis comes up from the bottom and has a built-in need to laugh (among other things) at every facet of the established order. The simple fact of using slang is all we need. That is its usage and there are no gradations. Partridge attempted to define a hierarchy, wishing to show how slang words shifted in register – starting for instance as wholly taboo, then moving gradually 'upwards' towards colloquialism – but, really, it doesn't work like that. Look at some of the longer lists of citations: can you see where a word stops being 'low' and moves to 'general'? Me neither. Yes, certain terms start life as criminal terminology and move out into 'civilian' slang, but they are a minority. Using it is enough, and there is no 'correct' version of that. Cunt is a cunt is a cunt.

Where we might be seen as pronouncing beyond the simple definition A=B, though I prefer to see it as useful fine-tuning, is in the necessary discrimination between senses. This is not always simple. The problem is not variations on a theme. The first definition of 'piece of ass' (or 'arse') is a woman. That the phrase is open to various synonyms is not a problem, synonyms being the essence of the slang lexis. We can accept that what speaker A terms 'piece of ass' or 'arse', Speaker B will have as 'butt', Speaker C as 'cock' (that being the vagina in American South), and speakers D through O will have respectively as 'cunt', 'gash', 'honey', 'hump', 'pork', 'pratt', 'pussy', 'quiff', 'skin', 'snatch', 'trim', or 'work'; while Speakers P and Q prefer to substitute 'chunk' or 'hunk' for piece and give among much else a 'chunk of fanny' and 'hunk of hat'. The greater difficulty comes when these same pieces turn from person to activity, in this case sexual intercourse (usually, but not invariably heterosexual; the specifically anal version, again open to all genders, tends to a literal use of 'ass'). Fortunately there are clues. The copulatory piece of ass tends to be something one 'gets' or 'has', and one looks for the verb. It is not invariable: 'You got to ruin your life over a piece of snatch? It ain't sensible,' advises Charles Bukowski.* Could be a woman? Could be a 'bit of how's-yer-father'? Only the surrounding text can help, and one questions it accordingly: it's a fuck.

The more abstract the term, the harder it is to draw lines. Let us look, for instance, at the verb 'hang out'. There are two definitions, and one is simple: based on the image of a tongue hanging out with eagerness it refers to desperate need, usually of drugs, drink or sex. The other is more challenging. It comes from 'hang',

* *Erections, Ejaculations, etc.*, p. 349 (1972)

of which the primary meanings carry the literal or metaphorical image of 'to suspend' (which, strictly, also encompasses the pendant tongue). The *OED* has but a single slang definition: 'to reside, to lodge, to live'. My researches, while echoing the *OED* in definition 1, offer seven: 1 [early nineteenth century onwards] to live, to make one's home. 2 [mid-nineteenth century] (UK/US campus) to treat. 3 [late nineteenth century – 1940s] (Aus.) to endure, to survive. 4 [late nineteenth century] to meet, to collect together at a regular venue, to frequent. 5 [mid-nineteenth century] to idle away time with friends. 6 [twentieth century] to exist, to be situated, to be available, to happen. 7 [1980s onwards] to lie in wait.

All these are derived from the citations that I have encountered. The campus use, which is recorded in only two glossaries, seems anomalous but the image is of living somewhere and making oneself available to offer amusement to friends. (There is also, perhaps, the idea of 'hanging out' a virtual sign of welcome.) The remainder are all linked. The question is of bundling and again, only citations can help. The most problematic line is between 4, to gather, and 5, to idle. Both involve groups, presumably of acquaintances, but while 4 may well be accompanied by purposeful activity, 5 has an added 'moral' aspect: time is passed, but also wasted. Fortunately I have evidence. The first cite for 4 is this:

> 1855 *Yokel's Preceptor*: This is a Yarmouth mot. A very clean, sober, and honest piece. [. . .] She hangs out in Fleet-street.

We are helped by the specific geographical reference – which can be found in many subsequent examples – and the fact that the pamphlet is a guide to London lowlife. The girl is not wasting time, she is selling her body as a whore, sometimes known as a 'Fleet-street houri'.

The first cite for 5 is different:

> 1831 'Navy at Home' II 180: What has he been about? – look no further than the next lane – the handiest gin shop; there, amidst fumes of tobacco, he hangs out – in a happy fuddle, if not quite drunk, all day.

This is the use that would persist into the 1960s and beyond, almost synonymous with 'hanging around'. The 'happy fuddle' helps, as does the lack of geography. In addition, as further cites underline, this is not positive 'hanging' but aimless and self-indulgent. The Australian writer Henry Lawson makes it absolutely clear his 1895 reference to one who is: 'Lazy, purposeless, and useless – knocking around and hanging out.'

These choices have to be made almost continually. Slang speakers, while they may fall into deliberate codes, are not pausing for nuance. We fall back, as so often in this originally spoken lexis, on context but it is not always as welcoming to our knock as we might require and clarification becomes a subjective act. One makes assessment of the speaker, the scene in which they are acting, the larger plot. The problem is further compounded by the brevity of cites. We know that use X differs, however minutely, from use Y, because we have seen it as used. This is privileged knowledge, however: we know because we have done the research. The dictionary's reader lacks that background information and there is no space, as things stand, to offer it. There is no choice but to trust.

Trust can also lead to disappointment when it is seen to be betrayed. I am not subject to the wave of near-hysterical criticism that greeted one of the Webster generics, the *Third International Dictionary* of 1961. The lexicographers, accused of failing to lay down the judgments that were assumed to be their duty, were deemed to have abrogated their priestly role, and, that done, what could the congregation do but fall into sin. If the definer refuses to take his duties seriously, what is he encouraging but what one horror-struck adversary termed 'subversion and decay'? It was noted that 'to the swallower of the definition it never occurs that he can have drunk corruption from a well that he has every reason to trust as the ultimate in purity'. The primary point at issue, by the way, was the judgment-free inclusion of the word 'ain't'.

Ah yes, the Sixties. If those who sought change seemed at times hysterical, so too did those who stood, however impotently, in their path. The world as we knew it was ending. To arms, for the barricades beckoned and we had to fight. Now one laughs, but the publishers did not: deeply rattled, they resisted offering an update for the next half-century though, belatedly, one is on the way now. I do not know quite why American critics are so keen that their dictionaries be sources of social as well as linguistic instruction – how to learn lots of words and influence people – while British ones, faced with the *OED* and its lesser coevals, are unworried that the great work describes rather than proscribes. The whole descriptive/proscriptive thing is debatable in itself. Some say 'bullshit' and declare that there is no division; others see it as a trench that divides dictionary-making and ne'er the twain can meet. If I stick to definitions, then I have to go with the nay-sayers and agree that all is united, because, as I have tried to make clear, simply stating a definition – bearing the implication: 'this is true, believe me' – is to proscribe. Simply tapping letter one into a book that sets itself up as an authority, a showcase for facts over fantasies, is proscriptive. But if one strays beyond that, and starts to specify what is 'correct' and thus 'incorrect', then OK, the division exists and it is serious. It also nonsensical or at best ephemeral. Like the 'proper' way to rear babies (breast/bottle, feed on demand/feed at set hours, swaddling/freedom of movement) which seems to alter every time a new expert wishes to promote a book and has done so ever since such manuals began appearing in the eighteenth century, 'correct' is mutable. I commend readers to Henry Hitchings' 'Language Wars' (2011), which lays it all out. In the land of the linguistically deaf, he who shouts loudest is king, but kings are short-lived and so too is 'correct'.

4. Perfection

Slang does not like abstracts; nor do slang lexicographers. The lexis keeps moving and we keep chasing. We can no more corral its entirety than we finish our dictionaries. Nor, and I feel no shame in this, is there such a thing as perfection. The best I can manage is an informed approximation of what I, doubtless dangerously, term 'truth'.

I am not interested in 'beauty' (another concept slang eschews, other than coarsely and with beauty's sexual potential upmost in mind) but I am interested in 'truth'. My definitions aim at veracity, at accuracy. I am trying, quite consciously, to help. To cut the crap. What else is the dictionary for? Slang dictionaries very likely have more readers – readers in the traditional sense of sit down, open and enjoy – than standard ones, which for many users represent information over possible entertainment, but at bottom they are both tools. That is what I see when creating an entry, especially one that is long and complex and bears a number of nuanced definitions. Do I get it wrong? Sometimes, I have no doubt, and hope to get it (more nearly) right in some future edition.* If so I

* 'Sometimes' is, I confess, a cop-out. I have made errors where really I have no excuse, because I was not ignorant, merely slipshod, and they have been pointed out and I am laying myself open to those who can and will throw such blunders in my face. My hands are raised. *Mea culpa*.

echo Johnson who, when faced with the woman who asked how he could have defined 'pastern' (properly the part of a horse's foot between the fetlock and the hoof) as the 'knee of the horse', gave the candid response: 'Ignorance, Madam, pure ignorance.' Do I miss stuff? Oh, please. And sometimes it is conspiracy – I don't consider that every word qualifies – though just as often it is cock-up. Ignorance, Madam and indeed Sir, pure ignorance. Then there is the critics' favourite: I know a word that Mr G. does not. Well, good on you. Now do something positive: tell me and the readers something useful about the ones I have included.

If slang is, as claimed, the 'people's poetry' then that stops before its definition. Editing the book is smoothing, polishing, removing extranea, correcting blunders, reducing again. The aim is to reach for truth, as far as is possible, and to contain that truth in a minimal space. If that reduces its poetry, I am unmoved. The craft is not one for those whose fancies fly. Johnson, in his introduction and talking of his own fantasies of perfection, especially as in defining, explained wistfully how he 'resolved to show likewise my attention to things; to pierce deep into every science, to inquire the nature of every substance of which I inserted the name, to limit every idea by a definition strictly logical, and exhibit every production of art or nature in an accurate description, that my book might be in place of all other dictionaries whether appellative or technical.' Theory is kind, practice intolerant. The book must be 'finished' or at least research must pause and a text be published. 'So,' continues Johnson, 'these were the dreams of a poet doomed at last to wake a lexicographer.' He feared that he might never stop, and, having dropped his stone into the pond, never run out of ripples to pursue, and in so doing, 'would have protracted the undertaking without end, and, perhaps, without much improvement.'

If that were true of Johnson, then how much more so of me. We are doomed to fail. Such is the story: we try, we fail, we try again and as one attempt follows the last the only hope, as Samuel Beckett put it, is to 'fail better'.

Calling Names

Slang is quite literally *profane*, which translates from Latin as 'outside the temple' and, in the figurative uses that lay out its path from Latin to medieval French and thence to English, has been defined as 'not dedicated to religious use, secular, not initiated into a religious rite, ceremonially unclean, impious', and as a noun, 'a person who is uninitiated or impious'. In the context of language *profane* and its noun-form *profanity* began as blasphemy and irreverence, and moved on to a synonym for ribald, coarse and indecent. In this it resembles the progress of taboo language, which starts by mocking God with 'zounds', 'oddsboddikins', 'slids', 'snails' (respectively God's wounds, little body, eyelids and nails – and in all cases 'God' is of course Christ) and so on, and then, when copulation, defecation and the parts of the body that performed them replaced the deity as the source of terror, turned to terms that described them and what they did.

Nothing is 'unsayable': such is the message of slang. Mine too, at least professionally. I can be foul-mouthed but if I do not invariably bespatter my conversations it may be because I too am susceptible to that easing superficiality: politeness. It may also be that, bereft of database, I simply forget. At work they are wholly and for me easily sayable and writable and the dictionary is not a comforting place for those who fetishise restraint. I am immune. I can think of only two slang words that make me wince: 'oven-dodger', which is the Jew in the role of 'one that got away', and 'Kleenex' which, or so I have read and so I have chosen to note, refers to the victim of paedophilic assault: 'you blow once and throw them away'. But in they go too and there have been and will be no exceptions. No bouncers at my door for anything, however grotesque, and if I don't like the punters that's my bad luck.

All slang is the calling of names. (And as its recorder I, who am still wondering what my own surname might have been, spend my time giving names to others.) What else, boiled down, is any language or form of communication? In slang's case the names are usually derogatory, negative and sceptical. Slang is the great nay-sayer. The wide-spectrum critic with 117 synonyms for 'put down'. No courtier, its m.o. is jesting, brandishing its pig's bladder of verbal cruelty, gleefully thumping pomposity, self-righteousness and the certainties of true belief. It flinches from diplomacy, from euphemism (except for the literary, a bad sex award all to itself). It is not loved, but, failing to offer affection, it sees no need to seek it. It lacks a voice, being but twenty-six mute letters, but were it to speak it would revel in the longevity of its power, its lasting ability to cause alarm.

Lenny Bruce, fearless of anything that came in words, but equally repelled by some of what he might hear, believed that the way to deal with slang's cruelties, specifically the nationalist and racist ones, was repetition. Use them enough, out front and without mystique, bring them out of the shadows and into the spotlight, and the result would be that they slunk away of their own accord. That 'if President Kennedy would just go on television, and say, "I would like to introduce you to all the niggers in my cabinet", and if he'd just say "nigger nigger nigger nigger nigger" to every nigger he saw, "boogie boogie boogie boogie boogie", "nigger nigger nigger nigger nigger" 'til nigger didn't mean anything anymore, then you could never make some six year old black kid cry because somebody called him a nigger at school.'

Nothing works out as we expect. Bruce, like many ostensible cynics, masked a romantic view of human possibility. The arc of taboo has undoubtedly moved: Eric Partridge couldn't spell out 'f-ck' or 'sh-t' but in another era had no problems with offering unmediated definitions of 'wog' or 'nigger', while I, and many others, find things quite the contrary.* Political correctness, child of the 1970s, is in the ascendant. A two-term black president sits in the White House and I don't see him trying the hipster satirist's experiment any time soon. Bruce's question 'Are there any niggers in the house tonight?' delivered on-stage against a rush of indrawn breath in 1960 and with which he prefaced his theorising, is listed at the Comedy Quotes website. These eight words – no context is offered, no further explanation of the material that followed – are introduced thus: 'Please note: This quote contains offensive content and is only available to view by individuals 18 years of age or older. By viewing I hereby certify that: I am at least 18 years of age and I do not find explicit content to be obscene or offensive in any way.' Oh, for fuck's sake. Are we to proffer that

* Not everyone agrees and times do not invariably change, PC notwithstanding: Eric Partridge's successor Paul Beale could write of 'wog' in the 1984 edition of *A Dictionary of Slang and Unconventional English*, 'The term is not *always* used with rabid xenophobia – it's often a matter of "What else can you call them?"' and in November 2012 an Australian commenter in the *Guardian* complained that 'For the thousandth effing time, wog does not mean black person in Australia. If you say wog, and are referring to a black person, nobody will have a clue what you mean. Wog means person of Mediterranean origin and is in no way offensive.' It was also ANZAC troops, on adopting a stray Egyptian dog in 1945, who christened it 'Horrie the Wog-Dog' – which thereafter became the title of a popular 'biography'. There was no suggestion of wog's alternative antipodean meaning: the 'flu.

cowardly excuse: 'their heart's in the right place', or is it simply fear of a lawsuit?

Pieties are not going to work. The racist lexis is based on stereotypes, the foundation stones of this particular set of terms. Figurative stereotypes, literally 'solid types' with that suggestion of 'set in stone', are rarely accurate, but the desire to create them, to find some shorthand for 'the other' remains pervasive. I am good and to make that so, you must be bad and labelled as such. In this world of aggression, what matters is not the ingredients, but the brand name. Like the Goths or the Tartars, typified as invaders and transmuted to Standard English negatives, the Vikings, whose invasion broke the Anglo-Saxon hold on Britain, stood for the violent, unbidden outsider. The current *OED* etymology links Viking either to the Old Norse *vik*, a creek, from which they sailed, or the Old English *wic,* a camp or settlement, which they established on arrival. The proto-lexicographer Aelfric, compiling his *Dictionarium Saxonico-Latino-Anglicum* around 1000 CE, defined the word as 'pirata', a pirate. The *Anglo-Saxon Chronicle* (*c.* 891–1164), a continuing 'diary' of national events, opted for the unadorned 'heathen'. Neither creeks nor camps entered the story. We see what we want, define accordingly, and thereafter speak in unison.

If ever I believed Lenny Bruce, I lost that optimism long since. Slang sees that one off in every page of its dictionaries. These are not the words that have died away, the withered leaves of some long-gone variety of criminality. Or some archaic euphemism like 'Eve's pleasure garden' or 'shaking the sheets of Bogie'. There are perhaps 1,000 terms that slither from the toxic lake of racially and nationally based abuse. The latter are perhaps less vicious, merely disdainful. Nations and other groups can be delineated by clothes ('rag-' or 'towel-heads' for that loose catch-all Muslims, 'old clo' for Jews), by food ('Johnny peasoup' for

French Canadian, 'spaghetti-bender' for Italian, plus the religious 'mackerel-snappers' for Catholics), sexual predilections (take a look at pretty much anything that starts with 'French'); there is room for humour, or so I see in the wonderful 'as bilong sospen' (from Tok Pisin, the Papua New Guinea pidgin) which refers to the North Solomon islanders, who play the same scorned role as the Irish in the UK and the Poles in America. However, neither of those groups is accused of cannibalism, since the literal translation is 'your arse belongs in a saucepan'. I wrote a book on racial and national slurs fifteen years ago, throwing in a further 1,000 from various warring European vocabularies – which proved, if nothing else, that stereotyping is an international given and that those who write in English should be grateful for their language's lack of diacritics. The book went largely unreviewed – I sensed a certain pulling aside of the garments, of shielding the children's eyes and averting one's own – other than one that praised it, before noting that so depressing were the contents I really ought not to have bothered.

I did bother. I do bother. Let's call it completism, though who can 'complete' a language for which evolution is its stock-in-trade? I am the recording . . . what, devil perhaps, surely not angel, of centuries of hatreds. The whole slang lexis trades in stereotypes, how can it resist in the context of race, most productive of all. The Jew is always greedy and duplicitously self-seeking (and, perhaps as a result of immigration to the East End, productive of much rhyming slang: 'buckle-my-shoe', kangaroo; 'Cisco Kid', front-wheel skid); the black stupid and sexually predatory ('ape', 'buck', 'coon'); the East Asian a 'yellow peril' and of course 'slanty-eyed'. Most are simply dumb: Poles, Irish, Mexicans, the stoop labour of the lexis. There are, for instance, eight columns of terms based on the adjective 'Irish'. They include five wheelbarrows ('ambulance', 'buggy', 'baby buggy', 'chariot' and 'local'), six for tools – usually the shovel – used in manual labour ('banjo', 'fan', 'local', 'screwdriver', 'toothpick' and 'tumble-dryer'), eight for potato ('apple', 'apricot', 'fruit' and 'wall-fruit', 'football', 'grape', 'lemon' and 'root') and on. None are flattering. Mexicans and Poles are not dissimilar, simply tweaked to factor in, among other stereotypes, donkeys and poverty for the first, and lack of hygiene for the second.

As insults such terms may be expected in slang, but in one respect they are anomalous: they defy slang's usual chronological procession of synonymy. These are stereotypes and were established long since. Of the 300 words meaning 'black person' the oldies remain the baddies. The same for a hundred Jews, forty-six Italians, forty-two Mexicans, forty Irish and all the rest. If it ain't broke . . . and despite the most determined efforts, it ain't fixed either.

It is not just race. Slang scatters its shots and, like the playground bully, while happy to focus on the supposed shortcomings of time-honoured scapegoats, is even more at home in the wide-ranging world of general insults. These are as ever broad brush calculations, but such is slang's core. There are 430 of what I define as 'general terms of abuse'. This is not that select group whereby the penis, vagina or anus multitask as both organs and idiots (of which 'prick', 'cunt' and 'arsehole' are but the tip of a substantial iceberg), and terms for defecation or urination, and that other bodily fluid, semen, often in compounds, work a double shift as sneers. Nor the terms for fools and foolish which number nearly 2,500; the near 800 defined, in defiance of current professional practice, as 'mad' (housed in fifty-seven 'psychiatric institutions' which coy euphemism is definitely not how slang describes the 'loony bin' or 'booby hatch') , and of course those labelled 'unattractive', which dismissal notches up 280 and 'fat' which scores 250. Though the latter pair usher in the far more substantial lexis concerning the near 3,000 women (who in slang's judgmental male gaze lack much identity beyond the sexual, and that's not to mention the prostitutes, some 1,180 who in turn overlap with 'promiscuous/promiscuity', good for 345 more). Then there are those who slang cannot even pretend to love: a thousand apiece of gay men and of policemen.

Then, as we must, we reach the obscenity, If we believe the Federal Communications Commission, which adjudicated back in the 1970s, then there are only twelve or thirteen. The canonical four letter words which in one instance, the Oedipal polysyllable, requires a dozen. That phrase underlines the religion to rudery move. The first such word is the tetragrammaton, 'JHVH', the vowelless rendering of Hebrew's taboo 'Jehovah', God, and as such pronounced 'adonai', lord. 'Four letter word' is first recorded in 1934 and develops thereafter. 'Four letter man' – a 'S-H-I-T' – is noted a decade earlier, and 'three letter man' – originally 'F-A-G', now 'G-A-Y' – appears in 1941. The abbreviation as insult is not new: in *Aulularia* (The Pot of Gold) the Roman playwright Plautus labels a character *trium litterarum homo*, 'a man of three letters': they were F-V-R, a thief.

That they have pitched up in the slang dictionaries is as much luck as judgment. The early cant glossaries offered their synonyms, typically 'wap', to have sex, found in Thomas Harman and satisfyingly echoic of the slap of flesh, but not these words that were everyday, not criminal. Some had a reasonably lengthy career as colloquial if not exactly standard, before the early eighteenth century's demand from Swift and others that the language should be purged. Only 'cunt' failed to move beyond middle English and into early modern, around 1450. It is hard not to link this to misogyny, conscious or otherwise. This purgation was not particularly aimed at 'filth', which as ever dealt in copulation and defecation, but such was a knock-on effect of the desire to standardise a language that reflected properly on a newly important nation. The *Académie Française* had brought out its *Dictionnaire* in 1694; Britons must show the flag. An Academy found no takers; Johnson was commissioned to do the clean-up job; to his credit he stood by the infinite potential of the language, even as he purveyed his own Tory rigidities. He did not, of course, stretch that tolerance to the obscene.

Coincidentally or otherwise the *épuration* ran in parallel to the growing demand for some form of obscenity law. Lord Rochester's late-seventeenth century works – magnificently profligate even by modern standards, fearful neither of 'cunt' nor anything else – had appeared ungelded. His friend Sir Charles Sedley, drunk and 'excrementising' on a crowd of onlookers from a pub balcony in Covent Garden, was fined and jailed, because he was also blaspheming, for 'obscene libel'.* This meant a 'dirty little book' but the concept of obscenity remained a religious concept. In 1724 the bookseller Edmund Curll, coincidentally Pope's *bête noire* and butt of *The Dunciad*, escaped punishment for putting out a handbook on flogging and, in translation, a piece of classic French porn. Their Lordships were forced to admit that no law existed under which they could try him. (They tried him instead for libel: guilty, and pilloried; 'Curlicism' became a synonym for obscene publication.) In 1748 John Cleland's printers, but not the author himself, were tried for 'producing an obscene work', the *Memoirs of a Woman of Pleasure* but the joke was that Cleland had set out

* According to Pepys, Sedley 'showed his nakedness – acting all the postures of lust and buggery that could be imagined, and abusing of scripture . . . preaching a Mountebank sermon from that pulpit . . . that being done, he took a glass of wine and washed his prick in it and then drank it off; and then took another and drank the King's health.' On being sentenced Sedley complained that he was 'the first man that ever paid for shitting'.

to write a book that, while titillating, included not one obscene word. In this he wholly succeeded, though it is hard, two-and-a-half centuries on, to see the thrills in his tortuous euphemisms, starting with his heroine's name: 'Fanny Hill'.

The concept of 'obscene publications' appears in the eponymous Act of 1857, the first of its type (a revised version would appear in 1959, itself slightly modified in 1964, and remains in place). Its target was the thriving porn trade of London's Holywell Street, long buried beneath modern Aldwych. Here one could find a whole row of 'dirty book' publishers, even if the term seems to be a coinage of the 1960s (though Swift's works were described as 'dirty volumes' in 1850 and 'dirty postcards' and 'stories' appear in the 1910s, and 'jokes' in 1940). Foremost among them was William Dugdale, a one-man embodiment of Holywell squalor. His tumescent catalogues included classic and contemporary works such as *The Battles of Venus*, *The Bed-Fellows or the Young Misses Manuel* [sic], *The Confessions of a Young Lady*, *The Ladies' Telltale*, *The Lustful Turk* and *The Victim of Lust*. There was a good deal of fladge. There was a series, *Lascivious Gems*: among them 'The Diary of a Nymphomaniac', 'The Fanciful Extremes of Fucksters', 'The Pleasing Pastime of Frigging' and 'A Night in St John's Wood.' All offering the delights to be found in his *Nunnery Tales* wherein Dugdale, in a burst of alliterative puffery, promised his clients that 'every stretch of voluptuous imagination is here fully depicted, rogering, ramming, one unbounded scene of lust, lechery and licentiousness'.

He put out bawdy songbooks – 'The Tuzzymuzzy Songster' and 'The Wanton Warbler', where the 'humour' relied on heavy-handed double entendres of the 'Has anyone seen Mike Hunt?' variety and which among many similar others could be bought for 6d. in certain pubs where drinkers enjoyed a smutty singalong – and a pair of magazines, *The Boudoir* and *The Exquisite*, top-shelf titles *avant la lettre*. He was regularly prosecuted and ran up nine sentences by 1857. It was his trial that year which so appalled Lord Chief Justice Campbell – 'a sale of poison more deadly than prussic acid, strychnine or arsenic' – that My Lord drove through the first Obscene Publications Act. The idea of women frequenting Dugdale's shops was apparently the final straw. The stock was repeatedly seized and destroyed. No matter: there were always more, knocked out in the cobwebby back rooms of one of his half dozen shops. The books, illustrated with barely lavatorial daubs, sold at three guineas, approximately three times the price of a 'straight' three-volume novel and six weeks' wages for the average worker. He became rich. It didn't last. When he died in 1868 he was serving a sentence in the Clerkenwell House of Correction and the death certificate hints at syphilis. There are no portraits.

The first Obscene Publications Act finally appeared in 1868 but the 'dirty words' – a term first used of 'popery' in 1842, and in the modern sense from 1855 – had long since left the mainstream dictionaries. They had taken sanctuary with such as Francis Grose, happy in his 'classical dictionary' of 1785 to include 'cunt', even if unable to resist a judicious hyphen and to define it as 'a nasty name for a nasty thing'. Pierce Egan, who revised him in 1823, was at pains to wash out Grose's mouth, although his own circle – hard-riding, fighting, gambling men, must have also been hard-cursing and hard-fucking. In 1859 James Camden Hotten, the pornographer of *Lady Bumtickler's Revels* and the *Library Illustrative of Social Progress* (which included Edmund Curll's old thrashing manual), compromised with a clean dictionary (given the contemporary anti-porn furore this was judicious). By the end of the century John S. Farmer was listing all dirty words that had been recorded and many more. He took his printers to court for their refusal to take on 'cunt' and 'fuck':

he lost and was forced to take his manuscript abroad. The slang dictionaries remain their home of choice, although the *OED* has repaired its nineteenth century omissions. (Jesse Sheidlower, the dictionary's former US editor-at-large, in his magisterial *F-Word* (2nd edn 2009) has surely written the last word necessary on these particular four letters.)

It is ironic, or if not ironic then infuriating, that, having given the obscenities shelter, the slang lexis has seen them come to typify its entirety (other than that perennial tourist trap, rhyming slang). Like some invasive insect that has decimated a native species, 'swear-words' (recorded in 1883 and so anodyne: perhaps one might bring back a pair of lost one-offs: 'tongue-worm' and 'shit-word') are the popular synonym for all slang. The search for such is as far as most are willing to go. It is a mistake: the list takes in some basic themes, but these are not all, and those who enquire of slang should see the flourishing wood, not merely a few rotting trees.

They are, of course, the unarguable denial of the supposed power of sticks and stones over that of language. They remain taboo for many and as such they are powerful. They are available in the *OED*, as well as in slang dictionaries, but scholars, like those who campaign against pornography, are deemed immune to exposure. Joe Public, the great unwashed, the habitué of whatever currently qualifies as the 'Clapham omnibus', in other words the actual users, must be shielded. They also crop up in the press (though more likely in what were once broadsheets than in tabloids), on television, radio, in movies, online – it is all symptomatic of profound denial. Of double standards and hypocrisy if one wishes to go that way. Or, in America particularly, of the stifling ascendancy of religious delusion. (That the great exceptions are unfettered scripts of material – typically the TV series *Oz* or *The Wire* – merely adds a pleasing twist to those much-touted 'family values'.) Popular justification is in terms of age: would you want your grandmother to hear you, or your children? (Servants, once another endangered species, seem to have been forgotten.) Granny is probably too busy sucking eggs and, if dementia has not set in, is probably far more liberal than might be assumed. As for children, my own experience was learning the core vocabulary on my first afternoon at boarding school. That was 1959; I somehow doubt that those who might be my grandchildren have taken to a diet of soap and water.

Reading for Pleasure

> A book, which one reads alone, is something else again . . . an unbelievably complicated task that gets done in a thousandth of a second. First, one deciphers some cabbalistic signs that one transforms into sounds and, from syllables into words, from words to meanings, one uncovers the sense. And all that while talking. Talking silently. In one's head one plays, one creates all sorts of voices, and then one imagines the decoration, the music, one creates the images. All that in a thousandth of a second.
>
> J.-B. Pouy, *1,280 Âmes* (2000)*

If I remain undecided about the precise definition of my 'love' of language, I have no doubt about my obsession for the printed word. The sensual, almost tangible beauty of letters ranged across a page. (There are many examples, but I would take a spread of six columns of *OED* citations, line after line of unbroken six point, above many.) The physical impression that remains when inked metal has invaded a plane constructed of compressed rags (or latterly, and less delightfully, the dried sludge of wood chips that has rendered my own recent efforts so much less white than those older works remain). The elegance of the typeface. The

* Author's translation.

argument with digital is too dull to join, and we have no choice but to submit to what Max Hastings, talking of weapons systems, terms the dynamism of technology: use it or lose it, and use it we always do. So the pixels will march on and the job is to utilise them for our benefit. The computer, I was told long ago, is only as bright as the user. We have to be bright, which, for me, means redesigning the way I work. Or at least the way I offer up the end product. But pleasure? No one offered, no one even mentioned pleasure. Will anyone ever sniff luxuriously at a discarded tablet, an outmoded Kindle? You cannot download the evocative mildew that impregnates books crammed over-long in backstreet second-hand bookstores, though you can access it fastest through bookfinder.com.

I remain in ignorance of my family surname but I do know what my signature looks like. Now, of course, but for every one of more than fifty years before that. I obsessively sign the books I buy. Almost before I've carried them away from the shop or, these days, removed the shipper's cardboard. Is someone going to snatch them back? One never knows. Like all happiness, my first thought is 'ephemeral'. I can see my scratchy eight year old efforts, replete with a middle name I long since abandoned. I can watch as I experimented with inks – school's obligatory, innately dull blue-black; a snappy red from Waterman that had a green tinge when in the bottle; the arrival of a Rotring designer's pen which turned my florid 'J' into a minimalist slash; the adoption of biros, markers, the rest. The acknowledgment of addiction when, once at thirteen and again with a new design a few years ago, I started pasting in my bookplate, though only hardbacks qualify. I add the date and, other than in London, the place. In France, shamelessly, I write the month in French. Occasionally I add an event. It seems natural, inevitable, above all necessary to me. They are, after all, my books. At least I own them. But mine in a deeper sense? Not at all. I didn't write them. Just purchased an open-ended licence to read. What am I doing, attempting some proxy authorship? Am I thinking theft? Probably not. And as for loans, bending to entreaties from those one had hitherto trusted, we all know where that leads. I will trust you with my life, perhaps, but never my books, Even the lowliest. Selfishly, too many times bitten and henceforth implacably shy, I no longer succumb to such foolish generosity. But like the books that are truly mine, the ones I do write and which, deliberately, I do not sign, they are a part of myself. Extensions of my existence. The signature is only a coincidental badge of ownership: its real signification is absorption. The embrace of four walls of ceiling-high shelves offers an unrivalled level of security.

Gathering in new books almost every day, is it paradoxical that I have never really collected? I pursued Wodehouse for a while, and enjoyed my finds, even joined a PGW dining club – black tie, squatting for the evening in a succession of gentleman's clubs, port passed left as per regulations – then sold the lot at auction. I have turned to dictionaries although those too, as did those Wodehouse titles I lacked, have come to defeat my limited pockets. And seeing someone else's Wodehouse, someone else's precious lexicon, I have felt the true collector's vice: that book, on someone else's shelf, and surely unappreciated there, that book belongs with me.* But I do not steal. I treasure books too much. I merely covet. Or, as I see it, love. Bibliophilia. The love of books. And as compensation make a life of reading.

* Meeting the great Madeline Kripke, the unrivalled doyenne of slang collectors, on whose West Village shelves reside some 15,000 slang-related volumes, the evil thought was magnified exponentially. One could probably, since she is not a large person, deal with *her* . . . the problem was extracting the tomes unnoticed.

If I were to offer my own version of Kane's Rosebud, the never-forgotten sledge abandoned alongside his impoverished, anonymous past, I would opt for the torch, with its flat olive green body and strangely bulbous tulip-shaped light with which, prior to departing for prep school for the first time in January 1959, I read beneath the blankets. There were ancillary pleasures – flashing it round the room to play with shadows, illuminating one corner or another in a literally new light – but it was the text that mattered. Do children still read in this – to them at least – surreptitious and thus exciting manner? Do children still read? That reviewer's cliché – I couldn't put it down – was quite literal for me: I couldn't, and since my bedroom light was extinguished at some long-forgotten time, I clicked the torch and read on. A year into prep school and I lost sight of the blackboard. I continue to wear glasses fifty plus years later. Whether the one pursuit led to the other has never worried me.

So would I do this even if they didn't pay me? Setting aside the thought that by many standards 'pay' is not a word the lexicographer prefers to ponder, I'm afraid that actually, no I wouldn't. I'm fascinated by what I do, but as Johnson pointed out, nobody but fools write merely for love, and while I remain prone to infatuations, they are not of the professional kind. One slang use of 'bread' means money and the former is necessary, if only to put the generic latter on the table. So no cash, no Swiss. (And the reference to mercenaries is quite deliberate.)

But I would read. I cannot not read. I cannot pass a bookshop without entering and browsing. I have barely entered a new acquaintance's home than I am assessing their books or if, bizarrely, they have none, dismissing them as worthless. I read in the street. I read in the bathroom. (So does everyone, but possibly not when peeing or brushing their teeth.) Left in the car as a child I read the AA guide or, as last resort, the car's manual. The idea of a bookless trip on public transport fills me full of terror, a junkie deprived of the sustaining narcotic. Trains pose no problem for the reader but if I'm loath to fly it is not because of claustrophobia or my tense anticipation of life after landing, though both apply, but my inability to concentrate on the pages five miles above the earth. And of course I have never learned to drive. I read, perhaps, because burying oneself in the thoughts of others is the best way of escaping from one's own. So the answer to that perennial question, which faculty would you be least willing to lose, is simple: the eyes. I need them to check out the permutations of those infinitely inventive twenty-six letters. The loss of any sense is undesirable but I know which bodily bits I've been working hardest, and I cannot live without them. No words: no life. And, albeit obvious, no words, definitely no dictionary.

Yet the reading one does for a dictionary – whether in search of headwords or the citations that underpin them – is not quite (perhaps not at all) like that which one does for recreation. Not all my reading is for slang, but if I do want to read 'non-professionally' it has to be some volume, typically non-fiction (since as much as anything I have become increasingly defeated by quite what I might enjoy in fiction's current incarnation) that guarantees me a wholly slang-free zone. Or translations, from which I will not permit myself to sample, other than on very rare occasions (Urquhart's *Rabelais*, McGinn's version of the French crim-turned-thief-taker Vidocq's memoirs), when the translator is introducing a whole new variety of English slang. (Urquhart, for instance, offers some forty-three new-minted coinages for penis, among them 'cockatoo', 'coral branch', 'flip-flap', 'John Thomas', 'nimble-wimble', 'sugar-stick' and 'trouble-gusset'.) If I do allow myself fiction, the task is impossible – I dare not chance that anything might escape – without a conveniently handy block of Post-it notes and a pen that will write horizontal to the ground – since I tend to do such reading lying down.

Reading in search of terminology requires one to read not so much 'for' (pleasure, information, the plot) or 'with' (the narrative, the characters, the author), but 'at' (focusing on possible extractions). It makes no difference: the book may be as complex as *Ulysses* (a remarkably fertile source of slang, since Joyce was voracious of all sources – and how I wish I had the skills and patience to tackle the next step: unravelling *Finnegans Wake*), as canonical as Dickens or Thackeray, or as out-and-out gutter-scraping (but so wondrously productive) as one of Donald Goines' ghetto potboilers (*Whoreson*, *Daddy Cool*). It may be one of the obscene sixpenny song-sheets ('The Gentleman's Spicey Songster', 'The Lummy Chaunter') that were flogged around the prototype music halls of mid-nineteenth-century London, the aptly named 'free-and-easies', like pornographic predecessors of the Jehovah's Witnesses' *The Watchtower*.

It may not even be a book, but a ballad, a modern lyric sheet, a script, a blog, anything that sources slang. Whatever one is looking at, that's the point: one is looking *at*. Not plots nor pages, nor paragraphs, not even sentences. Just words. Words and phrases. One learns to pick them from the greater mass. And zero in on the choicest paragraphs. So we bypass, to take *Ulysses* again, the much-evoked sensuality of Molly Bloom's soliloquy (other, heretically, than to breathe a relieved sigh in the knowledge that one can finally see the end to some 950 pages of difficult research), and instead alight joyfully on The Citizen's declaration that someone, was it Mrs Bloom's husband, can 'K. M. R. I. A.: Kiss My Royal Irish Arse'. Cite for 'kiss my arse', cite for 'royal' used other than in the context of crowned heads. Likewise while Goines may wish us to be shocked by the fact that the pimp Daddy Cool has put his own daughter on the street, we note only the fact that the unfortunate child is of course 'jailbait' and that her degradation takes place in the 'Motor City', slang's nickname for Detroit. The effect of all this is that quite often I find myself reading books twice; once for work and then, free of duty, for pleasure. Though even then constantly re-checking to see that such-and-such a term has not been overlooked on the first read. As, of course, it all too often has.

It is painstaking. The process requires close attention and for a fast reader such as myself, a forced and unusual level of concentration. One reads, a slang word appears and must be checked against the database, then entered (and tagged for search and, in time, printing). Then on to the next. It took, I think, two weeks to see off Irvine Welsh's *Trainspotting*, where one is not merely 'translating' slang but first disinterring it from the author's phonetic transcriptions. The recent prequel, *Skagboys*, was equally demanding. Niall Griffiths, garlanded as the Welsh equivalent of Leith's anatomist, is even more daunting. *Grits*, his debut novel, has representatives of every British localism: not merely the Scots, Welsh and Brits, but Scousers, Geordies, Cockneys, Brummies and so on. Every speaker filtered through the blurred, attenuated syllables of their region. What it was like to write I cannot say – I assume epic concentration was required – but disentangling such ventriloquy is exhausting. But, like Irvine Welsh, always worth it. At least with reading you can set your own pace. Watching sixty back-to-back episodes of *The Wire* took even longer, with heavy emphasis on pause/replay, and not perhaps helped by an arrogant refusal to use a version with subtitles. Painstaking but not in any way drudgery. This, for me, is fun. Its essence is the hunt, figurative of course – though Robert Smith Surtees' raffish world has been mined and Messrs Jorrocks, Soapy Sponge and Facey Romford have contributed generously to the lists – and the 'field' remains indoors and the 'kill' is bloodless.

So what does one read (and as I say, by 'reading' I am not merely talking of books, though the late arrival of other media, however welcoming to slang, does ensure that the majority of one's examples are drawn from print and not from radio, television, movies, lyrics, and of course the Internet). There are over 6,000 titles in my bibliography (and that includes only sources that have produced five or more citations). And while I have combed a number of canonical authors, there is undoubtedly what one might term an 'anti-canon'. For marginal language one requires marginal authors. My literary pathways tend to the dark and narrow, and not, in the strictest sense, to the overly literary.

It is chicken and egg, no doubt, but slang embraces many of my favourite authors, and many of my favourite authors are those who find a place for slang. To a man, because too few of them are at least as yet women, they are the cynical, the deflatory, the jesters in the ear of power, murmuring in Caesar's ear as he processes before his captives and loot. The majority are outsiders: sneered at by their *soi-disant* literary superiors, ineligible for canonisation (in every sense), they offer wit, satire, parody, playfulness and cruelty, and disdain without mercy the pompous and self-regarding. Like slang itself.

The fiction I have gutted (which is one way that I see it: an anatomist of illicit words, with publishers, libraries, online databases and Google Book Search as my resurrection men) is not usually good, nor indeed 'good'. No moralising, other than that of authors who usefully cite the use of slang as yet another proof of degeneracy. Quite the opposite.

Much of what I have read will be defined as third-rate, mediocre, crap; though not by professional reviewers who wouldn't have entered the picture in the first place. Are there no limits? Perhaps not – but certainly prejudices. Some names I simply don't wish to see on my pages. There are always alternatives.

If I have touched the canon – for example in its UK dimension – then there may be Dickens but no T. S. Eliot, Joyce but no Yeats, no Woolf, no D. H. Lawrence (the teeth-clenching references to 'John Thomas' and 'Lady Jane' aside, and of course his thirty instances of 'fuck' or 'fucking', fourteen of 'cunt', thirteen of 'balls' and all the rest so lip-smackingly cited when *Lady Chatterley's Lover* went on trial),* and no Hardy. T. E. Lawrence, yes, but only for *The Mint*, a scabrously obscene recreation of his training as 'Aircraftsman Ross' which offers first examples of such as 'fuckpig', 'shitbag', 'map of Ireland' (a semen stain) and 'twat' (as in 'the silly twat didn't know if his arse-hole was bored, punched, drilled, or countersunk'). There is a little Orwell, but mainly from his slumming days. Nor, to note the contemporary, have I bothered the pages of McEwan or Barnes (though Martin Amis, who is currently recorded as the first author to have chronicled that menacing enquiry 'Do you like hospital food?', has helped, even if nothing like so productively as has the admirably vituperative tone of his father's letters: 'Here I am and here I bloody fucking bastard buggering sodding pissing shitting stay' as he put it to Philip Larkin in 1951, and there is more, so much more). There are few Booker winners or Nobel laureates though some – Peter Carey

* This wrote well, or at least usefully, but is not strictly true, other than in sentiment: that such canonical figures are not first among the reading lists one must prepare, where authors are judged by their possible slang productiveness. In fact Mrs Woolf gives us 'poop', a fool, the first recorded use of 'bumf', lavatory paper, and 'fuck', albeit as *f*—. D. H. Lawrence has thirty-three citations of which fifteen, including 'arse-licking' (as a marginal comment on a letter) are first uses. T. S. Eliot, the terms garnered from a collection of obscene verses penned at Yale and long suppressed, twenty-nine (seven originals, among them 'whanger', a large penis, and 'breechloader', a 'catcher' in modern gay use). It remains down to priorities: any writer may be slangy but some are definitely slangier than others and it is to them we must turn first.

('piss-faced', 'stickybeak', 'ripperty man'), Saul Bellow ('ass-wipe', 'quickie', 'snotnose') – have appreciated the beauty and necessity of the non-standard. Nor are there poets, or precious few. Doggerel galore (typically Australia's much-loved but hardly first-rank 'Banjo' Paterson, whose collected work came with a lengthy glossary and to whom is attributed the song 'Waltzing Matilda'*), and ballads a-plenty (a succession of collections starting with 1660's *Choyce Drollery* and on to those of Samuel Pepys, the playwright Thomas D'Urfey and the antiquary Charles Hindley; all nine folio volumes of the nineteenth-century Roxburghe ballads, every one a generous repository of smut and double entendre – think tinkers and their 'hammers', tailors and their 'needles'), but 'proper' poems rarely qualify. Slang requires a harder edge, it doesn't indulge lyricism, though this absence may betray my own less than romantic tastes. And, as noted, some, though perhaps not me so much, see poetry in slang. Read the dictionary, read the citations. Not however in slang's Cockney rhyming variety in which, one must remember, it is the rhyming half that is always left unspoken. And women? Shamefully few as authors but my dictionary is hardly alone in that. And slang can claim some justification: in this most man-made of languages women are always objects, never subjects.†

* 'Waltzing Matilda' is Australia's 'other national anthem' (as 'bloody' is its 'national adjective'). Why 'Matilda'? The jury remains out and its popularity seems to have come with Paterson's lyrics. His fellow-writer the acerbic Henry Lawson noted sharply that 'A swag is not generally referred to as a 'bluey' or 'Matilda' – it is called a 'swag' [. . .] You do not 'hump bluey' – you simply carry your swag.' 'Swag' itself descends from fourteenth century English, meaning a bulgy bag.

† My friend Professor Michael Adams, who has written an entire book on the language of *Buffy the Vampire Slayer*, would and does disagree, and in his *Slang: The People's Poetry* cites not merely *Buffy* (even if her creator and most of her scriptwriters are male) but the language of teen magazines (whose readers tend

My researches have undoubtedly left me with a less than positive image of the world. You read *noir*, you watch *noir*, you cite from *noir* and after a while all you see is *noir*. Your horizons are lurid, melodramatic. The lexicographical voyeur does not indulge *noir*, but it colours his or her worldview. The street is full of those for whom I conjure stories. Areas give off slang-heavy histories. In London I live in Clerkenwell; there have been brothels in nearby Turnmill Street since 1200 when the area was the original 'suburb' (outside the city walls and thus less subject to City morals) and prostitution the 'suburban trade' – if there aren't any now it will not be the fault of my imagination. The 'Picked-hatch', from its sign of a spiked half-door, which was one of them, became a general term for 'such religious places, where Venus Nunnes are cloystered' and the area, given its breeding of candidates for the gallows, was known as 'Jack Ketch's warren'. Falstaff called it Turnbull Street and name-checks the Picked-hatch; a 'Turnbull-street bee' was a diseased whore, and Pepys used 'Turnbull-street Flea' to mean the pox: both, it was acknowledged, 'stung'. The sociologist James Greenwood set a whole novel, *The Little Ragamuffin*, in its alleyways. Walking home I see the whores and pimps even if everyone else registers only Farringdon tube and its commuters. Nor is the past necessary, nor psychogeographic wanderings: watching sixty back-to-back episodes of *The Wire* or fifty-six of *Oz* tend to have me slightly nervy when next I go out. Reality is heightened, but of course reality it isn't. Smithfield, however bloody its history, ranks low on drive-bys or drug corners; the London Library, under-lit basements notwithstanding, has no 'death row' or 'hole'.

---

to be female). My argument remains: slang is rooted in the male eye and takes its themes therefrom. The UK's ladettes of the 1990s certainly upped the visibility of female slang use, but the lexis was still that of the lads.

Sometimes it seems as if all the books run into one. All the PIs, all the villains, whores, junkies, boozers, tough guys, victims, spics, micks, kikes, niggers, dagos . . . All the cars and guns and drugs. All the hard-assed cops and bent authorities. The screws and the cons. The queens, the fags, the punks. All the violence. One writer blends into another. Algren's whores become Morgan's or Vollmann's. Chandler's hard boiled dick turns up again in Harry Whittington or Derek Raymond. Jim Thompson's broken psychotics mate and reproduce across the decades, spawning James Ellroy's grotesques.

Or slang jumps out in three dimensions. I am walking past the Louvre. A man approaches, then drops something, stops, bends, and registers surprise. He brandishes a gold ring beneath my nose, explains that it is a fortunate find, that he has no time to take it for valuation, and offers to sell it to me. I refuse. He pockets it and moves on. I am consumed with delight. Did that just happen, did I just encounter a twenty-first century equivalent of the 'ring-dropper', a character first encountered, by me, around 1560. And he tried his games on me. Synchronicity. Heaven. And fifteen minutes later, on the Left Bank, it all happens again. I am not a good target for beggars. Call it meanness; I call it been there, read that and got the citation.

No one cares to ask, but I do wonder on occasion about the effect of all this reading. This day upon day consumption of what, slang being what it is, exists in general at the sordid end of the street. Have I rolled through the gutter so long that my vision is occluded by its filth? Is my vocabulary attenuated, my mindset coarse, my syllables invariably mono? Am I, as the moralists claim of those who consume pornography, corrupted? Have I auto-propagandised myself into adopting a twisted worldview? Immune to optimism, disdainful of the positive. Cynical, sceptical, price of everything, value in nothing. A form of language-driven Stockholm syndrome: so identified with what I do that I have come to take on the world it projects. No. I think that was always there. It is doubtless what drew me to slang on day one. No one is more impassioned in their defence of slang's variety, its vast extent beyond the clichéd 'four-letter words', its wit, its ludic creativity, its pertinence. If I have been changed it is simply in a disinclination to waste time on unproductive texts.

This is not to say that at times the gutter does not depress. Thanks to digitisation the world's newspapers are open for those whose idea of a day's work is, like mine, paging (or is it screening?) through week after week of what would otherwise be yellowing, crumbled texts. John Bartlett, he of *Americanisms*, and James Murray of the *OED* were among many who came to appreciate that a nation's language can usefully be hunted through the columns of its popular press. This is not always the case for slang, which many newspapers affect to despise, but one comes to sense a candidate. Thus my trek through the *Sunday Times* of Perth Australia *c.*1905. The *Sunday Times* was a campaigning paper, the campaign in question known as 'White Australia'. Which means what it says. 'Two Wongs,' as the Forties' pol Arthur Calwell would put it, 'don't make a White.' It was not alone: the Sydney *Bulletin*, not for nothing known as the 'Bully', ran in harness. There are no blacks in the paper, they know only 'niggers'; no Chinese, merely 'Chinks' and 'Chinkies' though here there is a colour: the inevitable 'yellow'; no Jews, merely some entity known as 'Cohen', with his cousin 'Boodle'. (Though moneylenders are simply 'Jewmen').*

* For instance, from a pro-White Australia poem published November 19, 1905: 'Throw open your gates to the leprous Chow and the crimping pimping Jap [. . .] Shall we borrow the drama staged from life that another clime knows well / The outrage wrought on the lone white wife – the Fate that is worse than hell? / The hunt in the track of the lecherous black, while the toils close inch by inch' etc. ad nauseam.

Each is gifted with the predictable stereotypes. There is a gossip column, mini-paragraphs each headed 'They Say . . .' which skates so near to libel as one might believe to have cracked the ice. All this in a paper, do not forget, that sold in tens of thousands. I treasure slang's refusal to acknowledge the politically correct but this, the poujadist vomit of the politically motivated, leaves me feeling soiled. Please spare your pity. Two years of the *Sunday Times* offer over 1,000 citations; more important, over 250 of these predate any yet recorded use. There is 'sausage wrapper', for a newspaper, seventy years before the modern version, 'fish wrapper'; there is 'peter school', missed by the *Australian National Dictionary*, considered but rejected by Australia's Eric Partridge, Sydney Baker, and signifying a form of gambling, either with dice or, as a form of the coin-tossing game two-up, with three-penny bits ('trey-bit peter' as that's called). There's 'on one's ace', by oneself; 'amber fluid' for beer (beloved of Barry Mackenzie sixty years on), there's, no surprises, 'baboon' for a black person, 'blimey', a Briton, 'bonzer' for a female beauty, 'boob' for a prison, 'brummy' for second-rate, 'sure cop', a certainty, 'go down', to be imprisoned, 'get your head read', 'hot stuff' for sexy, and on it goes. Get in there, my son, get your hands dirty; you can always wash.

You start research with what you know, plucking down a book that guarantees you slang. Kerouac's *On the Road* in my case (605 citations and every one a winner – but they had to be, I hadn't searched elsewhere yet; only ninety-one would turn out to be first examples), and off you go. Scour your own shelves. Then the libraries. Buy from the bookshops. Order online. Drop that stone in the pond and follow the ripples. Rightly or wrongly I'd claim a degree of skill at scraping the barrel. A sort of divination for slang. At school I claimed the knack of opening any volume and cutting straight to the dirty bit. (OK, it worked for *The Carpetbaggers*, but then it wasn't hard with that one.) Nothing changes. Of course the covers help – just as gardening books tend be green, slang attracts rather more lurid tints. The presence of a young woman (invariably *pulpeuse* as the French slang has it) always helps: all the way from clothed, if revealing of a stocking-topped leg and a smidgeonette of cleavage, to the full fur-coat-and-no-knickers/tits-out-for-the-lads display. Or a gun. Or just the title or its typeface. But that's not going to work in 1750. Or for most of the next couple of centuries. Immature poets borrow as we know and mature lexicographers steal, not just from other people's lexicons – though that's a necessity – but from their bibliographies. A process that takes you to places you'd never have known. And an anti-canon begins to emerge.

Thus I came across the likes of Goines, whose brief career was coupled with his own drug addiction and a hands-on involvement in the world of pimping, an existence that led to his death, aged only thirty, when someone, never identified, pressed the barrel of a large pistol to his head and pulled the trigger. Or, mid-nineteenth century, *Leaves from the Diary of a Celebrated Burglar and Pickpocket*, whose anonymously penned memoirs anticipate the current crop of self-promoting sociopaths and which, how grateful I am, surrounds every single example of slang, some 871, with quote-marks. *Leaves* is lexicographical gold, with nearly half of its slang never previously discovered, and substantial pre-dates for such staples of the modern cops and robbers story as 'Death Row', 'have it off' (to commit a robbery), 'no bottle' (cowardly), 'porridge' (a jail sentence), 'screwing' (housebreaking), 'tumble' (a discovery) and 'turn over' (to search). Or the early twentieth-century suffragette and journalist Helen Green, later Helen Green van Campen, with her tales of the junkies, con men and vaudevillians at the fictional Broadway theatrical boarding house, the Maison de Shine, regular episodes of 'Life on Broadway' for *McClure's* and even a piece on 'What they read in the Klondyke' (the 'wide-open' towns of the

Alaskan gold rush). Consciously or not, Green is part of a literary world that, with its assumption that slang could provide the basis of any story, cannot be found in the contemporary UK. Others include C. L. Cullen, writing *Tales of the Ex-Tanks*, 'tanks', that is, as in alcoholics; George Ade, whose *Fables in Slang* and its successors made him a millionaire, 'Hugh McHugh', whose tales of 'John Henry' seem to prefigure Wodehouse's Bingo Little (and Wodehouse, of course, was in New York at the time of publication) and many more. This is before one arrives at the sportswriters Ring Lardner and Charles Van Loan or comic strip creators like T. A. Dorgan* or his drinking partner Bud Fisher of *A. Mutt* and latterly *Mutt and Jeff*. Paradoxically – this is puritan America – there is a magnificent disregard for morality. Cullen's 'tanks' receive no hectoring lectures, Green's 'dopes' can indulge their 'habits' for 'morf', at least when they have the 'iron men' to spend. But how else would one cheerfully set slang so near the centre of one's stage. One cannot list them all – and the candidates grow every passing year – but the anti-canon must tip its hat to Seth Morgan whose *Homeboy* appeared in 1990. Seth Morgan? Janis Joplin's roadie and sometime lover, strip-joint barker and junkie, and having lived properly fast, died young of a motorbike crash, after just a single slang-dense surrealist quasi-memoir. Another one gone and pretty much forgotten, because slang's canon is often for initiates only. If you don't know you're never going to find out – unless you want to piece the books together from my cites.

* Dorgan who signed as 'TAD' is, like Wilde or Dorothy Parker for one-liners, one of those to whom, if in doubt, slang coinages were ascribed. The public were over-generous, but Dorgan undoubtedly moved much slang from the street to the page; around 50 per cent of his uses had not been seen in print before. As for coinages, if nothing else, he has 'cat's pyjamas'.

Not that you need to live that far out on the edge. To name but a fraction: mid-twentieth-century London's James Curtis (*The Gilt Kid*), Gerald Kersh (*Night and the City*) or Alexander Baron (*The Lowlife*); the nineteenth's 'Cuthbert Bede' (*The Adventures of Mr Verdant Green* whose unnamed but illustrated Oxford college looks, pleasingly, a dead ringer for my own) or 'The Pitcher', as in the pitcher of (usually) male-oriented tales, properly named Arthur Binstead (mainstay of the *Sporting Times*, better known as 'The Pink' Un' and staple of the junior officers' mess), and Australia's Edward Dyson (*Factory 'Ands, Benno and Some of the Push*). These and many similar have never gained a place amongst the first literary ranks. Neither then nor now. But their books, lacking literary ambition (or at any rate failing to show its signs) gave house room to slang and I am more than a little grateful.

So many candidates. How can I choose a favourite, but we live in a world of lists, so who would top mine? Jim Thompson? Barry Gifford? James Ellroy? I don't do heroes but if I can allow for one apostate Jew, Lenny Bruce, then I offer another: Nelson Algren, born Abraham, best-known as laureate of Chicago's working class and for the junkie-saga *The Man with the Golden Arm*. I cite him over 1,100 times, which, for me at least, testifies to his importance. A man of the margins – his literary reputation among them – he decided early on that recording as accurately as possible the language of the streets was as near as one could get to the character of those that spoke it, and that those speakers, those who live nearest the gutter, were those most worthy of chronicling. He saw 'no purpose in writing about people who seem to have won everything. There's no story there . . . Why write about happiness? There's nothing there . . . no conflict, no catalyst for discovering anything about humanity.' Instead he wrote of an America that existed 'behind the billboards and comic strips', and noted that 'a thinker who wants to think justly must keep in touch with those who never think at all'.

This was not romantic: the 'community leaders' of those he described regularly sought to have his portraits effaced from the public's eye, and his tales, whether short stories of bums riding the rails, or the junkies, alcoholics, whores and assorted losers of the urban mean streets, were uniform only in their lack of any vestige of a happy ending. His own life was difficult: like other flawed semi-stars – George Gissing, Patrick Hamilton – he had a problematic relationship with a prostitute, compounded in his case by her heroin addiction. He also tried to take Simone de Beauvoir from Sartre, but she, unsurprisingly, wasn't about to be 'taken' by anyone and made her own choice. He flourished briefly after *Man . .* , granted a brief acknowledgement at the edges of respectability, but faded: his last decade was spent writing for *Playboy* and other, lesser 'men's magazines', and he knew that one wrote as an audience desired, even if he could never disguise his anger. He failed to complete his last novel, which, from what survives, might have been his best.

Why keep it to the grown-ups? Slang, after all, is endemic to youth and teenage, even if usually written by the adults, and is good for more. The JD pulp. Juvenile delinquents. You want a good word? Here are three. 'Pepe ain't no chicken and he ain't a rat. But you know how those cats are.' Thank you Wenzell Brown, whose quasi-documentary, *Monkey on My Back*, charts the case histories of various young junkies *c.* 1953. Brown, long gone and lost to all but the collectors, but for me an exemplar of the counter-canon. His output mixes the non-fiction of *Monkey* and *Girls on the Rampage* ('the brutal, shocking truth about girls who go bad'), with novels like *Cry Kill*, *Run Chico Run* and *Jailbait Jungle*. Jailbait ('a young person, usu. a girl, who is under the age of sexual consent; intercourse with such a person may lead to imprisonment', first recorded use 1930) was a surefire sale around the Fifties. Harlan Ellison, often writing as Hal Ellson, has *Jailbait Street*, while William Bernard offers *Jailbait* unadorned. The covers are all pretty samey, even if, rather like that of the supposed 'schoolgirls' to be found in Seventies porn, the age of consent seems to be moving towards the late twenties; and if that hussy in skintight yellow is Ellison's 'sweet virginal Carol' she appears to have been around the block a few times. Maybe they never caught her: but a serious prickteaser at best. The boys, of course, look like prototypes for the Fonz.

After jailbait, pornography. Of the triumvirate of money, liquor and sex, slang's primary obsessions, it is the last that is most productive of terms. It is also, certain glossaries notwithstanding, the one most reluctantly allowed, even in works that are otherwise slang-laden. Too often you have to turn to your predecessors: in 1890 John S. Farmer's magisterial seven-volume *Slang and Its Analogues* offered nineteen columns of synonyms for 'greens' (sexual intercourse), and a dozen for 'the monosyllable' (the vagina). But quoting from other dictionaries, especially such usually unsubstantiated lists, is a sign of defeat. One needs the real thing. Thanks to the Internet much of it, from the eighteenth century onward, is on offer. It is, like all pornography, geared to a single purpose and as such repetitious, but it has words that no one else at a given moment can or wishes to offer. This is not always so: those who have read, for instance, the nineteenth-century magazine *The Pearl*, will know that its language is almost prim, other than a few well-worn terms. Fortunately there are exceptions. *My Secret Life*, thirteen mind-numbingly detailed volumes of supposed autobiography, makes not the slightest pretension to literature. Even the index is far beyond the norm: 'Anus, toothbrush up a man's while he's gamahuched'; 'Champagne and sperm, singular letch'; 'Cunts, felt in church by me and frigged'; 'Sodomites, put pestles up arseholes'; 'Thrusts of prick, number given when fucking'; 'Virginities, women want to piddle after defloration'. 'Walter' as the anonymous author has come to be known, was a man of many parts; I have dissected every one. Lacking Walter* where would we be for first appearances of 'belly-bump', 'donkey-hung', 'flat-cocking' (lesbian sex), 'minetting' (cunnilingus), 'pooper' (the anus and sixty years prior to the next appearance), 'go shit yourself!', 'sperm-sucker' (the vagina) and many others. All in all he uses around 450 slang terms. If I have dissected Walter so too I have plunged into the more modern productions of the US porn factories, the works of the prolific 'Neil Forit', 'Bill E. Goodhead', 'Dick B. Long', 'Atza Nice', and their colleagues. Not that creative, pretty rote as to creating what Walter would have termed a 'cockstand', and the 'spending' that should follow, but needs must. As I say, I love to read.

And then, though still with sex, there are authors who defy easy categorisation other than that they must be assayed. Is this porn? Is it shock for shock's sake? Might it in some abstruse way be political? 'Rouse stately Tarse / And lett thy Bollocks grind / [. . .] / Heave up, faire Arse, / And lett thy Cunt be kind / To th' Deed. / Thrust Pintle with a force, / [. . .] / Spend till my Cunt overflow.' John Wilmot, Earl of Rochester, perhaps the most debauched member of Charles II's notably degenerate court, wrote many such poems. If they aroused then they might qualify as porn, but what Wilmot displays is only disgust. That and, dare I suggest, his sheer delight in the power of obscenity. He also offered a play,

* The author is in fact anonymous but such is the name which he has been given; best bets point to the businessman Henry Spencer Ashbee (1834–1900), who, as the obscenely punning 'Pisanus Fraxi', wrote a three-volume annotated catalogue of pornography and whose personal collection of 'facetiae' formed the foundation of the British Library's Private Case.

Sodom, whose cast-list includes Bolloxinion and Cuntigratia, 'King and Queen of Sodom'; Pricket and Swivia, 'young Prince and Princess'; Pockenello, 'Pimp, Catamite and Favourite to the King'; Buggeranthos, 'Generall of the Army'; and the 'maids of honor' Ffuckadilla, Clitoris and Cunticula. That is, 'bollocks', 'cunt', 'prick', 'swive' (an early synonym for fuck), syphilitic 'pocks' or pox, 'buggery' and 'fucking'. The play may not be much cop – and it may not even have been performed – but this is seriously hardcore stuff, and the lexicographer's delight.

On the other hand, and fifty years on, there is John Cleland. Cleland set out to create what must be a one-off: a porn-free porn book. A dirty book without a single dirty word. Instead a vast lexicon of alternatives. To offer just his vagina synonyms, there is the 'ready made breach for love's assaults', the 'furrow', which the lover 'ploughs up', and the 'saddle' ('He was too firm fix'd in the saddle for me to compass flinging him'). There is the 'central furrow' and the 'centre of attraction', the 'soft, narrow chink', the 'tender cleft of flesh', the 'cloven stamp of female distinction'. As a site of sexual enjoyment it can be 'mount pleasant' (and Cleland used the plural form to mean the breasts), the 'seat of pleasure', the 'pleasure girth' and 'pleasure pivot'. It is a 'jewel' (though 'lady's jewels', like the later 'family ones', are the testicles), the 'maiden-toy', the 'main spot' or 'main avenue' and the 'mouth of nature', the 'delicate glutton' and 'nether mouth'. At the time Cleland was prosecuted for his improprieties; today he's an Oxford Classic.

If slang gives us a vocabulary for sex, then so too for its bedfellow violence. Not just the endemic violence of *noir*, host to many of the 700 plus terms for 'hit' or 'beat', the 500 plus meaning 'kill' and the hundred for 'shoot', but its formalised version, war. Like politicians wearied of the intractability of domestic policy-making, and career military men eager to accelerate promotion, slang loves war. Bursts of psychotic combat interspersed with the tedium of lengthy waiting. Tedium that must be filled, ideally by slang-laden talk. War that persists. The modern variety offers little: the wars are far too short. The Falklands gave as us only 'yomping' and stole 'benny' from television's soap *Crossroads* to tease the locals. Beyond in-country militarisms Iraq has offered only the all-purpose 'hajji' and popularised 'sand nigger' but World War I, and particularly the Western front, gave four years of trenches: that's what slang calls a war and takes from it 1,000 terms. (And this is not the combat-specific stuff, the names of shells, vehicles or the manglings of French and Belgian place-names, just the soldier-to-soldier chat.) Diminuendo, but still usefully protracted is Vietnam. How else might I have encountered Ernest Spencer's *Welcome to Vietnam, Macho Man*. And thus such current first examples of 'pussy', to mean the real thing (as opposed to 'synthetic' jerking off), 'dream on!', 'bench', to criticise, and 'pimp', to nag.

Non-fiction, especially when mixed with sociology, can be hugely useful. And goes back a good deal further. (The very first slang 'dictionaries', properly glossaries, were after all as much sociological documents as lexicographical ones: primarily aimed at acquainting the uninitiated with the lives, and thus the language, of the criminal classes.) John Taylor, the mid-seventeenth-century Thames boatman and otherwise known as the 'Water Poet', worked at a vital employment when the capital city still had but a single bridge. In addition he wrote widely and wittily – and always slangily – of the city and country he knew. As the seventeenth century turned to the eighteenth two more observers were wandering London and noting what they encountered: the publican Ned Ward (*The London Spy*, *The Rambling Fuddle-Caps* and much besides) and the lesser known Thomas Brown (*Amusements Serious and Comical*). Ward, for it is not necessary to create a dictionary to introduce the world to unrecorded words, offers readers a score of whores who had yet to walk the printed street: 'bangtail', 'belfa', 'bunter', 'carrion', 'daggletail', 'duchess', 'flapcap', 'lechery-layer', 'market dame', 'molly', 'mumper', 'sportswoman', 'stargazer', 'still sow' and 'tickle-tail' and mentions another longer-established seventy. They were both connoisseurs of slang and the benefit has been all mine.

Unalloyed sociology (the slang was only a by-product, even if it seems to permeate every page) comes with Henry Mayhew. Mayhew, that indefatigable circumnavigator of London's 'other half', produced a decade's worth of pieces on its characters for the *Morning Post* between 1841–51. (That they appeared thus is somewhat paradoxical since the *Post* was a good way to the right of its contemporaries and its week on week interest in the great unwashed is surprising. Perhaps Mayhew's interviews were seen as an awful warning.) Like Dickens, who seems on occasion to be Mayhew lightly fictionalised, albeit by a genius, Mayhew walked the streets of the metropolis; in his case adding to his wanderings the interviewing of those who represented what his great work, published in four volumes 1861–5, called *London Labour and the London Poor*. Few resisted slang and Mayhew conveniently points up each instance with 'beware non-standard speech' apostrophes. And if Mayhew recoiled from certain topics – the murder of rats for 'sport', London's thronging whores – then his brother Augustus, who preferred fiction, ironically entitling his London novel *Paved with Gold*, was happy to fill in. Nor was Mayhew alone: the less-feted James Greenwood (*The Seven Curses of London*, *Low-Life Deeps*) followed loyally in his footsteps, while across the Atlantic Edward Judson, writing as 'Ned Buntline', offered *The Mysteries and Miseries of New York* (ripping off Eugène Sue who had already used the title for Paris) as well as a bunch of blood-and-thunder melodramas featuring the 'Bowery B'hoy' Mose, his girl Lize and their friend – a tip of the hat to transatlantic Bill? – Sykesy. G. G. Foster has *New York in Slices*, while in the next century Herbert

Asbury set about tearing apart hundreds of yellowing newspapers to cut-and-paste his way through his chronicles of the *Gangs of New York* (stick with the book: even Scorsese nods), as well as those of Chicago, San Francisco and New Orleans.

Meanwhile we still need the canon. Slang is on the margins and the margins don't always attract publishers, especially when prevailing moralism tells them to keep clear. Hence one must, especially when ferreting through the past, acknowledge the greats and submit them to the scalpel. But it comes with problems. The characters of the anti-canon need slang: it is the way that they speak. The author, having taken the plunge downmarket, has no choice but to allow it them. The problem with 'literature' is that too often one cannot escape the feeling that the slang is artificial; the dictionaries have been consulted and regurgitated. Authors of mid-nineteenth-century 'Newgate novels' such as William Harrison Ainsworth and Bulwer-Lytton are typical. Harrison Ainsworth, congratulated on his research, admitted to taking it all from a single glossary (compiled by the 'lag' or transportee, James Hardy Vaux, whose compilation of terms, appended to his autobiography, stands as Australia's first ever dictionary) and was unashamed. But *Oliver Twist* was vilified as a Newgate novel too, and even Dickens cannot escape suspicion. (And where did Nancy, so far from the middle classes, get her impeccable Standard English? Not from Sykes or Fagin, whose patter makes it clear that Dickens had read his Egan. But Dickens couldn't sully a woman, even a 'fallen' woman's syllables, with aught but Standard English. Bill Sykes and Fagin display the Master's absorption of the slang dictionary; Nancy drops nary an aitch; in real life they'd have called her a 'twopenny upright'.) If one moves further back in time, say to Middleton's *Roaring Girl* of 1611 or Shadwell's *Squire of Alsatia* of 1688 there's no argument. The plays trip along until suddenly one falls into a scene that's little more than an animated glossary; that finished, it's back to the Standard. Look, says the playwright, I've plumbed the depths and here they are for you. Like the old *News of the World*, the writer gets up close but not too personal, then makes his excuses and leaves.

Shakespeare, being, like Dickens, a superstar, makes sure you rarely see the seams. And he can be remarkably modern (or is modernity Shakespearian?). There's this exchange: 'Lady, shall I lie in your lap? No, my lord. I mean, my head upon your lap? Ay, my lord. Do you think I meant country matters?' And there's this one: 'It has been my experience as once young people sample the delights of country life and the wonders of nature they just can't get enough of it. Exactly. Well I was thinking of the girls. So was I.' Hamlet and Ophelia; Hattie Jacques and Kenneth Williams. *Hamlet* meets *Carry On Camping*. Shakespeare's use of puns and double entendres rivals anything Talbot Rothwell, the *Carry On* scriptwriter, might have achieved three and a half centuries later. *Romeo and Juliet* and *Love's Labour's Lost* are bowed beneath them. So is *Henry VI* where 'Pistol's cock is up and flashing fire will follow'. Boom! Boom! *Carry on Barding* anyone?

So reading for slang is a specialised art. And so many of these titles would never have come my way without slang and my need to read. One tries to read widely but there's just too much. I would always have encountered slang – my tastes have taken me to books in which it plays a necessary role – but never so widely, and never so much. If it is a delight to find that one can create a life and a career from the simple act of reading, then the discoveries that turn up as part of that career are a hugely pleasing bonus.

Of course I haven't, even with the help of researchers, read 'everything' that qualifies as a book. But I assess my bibliography and wonder how much more can be read. It is possible that as regards available books, not that much. This is not arrogant but practical. I do not want every instance of every slang term. I want an effective sample. In any case, I have many more cites than are displayed: space has determined cuts and I would like to offer a greater geographical spread. Online this may be possible. Why not? There are no limits any more, other than to the user's interest. Thus, the usual sidestepping of local slang, even that of big cities beyond a capital (or certainly so in the UK), may no longer be necessary. The rationalisation of non-metropolitan usage as 'dialect' – when at least a proportion of such usage is in fact local slang – has always been something of a cop-out. Why should the terminology of Manchester not equate with that of London, or Cork with that of Dublin? It is, like the vast expansion of potential research, down to the lexicographer.

I would like to root out the glossarial entries, culled from someone else's list, and this is being done. Any cite is open to suspicion and I aim for perfect encapsulations of use. As for dates . . . I deal with them elsewhere. So what is good can be made better and maybe I have enough to time to make some inroads. I hope that, unlike my own cocky self, there isn't yet some pretender, dismissing my efforts with the same confidence as I mocked those of the man who predated me. On the other hand, because I value what I do and see that it has never been dependent on any individual – other than that someone has to keep brandishing the flag – I hope that there is just some such young – I assume young – upstart (in the most literal sense) who believes that it's their turn to be the contender.

We shall see. I am not done yet. And while the theory will persist, the practice will be very different. It already is for me. Slang sources – at least as found between two covers and a colophon – once seemed so all-encompassing, so unassailable. Now I experience them as finite. We have, exult the technically besotted, arrived at the end of such publications. Gutenberg is dead, along with his hecatombs of slaughtered trees. For every new book I go back to a hundred old newspapers. I could have read them long ago, but, lacking easy access, too often I did not. Now, Internet-armed, the only problem is time and achieving that vital triage that makes research feasible. That and the means and skills to turn what once appeared in 12,500 columns into however many necessary ones and zeroes.

Citations: The Chase Is On

The etymology provides proof of origin. It does not reveal the ways in which a word is used, and as such cannot help us disentangle the nuance of sense even if it often points us towards a primary definition. For that one must look at 'slang live'. For examples of slang as it was spoken and recorded. These are known as citations: let us ponder.

'We begin by loving our parents; later we judge them; rarely, if ever do we forgive them.' I remember smugly copying that out from dear Oscar's collected works and committing it to some scrap of paper or another. I don't know: maybe 1964. I always enjoyed a bit of expert guidance. '*Erst kommt das fressen, dann kommt die morale*': eats first, morals after, to translate Brecht in the *Dreigroschenoper*. Tart, witty, that kind of thing. No candidates for the *gros point* sampler, but good life advice for the adolescent. Didn't give much help as to putting words into deeds, but that wasn't the point. More a framing procedure for life.

Lying around on my desk it was seized upon by my mother and read. No comment but what I believe used to be termed an 'old-fashioned look'. But the problem with this, and any other such aphorism, is (and I speak as a not wholly proud veteran of writing dictionaries of quotations) that it all seems terribly glib. As to its accuracy, let the reader interpret as they wish. With notable exceptions – Shakespeare being the obvious example – too many supposedly important quotes are only one step away from the kind of mottoes we find in our Christmas cracker, sometimes not even as perceptive. Other than writing for the underground press, ventures into 'top shelf' magazines, a pseudonymous softcore *Diary of a Masseuse* ('A Bishop learns the real meaning of "the laying on of hands"'), and some monthly puffery for the salesmen of a music biz company ('Jubilee've in Profits?' asked one of my headlines in 1977, a year of royal jamboree), dictionaries of quotations were my first published efforts. From the late 1970s to early 1980s I published books gathering supposedly memorable remarks from rock 'n' roll, food, sport, the royal family, politics and love, as well as collecting and retailing 'famous last words' and a large agglomeration of 'contemporary quotations', coined post 1945. In a high percentage of cases what was considered quotable was wholly of my own idiosyncratic choosing. (The 'contemporary' collection sold, but I winced at Anthony Burgess' review which was, no doubt justifiably, less than kind.) There was also one that dealt with the supposed origins of the 'great quotes of all time'. I planned a history of the world in quotations but by then I was bored and dropped it. One that I also wrote – predictably – was 'cynical quotes'. It appeared in the mid-1980s and a revamp was commissioned by Cassell in 1993.

I still gather quotes, in lexicographical terms: 'citations'. The word parallels the French *citation* which is synonymous; both come ultimately from the Latin *citare*, to move, excite or summon. The semantic journey begins around 1300 as a 'citing' or summoning to a court of justice; thence to the written form of the summons, and thence to a printed reference to legal precedents. The first recorded use in terms of a literary quotation, irrespective of source, is dated 1548.

But while Oxford and Yale do quote, the form, function and content of lexicographical 'cites' is somewhat different to that of the supposed aphorisms enshrined in their *Dictionaries of Quotations*, in *Bartlett* and elsewhere. Like the books from which they come, they are another example of the tools of my trade. There are well over 600,000 to choose from in the database (and the total expands with research), although a good percentage were removed from the book as published. One of the small bonuses of the long-distance project is the ability to hone. (However there are also losses: there was insufficient space for a proper geographical representation, and that will be amended when the material goes online.)

I search for one cite per decade, per definition, per headword. Some only yield a single example; others, such as 'booze', may provide – factoring in its different senses, derivations, compounds and so on – dozens, even hundreds. But, the word's French etymology apart, citations are not simply quotes. Dictionaries that are prepared 'on historical principles', those whose chronological information is derived from citations such as the *OED*, are not simply dictionaries of quotations. The citation must focus, must illustrate, must work for its inclusion. It is the 'quotable' quotation's harder-working, tougher-minded, cousin. It grinds no axe, proposes no morality, nor indeed amorality. The ideal citation, drawn from a valid source, makes the usage crystal clear; the least is snatched, ungratefully and often for lack of something better, from a glossary.

If one were to count up the titles listed in my bibliography there are something in excess of 6,000 sources. In chronological terms they start very few and far between, but as slang grows, so do they and every century from the sixteenth onwards approximately doubles what is on offer. Though those of the twentieth and beyond are uncountable. In addition there are those printed sources that are not books – newspapers, broadsheet ballads, comics – and in due course, and as they come on stream, the scripts of movies and television. And sometime in the 1990s, while I was head down eviscerating some book, the world turned upside down. The Internet arrived and that also continues to double in size, though that expansion should probably be judged by minutes or at least days rather than centuries, and the mountain of material looms ever larger and the possibility of making any real inroads, wielding the plastic spoon of one's most assiduous researches, grows less and less feasible. When one starts – back around 1500 – one can quite possibly read the entirety of the contemporary slang lexis; by the time one finishes – but of course one never finishes – one must pick and choose and mourn lost opportunities. Why fool myself? I cannot keep up. Like every lexicographer I am running a marathon that never ends. It was ever so: a dictionary is 'finished' only to accommodate the dictates of a publisher's deadline and language merely laughs at the exhausted drudge and moves on.

Technology cuts both ways. Wonderful to have all this new material to hand, so much more easily accessible than spending long days in the stacks ferreting through yellow, brittle pages dense with faded six point. I have stood in the room that houses the original handwritten slips from which the first *OED* was composed. Drawer upon drawer, cabinet upon cabinet. Hundreds upon hundreds of thousands of pieces of paper. Requested and gained a view of that on which Murray himself, I believe, wrote the definition of 'slang'. There is the famous picture of Murray – gowned, bearded, benign, the parfit gentle scholar; the flat hat he's wearing is called a 'Canterbury cap', Protestantism's variation of the biretta – standing in his Oxford back garden shed that was known as the Scriptorium (literally 'writing room' and originally found in monasteries for the copying of manuscripts) and gave the *OED* its first home: you can see the jumble of slips bursting from the purpose-built cubbyholes. It was never done for slang but I have trod the path myself: when I bought my first computer in 1984 I binned a decade's worth of work, 44,000 5″ x 3″ cards. All those 'contemporary' and other quotations. They went into a skip. A passing tramp extracted one, read it and spat. I wondered whether it was a 'Famous Last Word' or a 'Cynical Quotation'.

So it is a wonderful thing, technology. Perfect for reference. No slips, just mute, unchanging desktop boxes linked cyberspatially to other boxes in another town, or even another country. You can do it all these days. It would have been literally wonderful for Murray, and remains metaphorically so for me, since I am old enough to remember other means. Of the very first collection of slips, before Murray brought order to what had started in splendid optimism but quickly plummeted into increasing chaos, some were lost, others nibbled by mice. You don't get that now, though computers still crash and I stay sufficiently earthbound to bridle at the thought of storing my life in some virtual 'cloud'. But technology and the ever more plentiful fruits of its tree of knowledge are also quite overwhelming. Lexicography, always challenging, now resembles the endless task presented to some mythical hero, never attainable, never achieved. But a task that must be essayed. Wonderful to see so many variations, so many styles, so many words on offer. And terrifying. Daunting beyond belief. I know, with sorrow and regret, that I shall die before I can make any substantial headway. The rampant plenitude is just too much: databases that bring us every newspaper ever cried on any corner; collections that parade the lyrics of the entirety of every musical genre; websites, blogs, tweets, the rest of the social networks. And that is today. Only today and I have a finite number of tomorrows.

But if there is no end then there is a beginning, though even that too is mutable. What I do and the *OED* does but pretty much no one else – or not those who make English dictionaries – does these days is called lexicography 'on historical principles'. Which is not making dictionaries that deal only with old words. Let alone words no one uses any longer. The *OED*, cussedly, fails to include the phrase. It should, it is its founding principle. For the *OED* was first the *New English Dictionary on Historical Principles*, 'founded mainly on the materials collected by the Philological Society' and this was how the Philological Society proposed what was still 'their' dictionary in 1859:

> IV. In the treatment of individual words the historical principle will be uniformly adopted; – that is to say, we shall endeavour to show more clearly and fully than has hitherto been done, or even attempted, the development of the sense or various senses of each word from its etymology and from each other, so as to bring to light the common thread which unites all together. The greatest care will also be taken to fix as accurately as possible, by means of appropriate quotations, the epoch of the appearance of each word in the language, and, in the case of archaisms and obsolete words, of their disappearance also; and the limits of the various phases of meaning exhibited by each individual will be defined, as far as possible, in like manner and by the same means.

Which, even if this citation comes in the orotund style of high Victorian scholarship, remains what I do. And in doing so sometimes get it right and sometimes get it wrong which, if nothing else, puts me on a par, for all their undoubted glory, with James Murray, his team and their scholarly successors. Let me not self-aggrandise. My comparison is simply of technique. Work. Research. Professional rigour. We make our best efforts and sometimes the best is not good enough. The dictionary remains, has to remain, subject to revision, to correction, to improvement. That's why such books have successive editions. Or, in digital terms, regular updates. Not merely, however keen their publicists may be to brandish them, to parade the inclusion of the latest 'edgy' word as used by the young. A decade previously.

Because the words are out there. And the search goes on. Chasing what William Cowper, who in the same poem 'Retirement' (1782) called for 'the strenuous use of profitable thought,' termed 'the panting syllables'.* And unlike the frustrating end, the mutability of the beginning is half its charm. The thrill of the chase? How can I convince you? It is. It is the antithesis of what populism demands. Especially of slang. The promotion, whether the publisher's or more increasingly one's own, that accompanies the launch of a new dictionary requests only the new and glittery. I provide it but it no longer excites. I may have begun this career in 1982, spurred by the knowledge that the current slang authority had fallen at the hurdles of teenage, of drugs, of 'now', and that I, believing myself to have experienced them all, could fill the gap, but the more I work the more I wonder whether he, like me, was perhaps not so much ignorant as otherwise preoccupied.

Slang has its focus, slang works in themes, and slang's essence is repetition. But how many words do we want for fucking or shitting or getting pissed? I don't know, though I can tell you how many there are to date. And there will be more, never fear, lots more. Interesting, creative, amusing, gross, but also much

* A phrase he seems to have borrowed from St Jerome who, referring to his arduous study of Hebrew in pursuit of Scriptural truth, had added 'hissing' to the 'panting'.

the same: the penis will remain a weapon, the vagina a snare, sexual intercourse a variation on man hits woman, and terms for stupid will still equate with 'not all there'. But if you do this the hard way, which is also for me the only way, then the fun, the excitement, the entire *point* is not the latest but the first. The earliest 'fuck', the first recorded 'shit', 'piss' on day one. And all the synonyms as well. And there is only one way to do this: and that is to read.

To read backwards. Read old. Read dead. Read, with grateful thanks but in the knowledge that one can only read a fraction, the digitised cornucopia of past records that every day grows larger and more daunting.

It is linguistic gerontophilia, this obsession with the past. A form of paleography of the gutter. This lust to uncover those moments when the worn artefacts of the slang lexis were still new-minted. Finding the first use is the holy grail, the gold medal, the Oscar of lexicography. We prize our 'first uses', polish them and display them for attention.* And the potential is of winning so many of them. Because whatever you have found, it's never enough. Because whatever you find, you look again, maybe harder and, reinforced by the new and ever-expanding facilities that the Internet has brought you, you may find that what was a first use is now only a second one – if that – and you go back even further. There is no such thing as a first use, only, as I am invariably, pettifoggingly, pedantically careful to

* This is not merely personal: when Sarah Ogilvie suggests Murray was 'paranoid' (see p. 145) it was not some fear – all too rational – that the OUP might be about to shut his project down, but that a rival lexicographer had ante-dated some of 'his' words and might have achieved this in some unknown but definitely nefarious manner.

write, the first 'recorded' use.* Because that paving stone is so skewiff, that rug so slippery beneath your feet. I look at my own work and squirm. Because I have put in many months of extra work since it was published and oh . . . how could I have let that stand, how could I have allowed the users, these users who trust me and quote me, how could I have misled them, how could I have failed them so badly? 'You haven't just let yourself down, boy . . .' I know. *Mea culpa. Mea maxima culpa.* And *peccavi* too.

The reality is that one has no choice. We do not compile our databases for the self-indulgent pleasure of watching the words and phrases trickle across the screen. Pure scholarship is alluring but untenured it is not feasible. This may be a craft but it is also a job, and jobs are there to achieve an end. There is a point: once it was print publication, the next stage is likely to be the establishment of a presence online. We must work to a deadline, which we might not have chosen but both we and the publisher hope, and indeed need to, make money. An advance, whether nugatory or munificent, has been paid out; editing and print costs have been factored painfully into that year's P and L assessment; there may have been a publicity budget, though rarely in these days when the more economical aspects of self-publishing have been adopted by the mainstream; expenditure must be recouped, or at least a percentage of it. Perfection, even an approximation thereof, does not matter. My database was frozen some fifteen months prior to publication,

* Even that, as noted by Murray in 1884, is evidence 'not that the word was coming into use, but that it was already established and known to readers generally'. This is true of slang but, given its nature, it may also be true that far from a term being 'known to readers generally', its appearance is an example of a writer, who'd done their street research, showing off.

eighteen months for the purposes of the book's North American appearance and two years for the ebook version. I found this agonising and still do.

Let me not overdo the exculpation. I do not pretend that every dictionary user cares; most will not even know nor need to know. What does the date matter if the spelling is right (as much as it can be in slang) and the definition and the etymology and, if one is offering Standard English (for who really knows how slang sounded when spoken out loud?), the pronunciation? What does all of that matter so long as it's 'in the dictionary'? I scourge myself and who's to notice, let alone bother. But it does matter: it matters enormously if what you are purveying is information, and there is a duty – your duty – to make that information as correct and authoritative and as *right* as possible. There are private games: pushing into the past have I leapfrogged the *OED*? Have I and my one peerless researcher unearthed something that their teams have as yet failed to find? How long will it take for them to leapfrog me in turn? Of course I specialise in slang and they do not, but we overlap. Wot larks, Pip, wot larks.

Yet, as I say, the beginning is mutable too. There is no established start line. Whatever you have found may, more than likely, be only temporary. The possibility of predating, always there if one only searched hard enough, is now within more feasible grasp. If slang was once hard to find, the arrival of online databases, especially of old newspapers, magazines and journals, has opened up vistas of exploration. Though even those, given the constant addition of new material, are temporary too. Like the ground beneath a great city the past is filled with discoveries if one is prepared and permitted to dig. And like physical archaeology what one finds changes the assumptions one may have happily maintained. If one can propose a 'truth' when it comes to etymology, it's impossible with cites. The focused searches permitted by the net make sure of that.*

I write in 2013 and since *GDoS* appeared I have altered over 11,000 of its entries. Around 40 per cent of these push the 'first use' backward. But it is not just time but place too. The term blithely labelled 'orig. US' or 'Aus.' cannot stand up when it appears fifty years earlier and recorded in the *Exeter and Plymouth Gazette*, the *Manchester Courier* or some other defunct nineteenth-century provincial newspaper. The earliest cites I had before this new discovery may have come from 'US' or 'Aus.' sources, but that was yesterday and in the end was serendipity: that was what I had read and that was what I had found. Or for that matter, when what seemed a cast-iron Anglicism turns up in the pages of Australia's mid-nineteenth-century 'sporting journal' *Bell's Life in Sydney*. Thus 'bad actor', a criminal, apparently an American coinage recorded in 1886, now turns up in *Bell's* in 1848; 'bagged', imprisoned and another purported Americanism, appears in Sydney sixteen years earlier and 'boys in blue', albeit as 'men in blue', predates the London *Sporting Times*' 1890 example by thirty-six years. However, there are times when the new citation does appear to confirm a real change in geographical origin. A 1906 issue of the tabloid *Sunday Times* of Perth offers an example of 'dis', otherwise first recorded in 1981. The meaning is undeniable: to disrepect or to disparage; the very same as found in one of the core terms of modern rap slang, the world with which it is generally identified. One is now facing two tasks: to find other early examples from Australia, which will confirm the geography,

* There is another side to this: hitherto if one found a lone cite, much earlier than those which follow, one assumed that the word had been coined once, and then, independently, re-coined. Electronic searching allows for such gaps to be filled, although that does not mean that they always are.

and to see whether, between 1906–81, there are any other examples.

Sometimes the new information demands more, some knowledge of the backdrop that moves beyond the purely lexicographical. Why, for instance, did Cumbria's *Kendal Mercury* (closed since 1917) decide in April 1852 to run a four-part series 'On Cadgers', and illustrate it with a detailed glossary of criminal talk that in many cases was elsewhere quite unrecorded? Was it perhaps a reprint from some London journal? The archives have no parallels. This is a one-off, responding, according to its author, to the county's infestation by wandering tricksters. So who was this lost, anonymous lexicographer who, knowingly or not, gives us this wonderful repository so filled with predates? For instance 'dona', usually a woman but here as a landlady, which would not reappear with that meaning until 1922 in Joyce's *Ulysses*; a 'dry-land sailor', posing as the victim of shipwreck, who appears alongside 'the escaped slave dodge,' 'the modest dodge,' '[the] journeyman tradesman's dodge', and 'the mud-lark's dodge' thirty years before its next appearance; the 'gospel cove', a clergyman's nickname not so far found again until Australia in 1914; and the 'professor', a variation on 'genteel con man', which would have to wait until a prison memoir of 1885.

All is flux and today's database has moved a good way from the published version.

Even so, as one retreats backwards the records grow sparse. For several centuries after English printing's fifteenth-century origins few would publish slang if there were more canonical works higher on the list. Such slang – and before that the criminal's jargon cant – that did appear was in lists, then dictionaries and on occasion trotted out by playwrights fond of displaying their insider knowledge. Their scripts read like lists too, not much better than the ploddingly contrived 'rogues' conversations' that the glossarists sometimes appended to bring their lexes 'to life'.

I cannot rid myself of a fantasy: that somewhere there is more. Not just instances of words of which we are already aware, but other words, lost words. Older than we know and not limited to the didactic monochrome of glossaries, or dictionaries, or thesaurus-like plays. It is hidden of course, and I lack the map, the spot marked X, but it has to be there. A golden hoard of grubby language; the vulgar tongue as spoken not just in tantalising fragments in *Piers Ploughman*, or by Chaucer's more lubricious characters, but by a whole world of living people who had no more use for Standard English than do their descendants. On the other hand . . . perhaps what we have is all there is. Slang demands a standard against which it can set itself and in Chaucer's day a standard didn't exist, and wouldn't for the best part of another century after the dialect of the London establishment drove out all rivals. The phrase 'Standard English' doesn't enter the language till the 1850s. 'Slang', in the sense of a subset of English, doesn't see print until 1756. Chronology doesn't matter: whatever the year not everyone spoke like a nob. There was a vulgar tongue, what the French call *la langue populaire*. Even this has been poorly served by the record-keepers and the early writers. Records are again sparse; if there are more they are buried. Perhaps I must accept what is on offer; certainly I cannot convey such speculations within a published dictionary where everything must display its pedigree. But in my heart I dig on.

Slang lexicography simply extends what I have maybe always been: a picker up of (un)considered trifles. Yet not exactly a collector. (In its sense of compiler, which does seem more germane, this term is marked as 'obsolete' by the unrevised *OED*.) This is not hobbyism. I have collected neither stamps nor butterflies (and yes, I do appreciate that these can also be the province of professionals). Or anything else. Only books and the words they contain. Is there something of the trainspotter here? If there is, and of course there is, I claim Irvine Welsh's version as well as Ian Allan's, since there is certainly an addiction in addition to an obsession. Nor am I merely ticking lists: lexicography requires motion, development, collection is static. I don't just gaze at my list of words. The making of dictionaries requires elucidation, explanation, information processing.

Not everything is obvious; some material seems wilfully to resist interpretation. One reads a text, say the anonymously written *Swell's Night Guide of 1846*. There were a number of these: louche guides for single gentleman on the mid-Victorian razzle. Another exemplar, published *c.*1830, boasts the title *The Flash Mirror; or, Kiddy's cabinet*: 'containing amongst many other rum goes, a famous guide to all the flash houses, meeting houses, boozing kens, and snoozing kens in London'. (A 'kiddy', it should be noted, was a raffish young man about town.) As well as offering the whereabouts of the best taverns ('boozing kens'), lodging houses ('snoozing kens') and brothels ('flash houses') with their inmates' specialities noted, the author lets us eavesdrop, or so he says, on the conversation of 'A Gonnof', who is a thief, and his girlfriend, 'A Shickster'. Both words come from Yiddish although the speakers are probably just East Enders. The great immigrations of the later century were still to come, but my people were already making their way to London and, as Henry Mayhew suggested, involving themselves, at least linguistically, in crime.* The Gonnof is reminiscing; let us listen in:

* And not just linguistically. Dickens' Fagin is thought to have been modelled on the era's top fence, the unarguably Jewish Ikey Solomon (1785–1850) who served time as a transportee in Australia. There had been five Jews included amongst the First Fleet of transportees in 1788; it may be assumed that there were many more. Yiddish-speaking cabbies introduced the term *shoful* for a Hansom cab, but there were less salubrious occupations on offer.

> I tells Bet to be on the wido, for a swell was sweet on me for a tail; officed Bet, she tumbled to the fake, and stalled off to the dossery. I take the swell to the tape shop, took our daffies, officed Lumming Ned and Scrapping George; they stalked off to the dossery, where I take my green'un; pinches his skin and ticker, darks the lumber, and planted Flabby Bet on him; she eased him of his fawney, tipped him the glue, officed her cullies, they pasted his nibs, and scarpered rumbo.

Of course it's fake, fake as whatever Flabby Bet pretends so as to pull the green'un. But it brims with examples of words that might not be so usefully crowded together elsewhere. As much as any contrived list of useful phrases appended to a Lonely Planet guide. Or, far earlier, a world in which hapless postillions are struck by lightning. What we need is a translation. I worry it terrier-like. Grasp visible threads. Tease out the easy meanings first. Ascertain some context. Reverse engineer. Make leaps, not too much in the dark. I am the tour guide, I must resist bum steers.

First the defunct, since slang, especially criminal slang, is not always made to last: 'office' means warn, 'fake' a confidence trick, 'fawney' a ring, 'daffy' gin, 'dossery' lodgings, 'skin' a wallet and 'ticker' a watch, 'cullies' are pals and 'rumbo' stands for quickly. Some persists: 'paste', 'scarper', 'tumble to', 'pinch' and 'plant'. And some defeats me. 'Tipped him the glue'. I know 'tip' which is an all-purpose word for 'give'. (There's 'tip the scroby for breakfast', to suffer a judicial whipping; 'tip the velvet' which is to kiss,* and 'tip the lion' which is to squeeze someone's nose

* As borne out by citations 'tip the velvet' has three senses: to 'French kiss', to scold, and to use flowery language in hopes of a seduction. It was been

flat against their face and either poke their eyes with one's extended fingers or place them in the person's mouth.) I know 'glue', it meant the pox. A good evocative image, reminiscent of the earlier, equally viscous 'gleet'. The drip. But surely not here. Does Bet fuck him? Even so, how does the Gonnof know the upshot. The green'un, the sucker, has surely not been back to complain. Tip someone the glue? 'Glue' can be found in south-western British dialects as an alternative to 'glow', as in 'glower', as in stare, but these are definitely Londoners talking. To my shame I cannot say other than a weak suggestion, based on 'glue' = 'stick' = 'stay', that she told him not to move. The past will have to keep this secret.

This is but one example of failure and the past, naturally, offers most of the great unknowns. I continue to agonise over this line, from the *Exeter Flying Post* of 10 June 1824: 'The Amazons exhibited on Saturday, the seconds, a knowing hoop driver for Bet and a lily cove of the swimmer for Sall, entered the ring.' This recounts a local girl-on-girl prizefight – the 'Amazons' being Sall Horse ('backed by the leary coves' at 5 to 4) v. Flash Bet (no apparent relation to Flabby Bet but who can truly say?). Most of the article is accessible: for instance the 'claret' that 'flowed in a deluge' following Sall's 'tremendous left-hander' to Bet's 'nasal organ' (a blow known as a 'snozzler' or 'nosender' in more orthodox prizefight reportage, while the

---

reinterpreted in a novel published in 1999 as to perform (lesbian) cunnilingus but this is based on a single 1684 reference to 'kissing and *tonguing*' the vagina, which in turn reflects the slightly more recent glossarial citation in B. E.'s *New Dictionary of the Canting Crew* (*c.* 1698): '*Velvet*, a Tongue. *Tip the Velvet*, to Tongue a Woman'. The problem remains that 'tonguing' did not mean cunnilingus until *c.*1890; the first slang reference to oral sex of any sort is 'suck', recorded for fellatio in 1631 and for cunnilingus in 1898; it was joined by 'larking' in the eighteenth century, and 'eat' and 'gamahuche' in the nineteenth.

impulsion of 'claret', or 'ruby', 'carmine', 'cochineal' and a number of others, is 'drawing the cork'). But brandishing such alternatives is merely to shelter defensively on the ropes: what about 'hoop driver', what about 'lily cove of the swimmer'? Any fule kno, chorus the Fancy's contemporary Molesworths, but I am not a contemporary, sources both printed and digital stay mum, and brains are to be wracked. A 'hoop-driver', says the *OED* (but only so far as written in 1899 and, for once, without a single illustratory citation) is 'a tool or machine by which the hoops of a cask are driven on'. Possible, very possible: never underestimate the presence of alcohol in such circumstances, and while the default analysis tends to assume some skewed approach to the standard, all may (for once) be as it seems. Though not the machine, rather the individual who operates it, or by extension at least an individual, e.g. a publican or barman. A better bet surely than the only alternative: a child driving its hoop along the road, though I wonder as to the use of 'hoop!' by Somerset carters to urge their horses into motion. So perhaps not an innkeeper, perhaps a farmboy? But the second phrase? 'Lily' is used in slang to mean white, e.g a 'lily benjamin', a white overcoat, a 'lily shallow', a white hat. There are noun forms, referring to character, to genitals, to effeminacy, but all come later and none would be useful here. The figurative use, defined as 'an outstanding example' and just feasible, is also anachronistic. 'Cove', as ever, is a bloke. And 'swimmer'? The term has various meanings: a counterfeit coin (too early, and in any case irrelevant unless the suggestion is of a counterfeiter), or various waterborne items: a bathing costume (far too late, and Australian), a dumpling (ditto, albeit British) or modernity's package of drugs, bobbing on the sea and awaiting pickup. Chronology permits only one possible candidate, which is recorded in 1819: a guardship or tender in which villains, given the choice of prison or an involuntary spell in the navy, were transported to their man o' war. A 'cove of the swimmer' could be a veteran of such a vessel and why, now at liberty, might he not work temporarily as a second? But we are left with 'lily'. Why specify his skin-tone, even if it suggests a post-prison pallor? My tools have taken me so far, but so far is not enough. This is not a matter of 'ety unknown', this is complete phrase unknown. Which is where, regretfully, I have left it.

The point of such worrying and evisceration is not simply to elucidate the meaning, though without that primary analysis where and how does one proceed? It is twofold: the meaning, but with that pinned down, the way in which such terms are used. The sense. Because the cite is, since we are looking for proof, for authority, its ultimate form. The cite is the nut and the bolt of one's research. No cites, no practical hands-on examples of flesh-and-blood usage, then no definitions, and no senses within them. Citations are not mandatory, but the background reading has to be done. Even my first, short effort of 1984 was drawn from books I had consulted. The penny-plain dictionary, offering A = word + B = definition, with maybe C = etymology as a useful bonus, can never achieve the informational subtlety of the one produced on 'historical principles'. One can, of course 'reverse engineer', doing the reading and drawing on usage examples that are never printed, but for those who want it, where's the proof?

Where indeed. One can never escape the orality of slang. The fact that even today there is much that escapes printed or even online record, that appears at best in glossaries compiled by those – academics, momentarily fascinated journalists – who have set themselves the task of finding out 'what the young people are saying'. This glossarising, these little lists, are in a long tradition, going back to the earliest of collections of sixteenth-century cant.

It is not satisfying. It lacks both flesh and blood, and the 'conversations' that the early collectors sometimes appended to their lists are equally inadequate.

We are not helped, of course, by the core nature of the language we are researching. Slang is innately imprecise. Its use suggests fluidity and malleability. It is why, perhaps, linguists find it so difficult to corral and so often shy away. Its speakers are not grasping at linguistic precision. Not so much a matter of that obscurantism, that in-group secrecy that allegedly underpins much of slang's vocabulary, but more a matter of who gives a fuck. Another reason for citations: context is all. The citation provides proof for a definition that might otherwise seem to have been plucked from mid-air. Not just a matter of what does it mean, but how is it meant *here*? The dependence of so much slang on tweaked Standard English is of no help. A 'pipe' may on occasion actually be just that: a pipe. But let us assume that it is definitely not, though, as we shall see, even that assumption is something of a false friend.

The first task is to group the various senses. There are those that deal with the reproduction of sound via the physical shape of the throat, a pipe, amplified by windpipe. It can be the human voice, the song that it sings and a story that is told. It can be a telephone or a saxophone. The next group tweaks the Standard English again, looking to the pipe as a tube, but this time depends mainly on double entendre for sexual reference: the penis (thus the compound 'pipe job', fellatio, which echoes the synonymous French *une pipe*) and the vagina; although the shape, presumably devoid of sniggering, also gives top-boots. Next come drug uses, where the pipe is, indeed, a pipe. A cigar, an opium pipe and which as 'pipe' or 'the pipe', represent the smoking of opium and as 'pipe' again an opium smoker, a marijuana or hashish pipe and a smoker of either; a vein into which a drug can be injected (which reflects the seventeenth-century 'pipe-vein', a human vein); and finally a pipe for smoking base cocaine or crack, by metonymy, the drug itself and thus the phrase 'on the pipe', using crack regularly. A fourth group uses the slang phrase a 'lead-pipe cinch', to give the meaning of a certainty or something that is easily accomplished. A fifth, based on the specific lead pipe, gives any form of clubbing weapon and finally, in London and constructed with 'the', the River Thames.

Obviously some of these are not going to be confused; the saxophone and the Thames, the penis and the certainty make their identity clear. But the variations on drugs uses, the fine-tuning of the meanings pertaining to sound, these require the sanctification of context and thus citation.

There is no escape with citations. No being smart. No intellectual suppositions or guesswork. No what one might wish for – just what the cites allow. There it is, as they say, in black and white. Not quite Occam's razor but undoubtedly no opportunity to embellish. You couldn't, as they also say, make it up. Which once said, demands a proviso. As far as anything in this world is able, cites keep you honest, but cites also deceive. The text can lie, or if not lie, mislead. Not in what it says – snapped up for the dictionary the quoted line is ripped from context and matters above all as a container of a given word or phrase; only as the niceties of sense follow does one reinstate the context – but as always comes first with cites, *when*. Each backwards discovery changes the historical picture, and one rejoices, but one cannot ever wholly trust. There are so many possibilities, so many governing vagaries, so much serendipity. Cites hide, cites go unrecorded, cites were never set down. Ghost cites, one might suggest. They (or first uses and indeed last ones) are always temporary. Objects of continuing desire; in this case the older the better. The linguistic past is a country without horizon and without borders. Looking for the grail, we turn away from the facility of research in the now and in search of the then we feel our way backwards in the dark. It is the best we can manage.

Cites: a Finder's Manual

1. Choose your source

Whether it's Shakespeare or Donald Goines or some blogger who has decided that slang is to be the basis of their communications, the first question has to be: is it worth it? Slang is universal, but some writers, be they authors, playwrights, lyricists, scriptwriters or whatever, seem immune, or virtually so. There is no point in hours of reading for the sake of a dozen cites or even fewer. I need slang-dense. Ideally I also need slang-new, or at least slang new for a given moment in time.

The TV series *Oz* was aired between 1997–2003 on HBO. I missed it at the time, not having access, and also knowing that without scripts it would be hard, if not impossible, to note down the passing slang. (I also laboured briefly beneath the delusion that it was another Australian soap, but I discovered otherwise.) This is now remedied by DVD sets, streaming and the like, although the ideal source, a book of scripts, has not materialised.

2. Will it deliver the goods?

Oz should be a prime candidate, being the first of a mini-genre of HBO cop/underworld series. It is written mainly by Tom

Fontana, who has form, among other things involvement in *Homicide*, taken from David Simon's book on the Baltimore PD. Simon, of course, created HBO's slightly later, and, most would consider, more successful series *The Wire*, which itself can be seen as a TV fusion of *Homicide* and Simon's study of a year among Baltimore's drug dealers and users, *The Corner*.* The show is set in a fictional, but heavily researched prison. A preliminary search on the label 'US prison' gives 1,113 terms in *GDoS*. Prisons love slang and vice versa. *Oz*, with its drug trade, hetero- and homosexual interactions including male-on-male rape, gangs of various loyalties – black gangbangers, Latinos, Muslims, the white supremacist Aryan Brotherhood – should provide a fertile range.

3. Is it still useful?

Given that I am watching it in year nineteen of my researches, am I too late? By 'late' I mean: do I have the material already? Do I, in addition, wish to devote what will probably be a month or so to watching fifty-six episodes (eviscerating *The Wire* took two months) given that the stop/check word/type in citation (if needed)/restart process adds many minutes to the programme time, and, since I cannot rid myself of a residual sense that 'watching TV in the afternoon' is in some way 'wrong' the process will therefore eat up many successive evenings. Still, familiarity breeds . . . familiarity and one soon finds that while certain characters are valuable, others are not. There's an unexpected amount of God-bothering (counterpoint to the gruesome

* Reading *The Corner*, one can see a number of episodes and characters that reappear in *The Wire*, but while between them the two offer nearly 800 slang terms, they overlap in only 10 per cent of them (*Homicide*, at least in book form, has relatively little slang).

depictions of violence?) – barring the Muslims the whole prison seems to be Catholic – and priest-nun interactions permit wandering attention, cups of coffee, whatever.

As for late? If the dictionary can't be 'finished', the researches can't be 'late'. The Internet means the problem is no longer worrying about where to find the stuff but when to allow yourself to take a pause in looking. I have to watch *Oz*.

I do not, on the other hand, need to watch *Deadwood* – notoriously awash with slang – let alone *Downton Abbey*. I also shy from all variations on the theme of 'historical fiction'. Set in the past and approximating some long-vanished 'reality', these all too often fall down on slang. The term 'anachronistic' rears up. If possible, one recoils, but sometimes, when nothing else is to be found, one surrenders. There are, throughout *GDoS* a number of citations modified by the tag 'context', which means, it may have been published yesterday, but the scenario is set long since. The eighteenth century seems particularly alluring, and a quick wander amongst the modern self-publishers of the Kindle store would bring up a wealth of archaisms, the linguistic equivalent of ruffles and stays, accurate but equally often not. We do not go there. Like copying from glossaries, accepting 'context' is to fail. The reader can be warned – there is the label – but the lexicographer is condemned to frustration. *Oz*, but a few years old, offers no such problems.

The Wire, with its primary focus on cops and corners, with forays into unions, inner-city schooling and journalism, gave me nearly 450 cites. My money is on *Oz*, even restricted to the limited world of prison, to make it worth my while, so I have to find out. Nothing ventured.

I also know that of my current examples of prison terms, far too many still come from glossaries. As noted, glossarial citing equals failure, or at best *faut de mieux*. I am hoping that *Oz* will provide some 'real' citations, even in its fictional environment.

4. What I See Is What I Get

To date I have watched forty of the fifty-six episodes. Score so far: 138 cites. This is not, I admit, up to *Wire* standards, but still worth the effort.

One subset – long since gutted – will not be required. Kipling described the British Tommy's lexis as '600 words and the adjective' which I believe to have been 'fucking'. ('Bloody', a possible challenger, had been snatched up as 'The Great Australian Adjective' and uncensored 1914–18 reminiscences, such as Frederic Manning's *Her Privates We* – the pun, taken from *Hamlet*, was quite deliberate – suggest that I am probably right.) All-male environments seem wedded to the term and *Oz* tests to destruction the theory that infinite repetition must defang verbal power. Or at least make it unremarkable. I cannot count the 'fucks', 'motherfuckers', 'what the fucks', the 'fuck withs' and the rest; I do not need to. These days it is not a set one needs to look far to find.

Assessing the words I encounter, I have two criteria: eligibility (in the case of words that I do not already list) and need (in the case of there being a gap in my stated one-cite-per-decade-per-definition rule). In many cases the language of *Oz*'s Hobbesian all-against-all world is common – obscenities, insults, and a leavening of general prison jargon – 'lockdown', 'shakedown' – which provides a necessary degree of authenticity. These present no problems and if I use them it is because they fill gaps in my current cite listing. Some I have not met, however, and give me pause for thought. I have to decide, in the same way as assessing any neologism, be it sixteenth century or twenty-first, whether they qualify.

'Prag', meaning a subservient prisoner, often young, who is exploited for sexual services, appears in the second episode and frequently thereafter. It is not a common word – the better known synonyms being 'punk', 'bitch' and 'maytag' – and all uses, since there are none to be found on Google other than via the Urban Dictionary and none of those predate the show, seem to refer back to *Oz*. Prisons do have local usage, but the question remains: is this an invention? Possible etymologies suggest an acronym: '*pr*ison *fag*', and the more contrived 'Punk's Really A Girl' or 'Prison Raped Ass Girl'. Rightly or wrongly, and mainly because it seems to have no semantic cognates, I do not include it.

Perhaps illogically I do include another possible invention: 'airhole', to stab. Again, I am unable to find any non-*Oz* uses, but here one has a number of cognates, all of which can be found in the nineteenth and even eighteenth centuries: 'let the air out of', 'let' or 'put the daylight into/through', 'let moonlight into', 'let sunshine through', 'hole' and 'ventilate'. Airhole is undeniably part of this imagery, It may be the writer's invention; it may have been one that hitherto has 'got away'. It will join the database for now, but still may not survive the editing process.*

Slang itself, as a word, 'slang', has to come from somewhere, even if to date we remain defeated by its source. Each of slang's words, 'the slang', is the same. It must have origins. Not simply lexical origins, etymologies, but chronological ones. Although my lexicon is not the place for searching down the ultimate origin of every word. Why do we call a dog a dog and so on. I simply wonder as to how a word enters the slang lexis and suggest that all the lexicographer can do is note the first recorded use, which means depending on something that at bottom is changeable and open to as many revisions as research, not to mention an inevitable

* An older version of 'airhole' is also listed among those terms once included, now excised: it meant a small London garden, usually sited in a former church graveyard; it played on the 'lungs of London' image, supposedly coined by an eighteenth-century Lord Chatham.

degree of serendipity. Occasionally that 'first cite' may come with a useful anecdote that lays out the whys and wherefores; on the whole it does not. This still avoids the question: how does one spot a comer, a staple of the slang dictionaries of the future. I doubt that Thomas Harman jumped on 'bouse/booze' and murmured gleefully, 'That's a stayer.' (Although given its meaning, he would not have been chancing his arm to any great extent.) But looking at 'prag' and 'airhole' I am, ultimately – since I have no supporting examples to steady my hand – tossing the dice. And if I have chosen to back the latter and excise the former, it is mainly because I can see semantic/thematic links for 'airhole', whereas 'prag' seems to be an artificial confection. And yes, I could ask the writer, and maybe shall.*

Fortunately one is not always gambling, even with a degree of insider info to help. 'Tits', meaning heroin, is cited in the first series and is one of the show's most common terms. They provide the phrase 'fiending for tits' which refers not to a 'breast man' but to a sufferer from withdrawal. (The phrase's drug sense dates only from the 1990s, but a more general use that focuses on sexual yearning can be found in Goines' *Black Gangster* in 1977.) It may sound local and invented, but it is not. The *Oz* use is so far the earliest I can find, but the word is used in a 400-word glossary published in 2000, and drawn from the US prison system at large. I can see no reason why the term is not genuine. The problem is finding further examples. Like 'airhole', 'tits' is a very common term, slang's plural for breasts, and in

* Such questioning is a definite upside of the Internet. Encountering the phrase 'low flying birdie' in the work of Scottish *noiriste* Tony Black I could see it meant Famous Grouse whisky. The problem: was it his creation or in wider use? A quick Twitter message and all was revealed: common Scottish use and I, quite literally, should have known better.

older texts for horses, and thus hard to isolate in an Internet search.

No problems at all with another set of *Oz* terms. 'Jism', with multiple spellings of which the most common is 'jizz', which in its 'literal' sense means semen, has in figurative use come to mean energy and spirit. (The long and on-going search for the origins of 'jazz', as music, sex and everything else, currently attributes its roots to 'jism'.) In series one, episode eight we meet the line 'You're going to have to take Beecher out, or you're not going to have any jizz in Em City.' Em City, the prison's special unit and focus of the story, seems at times to be awash with literal jizz, but this, it seems to me, merely adds another wholly acceptable figurative definition, in this case 'power' or 'influence'. 'Juice' offers a similar pair of linked meanings. Slang allows for these nuanced uses, and I would not be surprised to find others. So too the insults 'jizzbag' and 'jizzball', the first of which suggests a filled condom, the second a clot of ejaculated semen. The extension of a literal definition into a figurative, often insulting one, the use of 'penis' terms for 'fool' ones ('dipstick', 'dork', 'plonker', 'tool'), is common. The semen/condom/insult equation can also be seen in 'scum': 'scumbag' (first found in the 1950s), 'scumball', 'scumbucket' and so on. *Oz* uses some of these and adds 'scumhole', but here the use is literal: the anus, with its assumption of a context of sodomy.

5. If You Love Them, Let Them Go

Cite-gathering is not a game of finders keepers. Not, that is, if – and this is of course the whole point of searching – one tosses them, via print or digitally, into the public arena. Information may be power, but in this case the empowerment is of the users and cuddling such discoveries to your database is not going to help anyone. So out they go into the great, and hopefully interested, world and for a while, at least, they may even be re-cited, as in 'it now appears that X was first recorded in Y.' This will give a small glow of pride, further enhanced if the dictionary is permitted a name-check. The pride will be less if the older version of the same dictionary is quoted – in which case the glow will become a blush of shame – but then that's why one carries on searching.

Endgame

> When you've made your million, when you've cut your monsters, when your peak has been passed . . . what happens next? What about the fifty years before you die?
>
> Nik Cohn, *Awopbopaloobop Alopbamboom* (1969)

It appears that I have spent my life becoming good at the wrong thing.

Reference, I am informed on a distressingly regular basis, is dead. *Monty Python* fans could doubtless offer some synonyms, and slang gives me well over 800, but I shall not. Reference publishing – those damned thick square books – is finished. Which is a generalised way of explaining what is of course unpalatable but, like many disgusting experiences, must be choked down. You no longer have a job. You are not required on this or any other voyage. You are without value. Like the task to which you have dedicated the bulk of your professional life, you are effectively dead.

To date I have had two meetings with my current publisher. At the first they informed me they did not wish to publish the book; at the second, having performed the task nonetheless, they rejected my request that they support its furtherance. Such is that grim 'what if' and I do not blame them: they did not commission the book but had it thrust upon them by the multinational of which they are a part; its publication represented an expense they did not need. I do regret, however, that they seem to despair of its future. Times are tough.

So I am thinking of moving into a new world. One that I have never tried, nor ever wished to encounter, but one that seems to be a necessary and timely step. The small ad, the job-seeking small ad, to be precise. I see it as upmarket, I envisage a couple of hundred dollars worth of the *New York Review of Books*, the inside back cover, in there with the DJFs with their natural radiance, their love for white water rafting and Mozart sonatas, their deep thoughts and unimpeachably liberal values, their astounding (yet they have been told so, and it must be true) and near mirror likeness of some Hollywood beauty now, as are they, of a certain age (a euphemism used of women in English but also of men in French and which, how can I sidestep this one, almost certainly refers to me). On second thoughts, maybe not the *NYRB*. As much as ever I feel British, English even, it is on reading those cringingly self-congratulatory ads. No surprise, I always feel, that they are on the rebound from that 'D.' as in, to steal from Dolly Parton, 'I.V.O.R.C.E.'

But an ad it will have to be. 'Slang lexicographer, 65, widely published and acknowledged as among the best of his kind, seeks work. In his own field by choice, but all opportunities considered.'

What has happened is that, like the world that I affect to despise, I too, since *GDoS* appeared, have become all form and no content. Working to no end and no point. Pretending to utility while existing in a corner where what I do is irrelevant and valueless. Doing that which I promised, some chapters back, that I could never do: continuing my work even though 'they' no longer pay me. Such is the pessimistic view, but the most optimistic I can conjure is that I have come to resemble a first recorded use: temporary and definitely subject to improvement.

To be caught on the cusp of change is interesting in long shot but less appealing in tight focus. It is perhaps one of the less reported downsides of our increased longevity. One is not meant to be working at sixty-five. But to steal again from Cowper's 'Retirement', 'Absence of occupation is not a rest, / A mind quite vacant is a mind distress'd.' And so is mine. That I believe myself, perhaps by the particular nature of what I do, to be better now than I have ever been, is quite unimportant. Reference is dead.

Except that it is not. Just, it seems, on paper. People require sources of information. But they will no longer appear in print. It will no longer be mediated by expertise, it will no longer be reliable. It will be Wikipedia at best. At worst the Urban Dictionary. The dubious wisdom of the vapouring cloud. And because we must turn against what is termed elitism and because everyone has not just a novel but a dictionary or encyclopedia in them, everyone will have their say. All must have prizes, even if the prize is a confirmation of their own, and far worse – since what they peddle is too often trash – the encouragement of other people's ignorance. What the Internet provides, yes, amid other things that are good no doubt, is the best means yet of ensuring that everyone may be comfortably reinforced in their own invincible solipsisms, in their own mediocrity. The great equaliser, and what gets shot is culture. The Internet is an iceberg turned upside down: the tiny percentage of excellence is buried deep, the vast mass of dross floats via the self-proclamation of social networking.

At which point I must pause. Not merely because I will not permit this descent into the curmudgeonly. And what am I but solipsistic too. But more importantly because, to some extent, I am wrong. Yes, 99 per cent of the Internet, like 99 per cent of everything else, is crap, but that leaves an interesting if not important 1 per cent and it may just be that the Urban Dictionary is part of it. One cannot, after all, deny its presence – some 6,845,110 definitions (at time of writing) since its founding in 1999, and amassing more at the rate of 2,000 a day; with 2.2 million Facebook 'likes' and 13,691 Twitter followers. It is, without any doubt, the net's go-to lexicon. At least in the realm of fresh-minted terminology. It began life as a slang dictionary, slang being a loose synonym of 'urban' when it comes to language, but that adjective has been dropped. Journalists, some say of the lazier sort, adore it. It is regularly quoted. It is seriously down with the kidz. Indeed it is created by the kidz. Some 6.7 million hits worth of kidz each and every month even if, of every thousand users, only one offers up a new word. How can we not stand in awe?

We do. I do. I stand not just in awe, since as I must have said before, size matters in lexicography, but also at one side – the wrong side, naturally – of a generational abyss. No mere gap – which was how I saw the difference between Eric Partridge and myself – but a bottomless pit. If I represent one aspect of slang lexicography, the traditionalists who model themselves on the *OED*, then the Urban Dictionary legions, the majority of whom are aged 14–25, represent the antithesis. I am looking at the end, they have barely essayed the beginning. Its founder, Aaron Peckham, is thirty-two and he was eighteen when he launched his work; I admire his enterprise. Like many Internet creators he has conjured something substantial where once stood nothing at all. And it hangs in there. He funds the project through ads, but resists the many dubious supplicants – often politicians or tacky and not so tacky merchandisers – who offer him rewards for turning over Urban Dictionary to their exploitation. He founded the site to stand against what he saw as old people's hegemony of definition: why should you tell us what what we say means? It is a good Sixties conceit, the sort that underpinned the underground press for which I laboured. He maintains his position and thus his credibility. I very much doubt that he needs my approval, but I like his style.

But awe is one thing, intellectual trust is quite another. I am not a convert, never shall be I imagine – if nothing else it's far too late – but you cannot condemn by assailing motives that in fact don't exist. Credibility is admirable but nebulous: my problems lie in the concrete. Dictionary, even to my reasonably descriptivist self, still means authority. You want to know? Here's the answer. If it cannot provide authority, what is left to the dictionary? Spelling is simply not enough, especially in slang where one so often wonders as to the seeming randomness of orthographic choice. If its definitions cannot offer some form of accuracy, of 'truth', then what is their purpose? The dictionary is a tool, the tool should do its job and the job is providing information that the user can trust. It may err, but it is hoped that these are errors of omission not commission. Like the Fifties cop-show *Dragnet*'s hard-ass sergeant Joe Friday the lexicographer aims for 'the facts, just the facts'. New facts, of course, may overturn their predecessors, especially in the sphere of dating, which can always be pushed back a decade or more. Thus the traditional lexicon.

The Urban Dictionary does not, let us be quite blunt, give a fuck for all that. Look up an entry. See how it works. Here is a definition. Now here is another, and another and yet others too. They may jibe with one another, they may not. They may contradict. All that differentiates them is a pair of icons: thumbs up and thumbs down. One can see by the appended numbers which definition the UD-ers prefer. But other than by checking the respective counts (and 'downs' may challenge 'ups' quite closely even in what those of us who still trade in such value judgments might see as the 'right' definition) there is no verdict. Merely the varied opinions of the Urban Dictionary crowd. Far from offering the certainties of the traditional dictionary it is relativism epitomised. 'Define your world' it urges, and they do. All are qualified, all are welcome, there is no comment, and defining is free. Like the Internet of which it plays a part, no one has the right to mount a platform and dictate. Or if they do, no one else sees any particular requirement to listen. One might call it the wisdom of the crowd. One might call it the country of the blind, without even a one-eyed man to be king.

I have met Mr Peckham and railed at him on this account. I asked, and I was not alone because the environment was a conference and he was far and away the youngest there, how could he term his website a dictionary when by every standard it is patently no such thing. He was quite candid. The term 'dictionary' gave the website authority; the fact that it was consciously pitted against the traditional variants of that authority was a paradox which he fully appreciated. He had no intention of abandoning that useful noun. I have no intention of condemning him for such wholly judicious merchandising. 'Define your world' indeed, and that world, other than coincidentally, is no longer mine.

I have wondered who will succeed me in that parallel, infinitely smaller world that is slang lex. It is half a millennium old; surely it is not due for extinction. It may be that my answer lies in the Urban Dictionary, with its non-judgmental acceptance, its all-encompassing welcome for both contributors and language, its prizes – inclusion – for merely turning up. In a world of relativism (and who, we are informed, is responsible for that if not we proponents of 'the Sixties'?) perhaps 'authority' is due to become as outmoded a term as those which the sixteenth-century's criminals used for bread or milk. It may well be. But I hope, I do really hope, that it is not.

As for the alleged death of traditional reference: who says? as we would have put it in the playground. Who says those fat dictionaries are good for only propping up tables or holding open doors? Perhaps we all do. We have fallen prey not merely to the market and what for the majority are its cruel economics, but to a great tsunami of propaganda. Because as we have drummed into us on the hour and every hour, books are finished; the 'dead tree' has joined the Dead White European Male in the chamber of modern horrors. Digital is all, ebooks are the future and devil take the incomputerate. For traditionalists the bad is yet again driving out the good. Amazon parades its stats and notes that electronic downloads have surpassed paper. It does not note that the change does not represent addition, merely substitution. The reading public seems to remain as was. Only the list of writers has swelled. The slush pile has taken wing and flourishes. Some of these have and will triumph: naturally, since why should shit cease to float?

This is not luddism. I have used a computer since 1984 and would shudder at a world without my database. Nor is it even elitism. My shelves are crammed with titles that, dependent on slang, are far from 'literary'. Pulp fiction of one variety or another. I am biased, of course, but many such have style and wit and their authors had no choice but to fight for a place in the bookshops. Those who wrote them did so for money, to get money it was necessary to reach a certain standard – otherwise what exactly was the point? They could not simply announce themselves as authors and demand that the world assume it to be so. Is this cultural puritanism? Perhaps. The perennial debates inform me that I whinge too much. That Canute did not manage to withhold the incoming tide. If I make no money I have only myself to blame. Do it yourself: throw yourself into the arms of the social networks, promote yourself, interface with your readers. I see it all around me: authors who, day upon day, tweet their new releases and their backlists to a legion of followers. Perhaps, but life, surely and especially surely for me, is too short. And, I must ask, does this factor in a time for actual work?

Having used lex as my defence for thirty years – constructing my redoubt with every hwd/def/ety/cite – I find that it no longer works.

The bastion has become a Maginot Line, and the new world walks confidently round it without even dignifying it with a salvo. It is fine to make the rules of the game, in the confident hope that thereby you can win – so long as a parallel set have not evolved while you weren't looking. As I keep noting, what matters is not what should be but what is – unpalatable though it may be – and 'what is' is that around twenty years ago I popped out – not for a pack of fags but to write a three-volume dictionary of slang – and when, time having passed, my hair grown grey and the book finally published, I returned, I found the world turned upside down. The resourceful, the socially and intellectually limber, will of course spin with it, turning somersaults as required. I fear that my internal exile, however busy and I trust productive, has not equipped me for such acrobatics.

Much of my sorrow is, I must admit, aesthetic. Not literary aesthetic but simple sensuality. Nothing is going to reproduce the pure pleasure of my 1785 edition of Francis Grose's dictionary of 'the vulgar tongue'. The simple tactile enjoyment of handling such a book and others like it.* Nor, and perhaps this is it too, the sheer variety of physical books: shape, size, colour. For once form matters as much as content and if, as is the case with much pulp, there is homogeneity within the text, there is less in the cover and the dimensions. The electronic reader reduces everything to the same bland xerox as the retail chains have done with stores on the modern high street. High streets that of course no longer feel it necessary to include a bookseller.

* This has recently been intensified beyond infinity by my purchase of Grose's own interleaved and densely annotated edition of the book. In practical terms these browning, quill-inscribed amendments show how he revised and expanded his headword list for what would be the 1788 edition. In emotional ones, in the holding of this tangible link between my work and his, the effect is quite electric.

Enough. Old people: how they do go on.

In any case, there is the paradox. Reference and digital. Perhaps not love and marriage, but horse and carriage anyway. What bites our hand is also perfectly happy to feed us. I can, if you have a day or so, escort you through *GDoS* and reveal all of Joyce's cites; a little more time and we can find his borrowings from Thomas Harman or his use of slang terms for penis. But with the right search engine, I can find those figures instantly: the answers are 1,058, 6 and 13. I can also inform you as to those terms which, at the moment at least, he was the first to place in print: 197, and they include 'brekkie', 'jay!' (for Jesus!), 'shite!' and a figurative, non-sexual use of 'wet dream'. So can any user with sufficient commitment but I have the luxury of the database and who would trudge through 6,200 pages. It is time to move forward. If one has spent so long amassing this information, then make it available. Not only that: keep it up to date. The database was frozen in late 2009, with a year's proofing to follow prior to publication. Research restarted in late 2010. As I write (August 2013), getting on for one quarter of the book has to some extent been amended, revised, and corrected where necessary. There are over 30,000 new citations, plus new headwords and new definitions of words and phrases that appeared in print. For the scholars among you, I have now found earlier 'first uses' for well over 4,500 terms.

This has not followed an influx of unread books. One cannot read everything but we have read much and where we can we read more. What it reflects is the options available via the ever-expanding Internet. My own subset of what David Foster Wallace christened 'Total Noise': 'the tsunami of available fact, context, and perspective'. New material from blogs, websites and social media; old material from the continual arrival of scanned runs of old newspapers, magazines and journals. *GDoS* scratched the surface, now we are starting to burrow. Of course there is far too much. Overwhelmingly, inexhaustibly too much. Merely submitting every print entry to Google Book Search in the hope of tracing earlier examples of use would be enough and that holds merely a fraction and is notoriously untrustworthy. It is easier to pinpoint possibilities when they are available in digital form – give me an earlier use of 'endsville', and give it me now – but that has limits.* Slang lurks in odd corners, my headword lists are not all-conclusive. You cannot search for something you do not know exists. You can only disinter unnoticed material via the hard grind of reading.

So here I am, as that on-and-off slang collector W. E. Henley put it, feeling bloody but unbowed. One more dictionary published, a database to improve. Perhaps I should stop. Those who for years asked what I was doing, now ask me why I bother to go on. I am not stopping. Like a veteran copper who still arrives at the station every morning because he has nowhere else to go, I continue. I have no choice. This is ongoing work. It will not be finished in my lifetime. It need never be finished.

* For instance, monocularity: searching, for instance, for a cite for 'shallow cove', used by the nineteenth-century underworld, one focuses on its meaning in slang – a man who solicits alms by divesting himself of most of his clothes, especially on a day when the temperature demands the opposite. But once you look online for 'shallow cove' you find you're at the seaside. This tends to come as a disappointment, not to mention a reminder of wider worlds.

Acknowledgements

Despite the scope, at least chronologically, of what has been touched on here, I shall resist what I see as 'American' acknowledgements, starting with the thanks offered to one's mother's obstetrician, and moving on and ever-wider from there. In the end one makes one's own life and even if I were to thank my late parents for 'making me what I am today', I could never overlook the innate irony of so back-handed a compliment.

So I shall return to the present. As noted, this is my text and the thoughts on lexicography must be ascribed to their author. Nonetheless those thoughts have come from thirty years in 'the business' and have been stimulated by a number of individuals, whether I know them as colleagues or publishing professionals or as the authors of works I have encountered. If I describe them as 'the usual suspects' then I do so with co-conspiratorial admiration; and most have been named (and thus shamed?) in the introduction to *Green's Dictionary of Slang*. They know, as the cliché has it, who they are. The material has also been rehearsed in the introductions to various books, in lectures, essays and blogs, and my thanks go to all those who were involved, especially, as regards blogs, at www.thedabbler.co.uk.

On a more immediate level, I would like to thank my copy-editor at Cape, Clare Bullock, who asked only the *à propos* questions and even supplied some of the answers. Also my proofreader Myra Jones, indexer Vicki Robinson, and publicist Ruth Waldram. I have been working with Dan Franklin since 1986; this is our seventh collaboration. The publishing world may have changed; he remains a rock of excellence.

One figure is absent from the text, which was either an oversight or a disinclination to return to an often-told story. But if any single person has determined the possibility of spending so long immersed in slang, then it is my Uncle Jack Morris whose generosity conferred the near-obsolete role of 'gentleman scholar' (even if I would eschew the adjective and wonder as to the noun) on my role as dictionary-maker. Since this came as a legacy I cannot in any sense thank him enough, but at least on paper, I can do so again.

Finally I offer very sincere thanks to my dedicatee Patrick Hanks. He has been an unbidden supporter of my efforts for many years, a critical but always positive voice when assessing the work in hand, and consciously or otherwise a teacher of how better I might perform that work. Although lacking his intellectual skills, I can at least hope to emulate his enthusiasm for the task that, even at some professional distance, we share.

Index

Index

Index

Index

Index

Index

Index

Index

Index

Index